Coding Freedom

THE ETHICS AND AESTHETICS
OF HACKING

⤺⊚⤻

E. GABRIELLA COLEMAN

PRINCETON UNIVERSITY PRESS
PRINCETON AND OXFORD

Requests for permission to modify material from this work should be sent to
Permissions, Princeton University Press

Published by Princeton University Press, 41 William Street, Princeton,
New Jersey 08540

In the United Kingdom: Princeton University Press, 6 Oxford Street,
Woodstock, Oxfordshire OX20 1TW

press.princeton.edu

At the time of writing of this book, the references to Internet Web sites (URLs) were accurate.
Neither the author nor Princeton University Press is responsible for URLs that may have
expired or changed since the manuscript was prepared.

Library of Congress Cataloging-in-Publication Data
  Coleman, E. Gabriella, 1973–
  Coding freedom : the ethics and aesthetics of hacking / E. Gabriella Coleman.
    p. cm.
  Includes bibliographical references and index.
  ISBN 978-0-691-14460-3 (hbk. : alk. paper)—ISBN 978-0-691-14461-0 (pbk.
  : alk. paper) 1. Computer hackers. 2. Computer programmers. 3. Computer
  programming—Moral and ethical aspects. 4. Computer programming—Social
  aspects. 5. Intellectual freedom. I. Title.
  HD8039.D37C65 2012
  174'.90051--dc23   2012031422

British Library Cataloging-in-Publication Data is available

This book has been composed in Sabon

Printed on acid-free paper. ∞
Printed in the United States of America

1 3 5 7 9 10 8 6 4 2

This book is distributed in the hope that it will be useful, but
WITHOUT ANY WARRANTY; without even the implied warranty of
MERCHANTABILITY or FITNESS FOR A PARTICULAR PURPOSE

Coding Freedom

⁓◎⁓

We must be free not because we claim freedom,
but because we practice it.
—William Faulkner, "On Fear: The South in Labor"

Without models, it's hard to work; without a context,
difficult to evaluate; without peers, nearly
impossible to speak.
—Joanna Russ, *How to Suppress Woman's Writing*

CONTENTS

❧

ACKNOWLEDGMENTS

ℭ𝔬𝔊𝔳

This project marks the culmination of a multiyear, multicity endeavor that commenced in earnest during graduate school, found its first stable expression in a dissertation, and has, over a decade later, fully realized itself with this book. During this long period, over the various stages of this project, many people have left their mark in so many countless ways. Their support, interventions, comments, and presence have not only improved the quality of this work but also simply made it possible. This book could not have been written without all of you, and for that I am deeply grateful.

In 1996, at the time of my first exposure to Linux, I was unable to glean its significance. I could not comprehend why a friend was *so enthused* to have received a CD in the mail equipped with Slackware, a Linux distribution. To be frank, my friend's excitement about software was not only incomprehensible; it also was puzzling. Thankfully about a year later, this person clued me in as to what makes this world extraordinary, doing so initially via my interest at the time: intellectual property law. If it were not for Patrick Crosby, who literally sat me down one day in 1997 to describe the existence of a novel licensing agreement, the GNU General Public License (GPL), I would have likely never embarked on the study of free software and eventually hackers. I am thrilled he decided that something dear to him would be of interest to me. And it was. I was floored to discover working alternatives to existing intellectual property instruments. After months of spending hour after hour online, week after week, reading about the flurry of exciting developments reported on *Linux Weekly News*, Kuro5hin, and Slashdot, it became clear to me that much more than the law was compelling about this world, and that I should turn this distractingly fascinating hobby into my dissertation topic or run the risk of never finishing graduate school. Now I not only know why Patrick was happy to have received the Slackware CD back in 1996—and I found he was not alone, because many people have told me about the joy of discovering Slackware—but also hope I can convey this passion for technology to others in the pages of this book.

Many moons ago in graduate school at the University of Chicago when I proposed switching projects, my advisers supported my heretical decision, although some warned me that I would have trouble landing a job in an anthropology department (they were right). Members of my dissertation committee have given invaluable insight and support. My cochairs, Jean Comaroff and John Kelly, elongated my project in the sense that they always asked me to think historically. Jean has also inspired me in so many ways, then and now. She is everything a scholar should be, so I thank her for being such a great mentor. Nadia Abu El-Haj encouraged me to examine the sociocultural mechanisms by which technoscience can act as the basis for broader societal transformation. I was extremely fortunate to have Gary Downey and Chris Kelty on board. In 1999, I was inspired by a talk that Gary gave at the American Anthropological Association meetings on the importance of positive critique, and I hope to have contributed to such a project here.

Chris, a geek anthropologist extraordinaire, has added to this project in innumerable ways. Because of his stellar work on free software, his comments have been breathlessly on target, and more than any other person, he has pushed this project to firmer, more coherent ground. His insistence on not only understanding the world but also (re)shaping it is inspiring, and I hope that I can one day follow in his footsteps. Although Patrice Riemens was not an official adviser, he nonetheless, like any hacker would, shared freely. His advice, especially pertaining to hacker politics, was as indispensable as the guidance from my official committee members.

Fieldwork, of course, is where the bulk of anthropological research occurs. For me, most of that took place in San Francisco, with a short stint in the Netherlands, and throughout copious time was spent online. While there were countless people who made my fieldwork possible, I have to single out three who really went out on a limb for me, over and over again: Seth Schoen, Praveen Sinha, and Zack Brown. I think each one of you knows how much you have helped me start, proceed with, and finish this project, and I am grateful from the bottom of my heart.

Many others have helped me understand with much greater depth what drives people to write free and open-source software (F/OSS). Among those in the Bay Area, I would like to especially thank Brian Behlendorf, Rick Moen, Karsten Self, Don Marti, Mike Higashi, and Evan Prodromou. Also, all the folks at the Electronic Frontier Foundation and Online Policy Group provided me with the invaluable opportunity of interning at their respective organizations. Will Doherty, in particular, deserves a special nod (even though he worked me so hard). Quan Yin also gave me the opportunity to volunteer at its acupuncture clinic, and perhaps more than any other experience, this one kept everything in place and perspective. My Bay Area roommates, Linda Graham and Nikki Ford, supplied me with an endless stream of support.

My time in the Netherlands, in October 2002, was short but made a lasting impression. The Hippies from Hell were welcoming and helpful.

They also organize the best darn hacker conferences in the world, and a big thanks to them (and all the other volunteers) for putting in so much effort to ensure that others can have an amazing time. Niels Hatzmann was a gracious host, great biking partner, and now good friend.

A bulk of my work was with Debian and its developers. *I can't thank these developers enough.* Words can't capture how much I admire the ways in which you have managed to not only produce an operating system (OS) but also a stunningly vibrant online community—a word I rarely use for the Internet, and yet one that absolutely pertains to the case of Debian. I have thoroughly enjoyed my time with everyone as well, whether in person; on Internet Relay Chat (IRC), where countless folks have helped me answer questions and get through the many stages of writing and editing; and most especially, at the various Debconfs I have attended from Edinburgh to Porto Alegre. And after helping to organize Debconf10 in New York City, I was able to fully experience the unmistakable pride that swells when a collective works to conjure something into being. I am deeply grateful for the opportunity to have participated and look forward to attending many more in future times.

Though there are many developers who have taken the time to share their thoughts about Debian and other F/OSS projects, Benjamin "mako" Hill, in particular, has been a close friend and collaborator. I wish him well as he embarks on his own academic career and look forward to future collaborations. Martin Kraft, Clint Adams, Paul Wise, "vagrant," Joey Hess, Erinn Clark, and Daniel Khan Gilmore have also been great friends as well as teachers over this journey.

I returned to the University of Chicago in fall 2003 to write my dissertation, only to discover that really I had no idea how to proceed. Thankfully there were many others to teach me the ropes. An astounding range of people read different parts of my dissertation and gave me helpful feedback. There are a few who went beyond the call of duty, though. Alex "rex" Golub, who taught me more about liberalism than anyone else, really pushed me to think more systematically than I was used to at the time. Alex Choby has always been a steadfast long-distance interlocutor and also went for the extra mile to offer comments on my work on cleverness. James Rizzo was a fantastic editor with equally fantastic comments. Joe Hankins, Joe Feinberg, Jeff Martin, Andrea Muehlebach, Jessica Greenberg, Yarimar Bonilla, and Chris Walker also gave me copious feedback on this project. One of the reasons I have come to respect the University of Chicago is because of its student-run graduate workshops. I was known to make my rounds at various workshops, and the following students gave me great feedback throughout the last few years: Anya Bernsetin, Stephen Scott, Mike Cepek, Andrew Dilts. Alex Mawyer, Mihir Pandya, Anwen Tormey, Jason McGraw, Diana Bocarejo, and Tom Asher (and others who I don't know personally or may have forgotten). Many other professors in and out of the workshop system also read a few of the chapters and offered feedback, especially Tanya Luhrmann and Patchen Markell, who provided excellent advice on various chapters. Susan Gal, Manuela Carneiro Da Cunha, Michael Silverstein, Jessica Cattelinno, Joe Masco, and Judith Farquar at different points also read portions and provided helpful suggestions.

The dissertation formed the bulk of what became this book, which was written in diverse places and weather climates, from scorching summers in San Juan, Puerto Rico, to one of the coldest North American cities, Edmonton, Canada. While a postdoctoral fellow at the Center for Cultural Analysis at Rutgers University, I received useful comments from Meredith McGill, Michael Warner, Greg Lastowka, Paula McDowell, Ellen Goodman, Daniel Fisher, and especially Lisa Gitelman, and was also afforded a lively context from which to learn about intellectual property law from the angle of book history. At the University of Alberta, Rob Wilson, Kathleen Lowery, and my office mate Jeff Kochan also read various sections and chapters of the book. I finished a good chunk of the book thanks to the support (and amazing peace and quiet) provided by the Institute for Advanced Study. I would like to especially thank Didier Fassin and Tanya Erzen, whose insights have made their way into this book.

There are a few people who also have given important feedback on portions of this book, presented at conferences or other venues: Jelena Karanovic, Kathy Mancuso, Andrew Leonard, Nanodust, Martin Langhoff, Bill Sterner, Margot Browning, Jonas Smedegaard, Danny O'Brien, Cory Doctorow, Graham Jones, Thomas, Malaby, Alan Toner, Samir Chopra, Scott Dexter, Jonah Bossewitch, Marc Perlman, and Patrick Davison. Quinn Norton, whose expansive creativity and deep insight into all things geek aided me in toning down the academese, supplied great nuggets of wisdom and insight. Mary Murrell was kind enough to read the entire manuscript, and provide substantive insight and feedback on my arguments and the book's structure. I am so fortunate that I was able to teach material related to this topic and, especially, to such engaged students (and offer a hat tip to Parker Higgins, Max Salzberg, and Kevin Gotkin, in particular). Everyone in my "home away from home," #techfed, provided me with essential support throughout this process—humor—and many also offered their suggestions. Even if IRC has been known to draw my attention from writing, I could not have finished this book without it.

Two of my closest friends are everywhere in this book. Genevieve Lakier, the brightest woman I know, has read much of this book and pushed my thinking forward. Karl Fogel, an open-source developer and open access advocate, is not only featured in the pages of this book but read through many sections and chapters as well to make sure that my language, and thus arguments, were more precise.

For my first academic teaching position, I had the amazing fortune of landing at the Department of Media, Culture, and Communication at New York University—fortunate for the collegiality, commitment to excellence, and resources provided to junior faculty. I would like to thank my two chairs, Ted Magder and Marita Sturken, who went to bat for me many times, making New York University such a hospitable home from which to work. My New York University colleague Michael Ralph was one of the most engaging sounding boards, providing invaluable feedback especially on the question of cunning and craft among hackers. My research assistants, James Hodges, Parker Higgins, and especially Matthew Powers, helped enormously with making this book happen.

Various organizations provided me with generous funding, which has been essential for carrying out this research and writing. I graciously acknowledge support from the National Science Foundation Grant for a dissertation research grant, the Social Science Research Council for a research grant for the study of nonprofits, and the Woodrow Wilson National Fellowship Foundation's Charlotte W. Newcombe Doctoral Dissertation Fellowship for the study of religious and ethical values.

Parts of this book have also been published elsewhere, and have benefited tremendously from the anonymous reviewers and journal editors. The last section in chapter 1 was published as "Hacking in Person: The Ritual Character of Conferences and the Distillation of a Lifeworld," *Anthropological Quarterly* 83 (1): 47–72. An earlier version of chapter 5 was published as "Code Is Speech: Legal Tinkering, Expertise, and Protest among Free and Open-Source Software Developers," *Cultural Anthropology* 24 (3): 420–54. Sections of the conclusion can be found in "The Political Agnosticism of Free and Open-Source Software and the Inadvertent Politics of Contrast," *Anthropology Quarterly* 77 (3): 507–19.

I am extraordinarily fortunate that my book landed with Princeton University Press and Fred Appel. Fred has been such a lively editor and adviser, and I have so enjoyed our many chats over coffee and drinks, and look forward to many more in the future. To the anonymous reviewers: thank you for the kindness, generosity, and finely tuned comments that have been essential to completing this book.

One person has had the opportunity to see me through every last step of brainstorming, drafting, writing, rewriting, and complaining: Micah Anderson. For better and worse, he has experienced the public and private face of this project, graciously showering the pages with perceptive, lively, and especially humorous comments and edits on every last page, all the while providing steadfast support as we tromped from city to city under conditions that were for so many years often challenging. My gratitude is beyond words.

Finally, my family and adopted family have been an important source of strength. The Andersons were so patient and supportive as I hopped around cities all over North America, unable to see them as I spent so much time with my mother. My father has always placed great value on education, sacrificing many years of retirement so I could get a college education. In 2004, my sister made a significant sacrifice, moving in with my mother to take care of her, so I could finish my dissertation. From 2002–2010, my mother suffered a cruel illness that robbed her of her mind and soul. During those eight years, I traveled back and forth from wherever I was living to San Juan in order to be by her side. It was not always easy to live in a state of in-betweenness, in between cities, in between life and death, but I would not have had it any other way. Even though my mother is the one person close to me who will never be able to read any of this book, she made it possible in so many ways; I dedicate this book to my mother, Vera.

A Tale of Two Worlds

⤜∞⤏

Free and open-source software (F/OSS) refers to nonproprietary but licensed software, much of which is produced by technologists located around the globe who coordinate development through Internet-based projects. The developers, hackers, and system administrators who make free software routinely include the following artifact in the software they write:

> This program is distributed in the hope that it will be useful, but WITHOUT ANY WARRANTY; without even the implied warranty of MERCHANTABILITY or FITNESS FOR A PARTICULAR PURPOSE. See the GNU General Public License for more details.

While seemingly insignificant, this warning is quite meaningful for it reveals something important about the nature of free software and my subsequent representation of it. This legal notice is no doubt serious, but it also contains a subtle irony available to those who know about free software. For even if developers cannot legally guarantee the so-called FITNESS of software, they know that in many instances free software is often as useful as or in some cases superior to proprietary software. This fact brings hackers the same sort of pleasure, satisfaction, and pride that they derive when, and if, they are given free reign to hack. Further, even though hackers distribute their free software WITHOUT ANY WARRANTY, the law nevertheless enables them to create the software that many deem superior to proprietary software—software that they all "hope [. . .] will be useful." The freedom to labor within a framework of their own making is enabled by licenses that cleverly reformat copyright law to prioritize access, distribution, and circulation. Thus, hackers short-circuit the traditional uses of copyright: the right to exclude and control.

This artifact points to the GNU General Public License (GPL), an agreement that many hackers know well, for many use it (or other similar licenses) to transform their source code—the underlying directions of all software—into "free software." A quick gloss of the license, especially its preamble, reveals a more passionate language about freedom and rights:

> When we speak of free software, we are referring to freedom, not
> price. Our General Public Licenses are designed to make sure that you
> have the freedom to distribute copies of free software (and charge for
> this service if you wish), that you receive source code or can get it if
> you want it, that you can change the software or use pieces of it in new
> free programs; and that you know you can do these things.[1]

This type of language spills far beyond licensing agreements. It is routinely
voiced in public discourse and everyday conversation. Such commitments
to freedom, access, and transparency are formalized in a Linux distribution
known as Debian, one of the most famous free software projects. These
values are reflected in a pair of charters—the Debian Constitution and the
Debian Social Contract—that articulate an organizational vision and formulate a set of promises to the wider free software community. These charters' names alone unmistakably betray their liberal roots, even if they were
not explicitly created with the goal of "advancing" liberal ideals.

By liberalism, I do not mean what may first come to mind: a political
party in Europe usually associated with politicians who champion free
market solutions, or in the United States, a near synonym for the Democratic Party. Nor is it just an identity that follows from being a proud, card-
carrying member of the American Civil Liberties Union or Electronic Frontier Foundation, although these certainly can be markers.

Here I take liberalism to embrace historical as well as present-day moral
and political commitments and sensibilities that should be familiar to most
readers: protecting property and civil liberties, promoting individual autonomy and tolerance, securing a free press, ruling through limited government
and universal law, and preserving a commitment to equal opportunity and
meritocracy. These principles, which vary over time and place, are realized
institutionally and culturally in various locations at different times. Perhaps
the most famous of these are the institutions of higher education, market
policies set by transnational institutions, and the press, but they are also at
play on the Internet and with computer hackers, such as those who develop
free software.[2]

The small statement that prefaces the GNU GPL thus hints at two elements of this community: one is esoteric, and grounded in technology and
its material practices; and the other concerns a broader, culturally familiar
vision of freedom, free speech rights, and liberalism that harks back to constitutional ideals. We should not take either for granted but instead open
them up to critical reflection, and one route to do so is by bringing them
together. This ethnography takes seriously free software's visions of liberty
and freedom as well as the mundane artifacts that hackers take pleasure
and joy in creating. In considering them together, important lessons are revealed about the incomplete, sometimes fraught, but nonetheless noticeable

relationship between hacking and liberalism, and the transformations and tensions evident within the liberal tradition and computer hacking.

A LIBERAL CRITIQUE WITHIN LIBERALISM

The terms free and open as applied to software are distinct yet often come paired. This is in part because they designate the same alternative licenses and collaborative methodologies, but they differ in their moral orientation: the term free software foremost emphasizes the right to learn and access knowledge, while open source tends to flag practical benefits.[3] Many participants, whether they are volunteers or corporate employees paid to work on free software, refer to themselves with pride as hackers—computer aficionados driven by an inquisitive passion for tinkering and learning technical systems, and frequently committed to an ethical version of information freedom.

Although hackers hold multiple motivations for producing their software, collectively they are committed to *productive freedom*. This term designates the institutions, legal devices, and moral codes that hackers have built in order to autonomously improve on their peers' work, refine their technical skills, and extend craftlike engineering traditions. This ethnography is centrally concerned with how hackers have built a dense ethical and technical practice that sustains their productive freedom, and in so doing, how they extend as well as reformulate key liberal ideals such as access, free speech, transparency, equal opportunity, publicity, and meritocracy.

I argue that F/OSS draws from and also rearticulates elements of the liberal tradition. Rather than designating only a set of explicitly held political, economic, or legal views, I treat liberalism in its cultural registers.[4] Free software hackers culturally concretize a number of liberal themes and sensibilities—for example, through their competitive mutual aid, avid free speech principles, and implementation of meritocracy along with their frequent challenge to intellectual property provisions. Indeed, the ethical philosophy of F/OSS focuses on the importance of knowledge, self-cultivation, and self-expression as the vital locus of freedom. Hackers bring these values into being through an astounding range of social and technical practices, covered in detail throughout this book.

Because hackers challenge one strain of liberal jurisprudence, intellectual property, by drawing on and reformulating ideals from another one, free speech, the arena of F/OSS makes palpable the tensions between two of the most cherished liberal precepts—both of which have undergone a significant deepening and widening in recent decades. Thus, in its political dimension, and even if this point is left unstated by most developers and advocates, F/OSS represents a liberal critique from within liberalism. Hackers sit simultaneously at the center and margins of the liberal tradition.

The expansion of intellectual property law, as noted by some authors, is part and parcel of a broader neoliberal trend to privatize what was once public or under the state's aegis, such as health provision, water delivery, and military services. "Neoliberalism is in the first instance," writes David Harvey (2005, 2), "a theory of political economic practices that proposes human well-being can be best advanced by liberating entrepreneurial freedoms and skills within an institutional framework characterized by strong property rights, free markets, and free trade." As such, free software hackers not only reveal a long-standing tension within liberal legal rights but also offer a targeted critique of the neoliberal drive to make property out of almost anything, including software.

While most of this ethnography illustrates how free software hacking critiques neoliberal trends and reinvents liberal ideals by asserting a strong conception of productive freedom in the face of intellectual property restrictions, it also addresses the material, affective, and aesthetic dimensions of hacking. In pushing their personal capacities and technologies to new horizons (and encountering many frustrations along the way), hackers experience the joy that follows from the self-directed realization of skills, goals, and talents. At times, hacking provides experiences so completely overpowering, they hold the capacity to shred self-awareness, thus cutting into a particular conception of the liberal self—autonomous, authentic, and rational—that these hackers otherwise routinely advance. Thus, at least part of the reason that hacker ethics takes its liberal form is connected to the aesthetic experiences of hacking, which are informed by (but not reducible to) liberal idioms and grammars. Hacking, even if tethered to liberal ideologies, spills beyond and exceeds liberal tenets or liberal notions of personhood, most often melding with a more romantic sensibility concerned with a heightened form of individual expression, or in the words of political theorist Nancy Rosenblum (1987, 41), a "perfect freedom."

FIELDWORK AMONG HACKERS

For most of its history, anthropology stuck close to the study of non-Western and small-scale societies. This started to shift following a wave of internal and external critiques that first appeared in the 1960s, expanded in the 1970s, and peaked in the 1980s. Now referred to as "the critical turn in anthropology," the bulk of the critique was leveled against the discipline's signature concept: culture. Critics claimed that the notion of culture—as historically and commonly deployed—worked to portray groups as far more bounded, coherent, and timeless than they actually are, and worse, this impoverished rendition led to the omission of topics concerning power, class, colonialism, and capitalism (Abu-Lughod 1991; Asad 1973; Clifford 1988; Clifford and Marcus 1986; Dirks 1992; Said 1978). Among other effects, the critique cracked open new theoretical and topical vistas for anthropological inquiry. An anthropologist like myself, for example, could legitimately enter nontraditional "field sites" and address a new set of issues, which included those of technoscientific practice, information technologies, and other far-flung global processes stretching from labor migration to transnational intellectual property regulations.

Partly due to these disciplinary changes, in winter 2000, I left a snowy Chicago and arrived in a foggy San Francisco to commence what cultural anthropologists regard as our foundational methodological enterprise: fieldwork. Based on the imperative of total immersion, its driving logic is that we can gain analytic insight by inserting ourselves in the social milieu of those we seek to understand. Fieldwork mandates long-term research, usually a year or more, and includes a host of activities such as participating, watching, listening, recording, data collecting, interviewing, learning different languages, and asking many questions.

When I told peers of my plan to conduct fieldwork among hackers, many people, anthropologists and others, questioned it. How does one conduct fieldwork among hackers, given that they just hang out by themselves or on the Internet? Or among those who do not understand the name, given that they are all "outlaws"? Often playfully mocking me, many of my peers not only questioned how I would gather data but also routinely suggested that my fieldwork would be "so easy" (or "much easier than theirs") because I was studying hackers in San Francisco and on the Internet.

The subtext of this light taunting was easy enough to decipher: despite the transformations in anthropology that partially sanctioned my research as legitimate, my object of study nonetheless still struck them as patently atypical. My classmates made use of a socially acceptable medium—joking—to raise what could not be otherwise discussed openly: that my subjects of study, primarily North American and European (and some Latin American) hackers, were perhaps too close to my own cultural world for critical analysis, or perhaps that the very activity of computing (usually seen as an instrumental and solitary activity of pure rationality) could be subject only to thin, anemic cultural meanings.[5]

By the turn of the twenty-first century, although anthropology had certainly "reinvented" itself as a field of study—so that it is not only acceptable but one is in fact, at some level, also actively encouraged to study the West using new categories of analysis—Michel-Rolph Trouillot (2003, 13) has proposed that "anthropologists reenter the West cautiously, through the back door, after paying their dues elsewhere." As a young, aspiring anthropologist who was simply too keen on studying free software during graduate school and thus shirked her traditional dues, I knew that for myself as well as my peers, my project served as an object lesson in what constitutes an appropriate anthropological "location" (Gupta and Ferguson 1997) for study—in particular for graduate students and young scholars.

I myself wondered how I would ever recognize, much less analyze, forms of cultural value among a group of mostly men of relatively diverse class and national backgrounds who voluntarily band together online in order to create software. Would I have to stretch my ethnographic imagination too far? Or rely on a purely formal and semiotic analysis of texts and objects—a methodology I wanted for various reasons to avoid? Amid these fears, I took some comfort in the idea that, as my peers had indicated, my initial field-work would be free of much of the awkwardness that follows from thrusting oneself into the everyday lives of those who you seek to study, typically in an unfamiliar context. At the very least, I could communicate to hackers in English, live in a familiar and cosmopolitan urban setting, and at the end of the day, return to the privacy and comfort of my own apartment.

As it turned out, my early ethnographic experiences proved a challenge in many unexpected ways. The first point of contact, or put more poetically by Clifford Geertz (1977, 413), "the gust of wind stage" of research, was harder than I had imagined. Although not always discussed in such frank terms among anthropologists, showing up at a public gathering, sometimes unannounced, and declaring your intent to stay for months, or possibly years, is an extraordinarily difficult introduction to pull off to a group of people you seek to formally study. More difficult is describing to these strangers, whose typical understanding of anthropology stems from popular media representations like the Indiana Jones trilogy, our methodology of participant observation, which is undertheorized even among anthropologists.[6] Along with the awkwardness I experienced during the first few weeks of fieldwork, I was usually one of the only females present during hacker gatherings, and as a result felt even more out of place. And while I may have recognized individual words when hackers talked shop with each other—which accounted for a large percentage of their time—they might as well have been speaking another language.

At the start of my research period, then, I rarely wanted to leave my apartment to attend F/OSS hacker social events, user group meetings, or conferences, or participate on email lists or Internet relay chat channels—all of which were important sites for my research. But within a few months, my timidity and ambivalence started to melt away. The reason for this dramatic change of heart was a surprise to me: it was the abundance of humor and laughter among hackers. As I learned more about their technical world and was able to glean their esoteric jokes, I quickly found myself enjoying the endless stream of jokes they made in all sorts of contexts. During a dinner in San Francisco's Mission district, at the office while interning at the Electronic Frontier Foundation, or at the monthly gatherings of the Bay Area Linux User Group held in a large Chinatown restaurant, humor was a constant bedfellow.

Given the deep, bodily pleasures of laughter, the jovial atmosphere overcame most social barriers and sources of social discomfort, and allowed me to feel welcome among the hackers. It soon became clear to me, however, that this was not done for my benefit; humor saturates the social world of hacking. Hackers, I noticed, had an exhaustive ability to "misuse" most anything and turn it into grist for the humor mill. Once I began to master the esoteric and technical language of pointers, compilers, RFCs, i386, X86, AMD64, core dumps, shells, bash, man pages, PGP, GPG, gnupg, OpenPGP, pipes, world writeable, PCMCIA, chmod, syntactically significant white space, and so on (and really on and on), a rich terrain of jokes became sensible to me.

My enjoyment of hacker humor thus provided a recursive sense of comfort to a novice ethnographer. Along with personally enjoying their joshing around, my comprehension of their jokes indicated a change in my outsider status, which also meant I was learning how to read joking in terms of pleasure, creativity, and modes of being. Humor is not only the most crystalline expression of the pleasures of hacking (as I will explore later). It is also a crucial vehicle for expressing hackers' peculiar definitions of creativity and individuality, rendering partially visible the technocultural mode of life that is computer hacking. As with clever technical code, to joke in public allows hackers to conjure their most creative selves—a performative act that receives public (and indisputable) affirmation in the moment of laughter. This expression of wit solidifies the meaning of archetypal hacker selves: self-determined and rational individuals who use their well-developed faculties of discrimination and perception to understand the "formal" world—technical or not—around them with such perspicuity that they can intervene virtuously within this logical system either for the sake of play, pedagogy, · or technological innovation. In short, they have playfully defiant attitudes, which they apply to almost any system in order to repurpose it.

A few months into my research, I believed that the primary anthropological contribution of this project would reside in discussing the cultural mores of computer hacking, such as humor, conjoined with a methodological analysis of conducting research in the virtual space of bits and bytes. Later in my fieldwork, I came to see the significance of another issue: the close relationship between the ethics of free software and the normative, much broader regime of liberalism. Before expanding on this connection, I will first take a short ethnographic detour to specify *when* it became unmistakably apparent that this technical domain was a site where liberal ideals, notably free speech, were not only endowed with concrete meaning but also made the fault lines and cracks within liberalism palpably visible.

෴

It was August 29, 2001, and a typical San Francisco day. The abundant morning sun and deep blue skies deceptively concealed the reality of much cooler temperatures. I was attending a protest along with a group of about fifty programmers, system administrators, and free software enthusiasts who were demanding the release of a Russian programmer, Dmitry Sklyarov, arrested weeks earlier in Las Vegas by the Federal Bureau of Investigation (FBI) as he left Defcon, the largest hacker conference in the world. Arrested at the behest of the Silicon Valley software giant Adobe, Sklyarov was charged with violating the recently ratified and controversial Digital Millennium Copyright Act (DMCA). He had written a piece of software, the Advanced eBook Processor software, for his Russian employer. The application transforms the Adobe eBook format into the Portable Document Format (PDF). In order for the software to perform this conversion, it breaks and therefore circumvents the eBook's copy control measures. As such, the software violated the DMCA's anticircumvention clause, which states that "no person shall circumvent a technological protection measure that effectively controls access to a work protected under this measure."[7]

We had marched from the annual LinuxWorld conference being held in San Francisco's premier conference center, the Moscone Center, to the federal prosecutor's office. Along the way, a few homeless men offered solidarity by raising their fists. Two of them asked if we were marching to "Free Mumia"—an assumption probably influenced by the recent string of protests held in Mumia Abu-Jamal's honor. Indeed, as I learned soon after my first arrival in San Francisco, the city is one of the most active training grounds in the United States for radical activists. This particular spring and summer was especially abuzz with activity, given the prominence of counterglobalization mobilizations. But this small and intimate demonstration was not typical among the blizzard of typically left-of-center protests, for none of the participants had a way of conveying quickly nor coherently the nature of the arrest, given how it was swimming in an alphabet soup of acronyms, such as DRM, DMCA, and PDF, as opposed to more familiar ideas like justice and racism. A few members of our entourage nonetheless heartily thanked our unlikely though clearly sympathetic supporters, and assured them that while not as grave as Mumia's case, Dmitry's situation still represented an unfair targeting by a corrupt criminal justice system, especially since he was facing up to twenty-five years in jail "simply for writing software."

Once at the Hall of Justice, an impassioned crew of programmers huddled together and held up signs, such as "Do the Right Thing," "Coding Is Not a Crime," and "Code Is Speech."

There must have been something about directly witnessing such fiery outpourings among people who tend to shy away from overt forms of political action that led me to evaluate anew the deceptively simple claim: code is speech. It dawned on me that day that while I had certainly heard this assertion before (and in fact, I was only hearing it increasingly over time), it was more significant than I had earlier figured. And after some research,

FIGURE INTRO.1. Protesting the DMCA, San Francisco
Photo: Ed Hintz.

it was clear that while the link between free speech and source code was fast becoming entrenched as the new technical common sense among many hackers, its history was remarkably recent. Virtually nonexistent in published discourse before the early 1990s, this depiction now circulates widely and is routinely used to make claims against the indiscriminate application of intellectual property law to software production.

Early in my research, I was well aware that the production of free software was slowly but consistently dismantling the ideological scaffolding supporting the expansion of copyright and patent law into new realms of production, especially in the US and transnational context. Once I considered how hackers question one central pillar of liberal jurisprudence, intellectual property, by reformulating ideals from another one, free speech, it was evident that hackers also unmistakably revealed the fault line between two cherished sets of liberal principles.

While the two-hundred-year history of intellectual property has long been freighted with controversies over the scope, time limits, and purpose of various of its instruments (Hesse 2002; Johns 2006, 2010; McGill 2002), legal scholars have only recently given serious attention to the uneasy coexistence between free speech and intellectual property principles (McLeod 2007; Netanel 2008; Nimmer 1970; Tushnet 2004). Copyright law, in granting creators significant control over the reproduction and circulation of their work, limits the deployment of copyrighted material in other expressive activity, and consequently censors the public use of certain forms of expressive content. Legal scholar Ray Patterson (1968, 224) states this dynamic eloquently in terms of a clash over the fundamental values of a democratic society: "A society which has freedom of expression as a basic principle of liberty restricts that freedom to the extent that it vests ideas with legally protected property interests."

Because a commitment to free speech and intellectual property is housed under the same roof—the US Constitution—the potential for conflict has long existed. For most of their legal existence, however, conflict was noticeably absent, largely because the scope of both free speech and intellectual property law were more contained than they are today. It was only during the course of the twentieth-century that the First Amendment and intellectual property took on the unprecedented symbolic and legal meanings they now command in the United States as well as many other nations. (Although the United States has the broadest free speech protections in the world, many other Western nations, even if they limit the scope of speech, have also expanded free speech and intellectual property protections in the last fifty years.)

For example, copyright, which grants authors significant control over their expression of ideas, was initially limited to fourteen years with one opportunity for renewal. Today, the copyright term in the United States has ballooned to the length of the author's life plus seventy years, while works for hire get ninety-five years, regardless of the life of the author. The original registration requirement has also been eliminated. Most any expression—a scribble on a piece of paper, a blog post, or a song—automatically qualifies for protection, so long as it represents the author's creation.

Free speech jurisprudence follows a similar trajectory. Even though the Constitution famously states that "Congress shall make no law [. . .] abridging the freedom of speech, or of the press," during the first half of the twentieth century the US Supreme Court curtailed many forms of speech, such as political pamphleteering, that are now taken to represent the heart and soul of the democratic process. It is thus easy to forget that the current shape of free speech protections is a fairly recent social development, largely contained within the last fifty years (Bollinger and Stone 2002).

Due to the growing friction between free speech and intellectual property, US courts in the last twenty-five years have openly broached the issue by asserting that any negative consequences of censoring speech are far outweighed by the public benefit of copyright law. In other words, as a matter of public policy, copyright law represents an acceptable restriction on speech because it is the basis for what is designated as "the marketplace of ideas."[8] The theory animating the marketplace of ideas is that if and when ideas are allowed to publicly compete with each other, the truth—or in its less positivist form, the best policy—will become evident.

Given this historical trajectory, the use of F/OSS licenses challenges the current, intellectual property regime, growing ever more restrictive, and thus dubbed ominously by one legal scholar as the contemporary motor for "the second enclosure movement" (Boyle 2003). Many free software developers do not consider intellectual property instruments as the pivotal stimulus for a marketplace of ideas and knowledge. Instead, they see them as a form of restriction so fundamental (or poorly executed) that they need to be counteracted through alternative legal agreements that treat knowledge, inventions, and other creative expressions not as property but rather as speech to be freely shared, circulated, and modified.

THE AESTHETICS OF HACKING

If free software hackers render the tensions between two liberal principles visible, and offer a targeted, if not wholesale, critique of neoliberalism in challenging intellectual property law (but rarely using the language of neoliberalism), their commitment to free speech also puts forth a version of the liberal person who strays from the dominant ideas of liberal personhood: a self-interested consumer and rational economic seeker. Among academics, this has often been placed under the rubric of "possessive individualism," defined as "those deeply internalized habits of thinking and feeling [. . .] viewing everything around them primarily as actual or potential commercial property" (Graeber 2007, 3; see also Macpherson 1962). Among hackers, selfhood has a distinct register: an autonomous being guided by and committed to rational thought, critical reflection, skills, and capacity—a set of commitments presupposed in the free speech doctrine (Peters 2005).[9]

However important these expressive and rational impulses are among programmers, they don't fully capture the affective stances of hackers, most notably their deep engagement, sometimes born of frustration, and at other times born of pleasure, and sometimes, these two converge. Soon after commencing fieldwork, what I quickly learned is that hacking is characterized by a confluence of constant occupational disappointments *and* personal/collective joys. As many writers have noted, and as I routinely observed, hacking, whether in the form of programming, debugging (squashing errors), or running and maintaining systems (such as servers), is consistently frustrating (Rosenberg 2007; Ullman 2003). Computers/software are *constantly* malfunctioning, interoperability is frequently a nightmare to realize, users are often "clueless" about the systems they use (and therefore break them or require constant help), the rate and pace of technological change is relentless, and meeting customer expectations is nearly impossible to pull off predictably. The frustration that generally accompanies the realities of even mundane technical work is depicted as swimming with sharks in *xkcd*, one of the most beloved geeks' comic strips (figure Intro.2).

What this comic strip captures is how hackers, as they work, sometimes swim in seas of frustration. To tinker, solve problems, and produce software, especially over one's lifetime, will invariably be marked by varying degrees of difficulties and missteps—a state of laboring that one theorist of craftspersonship describes as material "resistance" (Sennett 2008). In encountering obstacles, adept craftspeople, such as hackers, must also build an abundant "tolerance for frustration" (ibid., 226), a mode of coping that at various points will break down, leading, at best, to feelings of frustration, and at worst, to anguish and even despair and burnout.

Despite these frustrations and perhaps because of them, the craft of hacking demands a deep engagement from hackers, or a state of being most commonly referred to in the literature as "flow" (Csikszentmihalyi 1990).

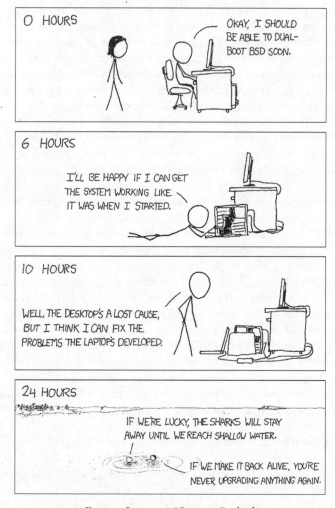

FIGURE INTRO.2. "Success," *xkcd*
Credit: Randall Munroe.

In its more mild and commonplace form, hacker pleasure could be said to approximate the Aristotelian theory of eudaemonia, defined succinctly by philosopher Martha Nussbaum (2004, 61) as "the unimpeded performance of the activities that constitute happiness." In pushing their personal capacities and skills though playing around with and making technologies, hackers experience the joy that follows from the self-directed realization of skills, goals, and talents. Indeed, overcoming resistance and solving problems, some of them quite baffling, is central to the sense of accomplishment and pride that hackers routinely experience.

Hacker pleasure, however, is not always so staid and controlled; it far exceeds the pride of eudaemonia. Less frequently, but still occurring often, hackers experience a more obsessive and blissful state. Hacker descriptions of immersing themselves in technology remind me of Rainer Maria Rilke's terse and beautiful depiction of the passion that drives his intellectual pursuits: "All the soarings of my mind begin in my blood." This form of pleasure approximates what Roland Barthes (1975) has portrayed as bliss or jouissance—a pleasure so complete, engrossing, and enveloping that it has the capacity to obliterate every last shred of self-awareness. In native hack jargon, the state of bliss is the "Deep Hack Mode." Matt Welsh, a well-known hacker and computer scientist, humorously describes the utter magnetism of this mode, "very few phenomena can pull someone out of Deep Hack Mode, with two noted exceptions: being struck by lightning, or worse, your *computer* being struck by lightning."[10]

Because hackers often submit their will and being to technology—and are famous for denying their bodies sleep, at least for short periods—the joy that hackers derive from attending to and carefully sculpting technologies are at times experienced as transcendent bliss. In these moments, utility is exceeded. The self can at once express its most inner being and collapse within the objects of its creation. In the aftermath of a particularly pleasurable moment of hacking, there is no autonomous liberal self to be found.

To be sure, these forms of pleasure and engagement were impossible for me, the ethnographer, to touch and feel. But I routinely witnessed the social markers of the joy of hacking, as hackers talked shop with each other, as they joked about technical minutiae, and especially during their festive hacker celebrations. The key point is that the multifaceted pleasures of hacking signal that utility is not the only driving force in hackers' creative acts. Although hackers are fiercely pragmatic and utilitarian—technology after all must work, and work exceptionally well—they are also fiercely poetic and repeatedly affirm the artistic elements of their work. One of the clearest expressions of technology/software as art is when source code is written as poetry, or alternatively when poetry is written in source code (Black 2002). For many free software hackers, the act of writing software and learning from others far exceeds the simple enactment of an engineering ethic, or a technocratic calculus for the sake of becoming a more proficient as well as efficient programmer or system administrator.

This is hacking in its more romantic incarnation—a set of characterizations and impulses that hold an affinity with liberalism, and yet also stray into different, largely aesthetic and emotional territory. Liberalism, as a body of thought, certainly allows for pleasure, but for the most part does not theorize the subjective and aesthetic states of pleasure, which the Romantic tradition has centralized and made its own. Romanticism, explains

Rosenblum (1987, 10), is a "lavish departure from sober individualism," but also "amounts to an exploitation of liberal ideals." Although it is important to differentiate liberal from romantic sensibilities, they nonetheless can co-exist without much friction, as Rosenblum contends in her account on Romanticism. She draws on various prominent historical figures, such as John Stuart Mill and Henry David Thoreau, to examine the compatibilities and symbiosis between liberalism and Romanticism. Hackers, borrowing from free speech commitments *and* also committed to aesthetic experiences, are a social group whose sensibilities lie at the interface between a more rational liberal calculus and a more aesthetic, inward-looking one.

Hackers are not alone in embracing this aesthetic, expressive sensibility, which philosopher Charles Taylor (1992) argues persuasively is a fundamental part of our contemporary imaginary, or what he calls the "expressive self." First visibly emerging in the eighteenth century, this sentiment formed the basis for "a new fuller individualism," and places tremendous weight on originality, sentiments, creativity, and at times, even disengagement. What must be noted is that expressive individualism and the moral commitments it most closely entails—self-fulfillment, self-discovery, and self-improvement—can be secured, as many critics have shown, through consumption, self-help, human enhancement technologies, and body modification (Bellah et al. 1985; Elliott 2003; Hogle 2005), and thus can converge seamlessly with elements of possessive individualism. Today to liberate and express the "authentic," "expressive" self is usually synonymous with a life-long engagement with consumption, fine tuned by a vast advertising apparatus that helps sustain the desire for a seemingly limitless number of consumer goods and, increasingly, human enhancement technologies such as plastic surgery.

The example set by free software (and a host of similar craftlike practices), however, should make us at least skeptical of the extent to which an ethic of consumption has colonized expressive individualism. Free software hackers undoubtedly affirm an expressive self rooted not in consumption but rather in production in a double sense: they produce software, and through this technical production, they also sustain informal social relations and even have built institutions. Given the different ethical implications entailed in these visions of fulfillment, expression, and self-development (consumerist versus productive self), it behooves us to analytically pry them apart.

While the liberal articulations made by free software hackers, notably those of free speech, carry a familiar political imprint, their material experiences, the frustrations and pleasures of hacking, (including the particularities of making, breaking, and improving software) might seem politically irrelevant. Yet the passionate commitment to hacking and especially the ethics of access enshrined in free software licensing, express as well as celebrate unalienated, autonomous labor, which also broadcasts a powerful political message. A number of theorists (Galloway 2004; Söderberg 2007; Wark 2004) have previously highlighted this phenomenon. Hackers insistence on never losing access to the fruits of their labor—and indeed actively seeking to share these fruits with others—calls into being Karl Marx's famous critique of estranged labor: "The external character of labour for the worker appears in the fact that it is not his own, but someone else's, that it does not belong to him, that in it he belongs, not to himself, but to another" (Marx and Engels 1978, 74). It evokes Marx's vision precisely because free software developers seek to avoid the forms of estrangement that have long been nearly synonymous with capitalist production. Freedom is thus not only based on the right to speak free of barriers but also conceived as (although primarily through practice) "the utopian promise of unalienated labor, of human flourishing through creative and self-actualizing production," as Barton Beebe (2010, 885) aptly describes it.

F/OSS hacker morality is therefore syncretic—a quality that is also patently evident in its politics. It enunciates a liberal politics of free speech and liberty that speaks to an audience beyond hackers as well as a nonliberal politics of cultural pleasure and political detachment, which is internally and intensely focused on the practice of hacking only and entirely for its own sake, although certainly inspiring others to follow in their footsteps. When assessing the liberal ethics and affective pleasure of hacking, we should not treat pleasure as the authentic face of hacking, and the other (liberalism) as an ideological veneer simply in need of debunking (or in need of celebrating). From an ethnographic vantage point, it is important to recognize many hackers are citizens of liberal democracies, and have drawn on the types of accessible liberal tropes—notably free speech—as a means to conceptualize their technical practice and secure novel political claims. And in the process, they have built institutions and sustain norms through which they internalize these liberal ideals as meaningful, all the while clearly upholding a marked commitment to unalienated labor.

ON REPRESENTING HACKER ETHICS

If I was comforted by the fact that hacking could be analyzed in light of cultural issues like humor, liberalism, and pleasure, and that I had some methodological tools at my disposal to do so, as I learned more about hacking, my ease vanished as I confronted a new set of concerns. I increasingly grew wary of how I would convey to others the dynamic vitality and diversity that marks hackers and hacking, but also the points of contention among them. To further illustrate this point, allow me to share a brief story.

Soon after ending my official fieldwork, I was having dinner in Chicago with three local free software developers. One of them asked me about some of my memorable fieldwork experiences. There were many stories I could have chosen, but I started to tell the story of a speech by Kevin Mitnick—a more transgressive hacker (for he had engaged in illegal behavior) than most free software developers and one of the most infamous of all time—that I heard during summer 2004 at Hackers on Planet Earth (HOPE)—a conference founded in 1994 to publicize his legal ordeals. Mitnick is known to have once been a master "social engineer," or one who distills the aesthetics of illicit acts into the human art of the short cons. Instead of piercing through a technological barricade, social engineers target humans, duping them in their insatiable search for secret information. Because of various legendary (and at times, illegal) computer break-ins, often facilitated by his social engineering skills, Mitnick spent a good number of his adult years either running from the law or behind bars, although he never profited from his hacks, nor destroyed any property (Coleman and Golub 2008; Mitnick 2011; Thomas 2003).

In July 2004, free at last and allowed to use computers again, Mitnick attended HOPE in New York City for the first time. He delivered his humorous and enticing keynote address to an overflowing crowd of hackers, who listened, enraptured, to the man who had commanded their political attention for over a decade as part of a "Free Kevin Campaign." He offered tale after tale about his clever pranks of hacking from childhood on: "I think I was born as a hacker because at ten I was fascinated with magic," he explained. "I wanted a bite of the forbidden fruit." Even as a kid, his victims were a diverse lot: his homeroom teacher, the phone company, and even the Los Angeles Rapid Transit District. After he bought the same device used by bus drivers for punching transfers, he adopted the persona of Robin Hood, spending hours riding the entire bus network, punching his own pirated transfers to give to customers. He found transfer stubs while dumpster diving, another time-honored hacker practice for finding information that was especially popular before the advent of paper shredding. Despite the way that lawyers and journalists had used Mitnick's case to give hackers a bad name, Mitnick clearly still used the term with pride.

When I finished my story describing what I personally thought was a pretty engrossing speech, one hacker, who obviously disapproved of my reference to Mitnick as a "hacker," replied, "Kevin is *not* a hacker. He is a cracker." In the mid-1980s, some hackers created the term cracker to deflect the negative images of them that began appearing in the media at that time. According to *The Hacker Jargon File*, crackers are those who hack for devious, malicious, or illegal ends, while hackers are simply technology enthusiasts. Although some hackers make the distinction between crackers and hackers, others also question the division. To take one example, during an interview, one free software hacker described this labeling as "a whitewashing of what kind of people are involved in hacking. [. . .] Very often the same techniques that are used in hacking 2 [the more illegal kind] are an important part of hacking 1."

To be sure, hackers can be grasped by their similarities. They tend to value a set of liberal principles: freedom, privacy, and access. Hackers also tend to adore computers—the glue that binds them together—and are trained in specialized and esoteric technical arts, primarily programming, system, or Net administration, security research, and hardware hacking. Some gain unauthorized access to technologies, though the degree of illegality varies greatly (and much of hacking is legal). Foremost, hacking, in its different forms and dimensions, embodies an aesthetic where craft and craftiness tightly converge. Hackers thus tend to value playfulness, pranking, and cleverness, and will frequently perform their wit through source code, humor, or both: humorous code.

Hackers, however, evince considerable diversity and are notoriously sectarian, constantly debating the meaning of the words hack, hacker, and hacking. Yet almost *all* academic and journalistic work on hackers commonly whitewashes these differences, and defines all hackers as sharing a singular "hacker ethic." Offering the first definition in *Hackers: Heroes of the Computer Revolution*, journalist Steven Levy (1984, 39) discovered among a couple of generations of MIT hackers a unique as well as "daring symbiosis between man and machine," where hackers placed the desire to tinker, learn, and create technical beauty above all other goals. The hacker ethic is shorthand for a list of tenets, and it includes a mix of aesthetic and pragmatic imperatives: a commitment to information freedom, a mistrust of authority, a heightened dedication to meritocracy, and the firm belief that computers can be the basis for beauty and a better world (ibid., 39–46).

In many respects, the fact that academics, journalists, and hackers alike refer to the existence of this ethic is a testament not only to the superb account that Levy offers—it is still one of the finest works on hacking—but also to the fact that the hacker ethic in the most general sense is an apt way to describe some contemporary ethics and aesthetics of hacking. For example, many of the principles motivating free software philosophy reinstantiate, refine, extend, and clarify many of those original precepts. Further, and rarely acknowledged, Levy's account helped set into motion a heightened form of reflexivity among hackers. Many hackers refer to their culture and ethics. It is an instance of what Marshall Sahlins (2000, 197; see also Carneiro da Cunha 2009) describes as "contemporary culturalism"—a form of "cultural self-awareness" that renders culture into an "objectified value." This political dynamic of self-directed cultural representation is suggested in the following quote by Seth Schoen, an avid free software advocate and staff technologist at the Electronic Frontier Foundation. In the first line of text that appears on his Web page, Schoen announces, with pride: "I read [Levy's *Hackers*] as a teenager. [. . .] I was like, 'God damn it, I should be here!' Then, about ten years later, I thought back about it: 'You know, if there was a fourth section in that book, maybe I would be in there!' That's a nice thought."[11]

As I delved deeper into the cultural politics of hacking, though, I began to see serious limitations in making any straightforward connections between the hacker ethic of the past and the free software of the present (much less other hacker practices). Most obviously, to do so is to overlook how ethical precepts take actual form and, more crucially, how they transform over time. For example, in the early 1980s, "the precepts of this revolutionary Hacker Ethic," Levy (1984, 39; emphasis added) observes, "were not so much debated and discussed as silently agreed upon. *No Manifestos were issued.*" Yet (and somewhat ironically) a mere year after the publication of his book, MIT programmer Richard Stallman charted the Free Software Foundation (FSF) ([1996] 2010) and issued "The GNU Manifesto," insisting "that the golden rule requires that if I like a program I must share it with other people who like it."[12] Today, hacker manifestos are commonplace. If hackers did not discuss the intricacies of ethical questions when Levy first studied them, over the span of two decades they would come to argue about ethics, and sometimes as heatedly as they argue over technology. And now many hackers recognize ethical precepts as one important engine driving their productive practices—a central theme to be explored in this book.

Additionally, and as the Mitnick example provided above illustrates so well, the story of the hacker ethic works to elide the tensions that exist among hackers as well as the different genealogies of hacking. Although hacker ethical principles may have a common core—one might even say a general ethos—ethnographic inquiry soon demonstrates that similar to any cultural sphere, we can easily identify great variance, ambiguity, and even serious points of contention.

Therefore, once we confront hacking in anthropological and historical terms, some similarities melt into a sea of differences. Some of these distinctions are subtle, while others are profound enough to warrant what I, along with Alex Golub, have elsewhere called genres of hacking (Coleman and Golub 2008). F/OSS hackers, say, tend to uphold political structures of transparency when collaborating. In contrast, the hacker underground, a more subversive variant of hacking, is more opaque in its modes of social organization (Thomas 2003). Indeed, these hackers have made secrecy and spectacle into something of a high art form (Coleman 2012b). Some hackers run vibrant technological collectives whose names—Riseup and Mayfirst—unabashedly broadcast that their technical crusade is to make this world a better one (Milberry 2009). Other hackers—for example, many "infosec" (information security) hackers—are first and foremost committed to security, and tend to steer clear of defining their actions in such overtly political terms—even if hacking usually tends to creep into political territory. Among those in the infosec community there are differences of opinion as to whether one should release a security vulnerability (often called full disclosure) or just announce its existence without revealing details (referred to as antidisclosure). A smaller, more extreme movement that goes by the name of antisec is vehemently against any disclosure, claiming, for instance, in one manifesto that it is their "goal that, through mayhem and the destruction of all exploitive and detrimental communities, companies, and individuals, full-disclosure will be abandoned and the security industry will be forced to reform."[13] There is also an important, though currently untold, story about gaming and hacking, not only because hackers created some of the first computer games, notably Space Wars, written in 1962, but because of the formal similarities between gaming and hacking as well (Dibbell 2006).

National and regional differences make their mark as well. For instance, southern European hackers have followed a more leftist, anarchist tradition than their northern European counterparts. Chinese hackers are quite nationalistic in their aims and aspirations (Henderson 2007), in contrast to those in North America, Latin America, and Europe, whose antiauthoritarian stance makes many—though certainly not all—wary of joining government endeavors.

Finally, while the brilliance of Levy's account lies in his ability to demonstrate how ethical precepts fundamentally inhere in hacker technical practice, it is important to recognize that hacker ethics, past and present, are not entirely of their own making. Just a quick gloss of the language many hackers frequently invoke to describe themselves or formulate ethical claims— freedom, free speech, privacy, the individual, and meritocracy—reveals that many of them unmistakably express liberal visions and romantic sensibilities: "We believe in freedom of speech, the right to explore and learn by doing," explains one hacker editorial, "and the tremendous power of the individual."[14] Once we recognize the intimate connection between hacker ethics and liberal commitments *and* the diversity of ethical positions, it is clear that hackers provide less of a unitary and distinguishable ethical position, and more of a mosaic of interconnected, but at times divergent, ethical principles.

Given this diversity, to which I can only briefly allude here, the hacker ethic should not be treated as a singular code formulated by some homogeneous group called hackers but instead as a composite of distinct yet connected moral genres. Along with a common set of moral referents, what hacker genres undoubtedly share is a certain relation to legality. Hacker actions or their artifacts are usually either in legally dubious waters or at the cusp of new legal meaning. Hence, they make *visible* emerging or contentious dilemmas.

Although hackers certainly share a set of technical and ethical commitments, and are in fact tied together by virtue of their heated debates over their differences, given the existence of the diversity just noted, my claims and arguments should not be taken as representative of all hacking, even though for the sake of simplicity (and stylistic purposes), in the chapters that follow I will often just refer to hackers and hacking. My discussion is more modest and narrow for it will stick primarily to the example of free software.[15] My preference for announcing the "self-conscious, serious partiality" (Clifford 1986, 7) of this account comes from witnessing motivations, ethical perceptions, desires, and practices far more plastic, flexible, sublime, contradictory, and especially fiery and feverish than usually accounted for in academic theories. The world of hacking, as is the case with many cultural worlds, is one of reckless blossoming, or in the words of Rilke: "Everything is blooming most recklessly; if it were voices instead of colors, there would be an unbelievable shrieking into the heart of the night."

OMISSIONS AND CHAPTER OVERVIEW

Some readers may be asking why I have not addressed Silicon Valley entrepreneurship and Web 2.0, both of which might further illuminate the ethics and politics of F/OSS.[16] For those interested in Web 2.0—a term that is bandied around to refer to nearly all contemporary digital tools and the social practices that cluster around these technologies—you might want to jump to the short epilogue, where I critique this term. It is a moniker that obscures far more than it reveals, for it includes such a wide range of disparate phenomena, from corporate platforms like Flickr, to free software projects, to dozens of other digital phenomena. In fact, by exploring in detail free software's sociocultural dynamics, I hope this book will make it more difficult to group free software in with other digital formations such as YouTube, as the media, pundits, and some academics regularly do under the banner of Web 2.0.

The relationship between Silicon Valley and open source is substantial as well as complicated. Without a doubt, when it comes to computers, hackers, and F/OSS, this high-tech region matters, as I quickly came to learn within weeks of my arrival there. For the last thirty years, hackers have flocked to the Bay Area from around the world to make it one of their most cherished homelands, although it certainly is not the only region where hackers have settled and set deep roots. At the turn of this century, open source also became the object of Silicon Valley entrepreneurial energy, funding, and hype, even though today the fever for open source has diminished significantly, redirected toward other social media platforms.

The book is thus not primarily about free software in Silicon Valley. In many respects my material tilts toward the North American and European region but, nevertheless, I have chosen to treat free software in more general than regional registers as well, so as to capture the reality of the legal transnational processes under investigation along with the experience of the thousands and thousands of developers across the world. Debian, for example, has developers from Japan, Australia, Canada, New Zealand, all over western and eastern Europe, Brazil, Venezuela, Argentina, and Mexico.[17] I decided on this approach as it is important to demonstrate different values and dynamics at play than those found in Silicon Valley, which are too often mistaken to represent *the* commitments of all engineers, computer scientists, and hackers.[18]

Coding Freedom is composed of six chapters, divided conceptually into pairs of two. The first two chapters are historically informed, providing the reader with a more general view of free software. Chapter 1 ("The Life of a Free Software Hacker") provides what is a fairly typical life history of a F/OSS hacker from early childhood to the moment of discovering the "gems" of free software: source code. Compiled from over seventy life histories, I demonstrate how hackers interact and collaborate through virtual technologies, how they formulate liberal discourses through virtual interactions, how they came to learn about free software, and how they individually and collectively experience the pleasures of hacking. I also offer an extended discussion of the hacker conference, which I argue is the ritual (and pleasurable) underside of discursive publics. Chapter 2 ("A Tale of Two Legal Regimes") presents what were initially two semi-independent legal regimes that over the last decade have become intertwined. The first story pertains to free software's maturity into a global movement, and the second turns to the globalization and so-called harmonization of intellectual property provisions administered through global institutional bodies like the World Trade Organization. By showing how these trajectories interwove, I emphasize various unexpected and ironic outcomes as I start to elaborate a single development that will continue to receive considerable treatment later in the book: the cultivation, among hackers, of a well-developed legal consciousness.

The next two chapters provide a close ethnographic analysis of free software production. Chapter 3 ("The Craft and Craftiness of Hacking") presents the central motif of value held by hackers by examining the practices of programming, joking, and norms of socialization through which they produce software and their hacker selves. Partly by way of humor, I tackle a series of social tensions that mark hacker interactions: individualism and collectivism, populism and elitism, hierarchy and equality as well as artistry and utility. These tensions are reflected but also partially attenuated through the expression of wit, especially jokes, and even funny code, whereby jokes ("easter eggs") are included in source code. Chapter 4 ("Two Ethical Moments in Debian") addresses ethical cultivation as it unfolds in the largest free software project in the world—Debian. This project is composed of over one thousand developers who produce a distribution of the Linux operating system (OS). I present and theorize on the tensions between Debian's governance, which blends democratic majoritarian rule, a guildlike meritocracy, and ad hoc deliberations. In comparing these three modes of governance, I unearth various ethical processes—informal, formal, pedagogical, and dramatic—by which Debian developers inhabit a liberally based philosophy of free software, and use it as an opportunity to revisit the tension between liberal individualism and corporate sociality explored earlier.

The final two chapters engage with more overtly political questions, examining two different and contrasting political elements of free software. Chapter 5 ("Code Is Speech") addresses two different types of legal pedagogy common among free software developers. First, in the context of Debian, I look at everyday legal learning, where debating and learning about the law is an integral part of project life. I then compare this with a series of dramatic arrests, lawsuits, and political protests that unfolded between 1999–2004 in the United States, Europe, and Russia, and on the Internet, and that allowed for a more explicit set of connections to be drawn between code and speech. These demonstrations were launched against what was, at the time, a relatively new copyright statute, the DMCA, and the arrest of two programmers. These multiyear protests worked, I argue, to stabilize a relatively nascent cultural claim—nearly nonexistent before the early 1990s—that source code should be protected speech under the First Amendment (or among non-American developers, protected under free speech laws). In contrast to the political avowal of the DMCA protests, my conclusion ("The Politics of Disavowal and the Cultural Critique of Intellectual Property Law") discusses how and why hackers disavow engagement in broad-based politics, and instead formulate a narrow politics of software freedom. Because a commitment to the F/OSS principles is what primarily binds hackers together, and because many developers so actively disavow political associations that go beyond software freedom, I contend that the technoscientific project of F/OSS has been able to escape the various ideological polarizations (such as liberal versus conservative) so common in our current political climate. F/OSS has thus been taken up by a wide array of differently positioned actors and been placed in a position of significant social legibility whereby it can publicly perform its critique of intellectual property law.

Finally, to end this introduction, it is worth noting that this book is not only an ethnography but also already an archive of sorts. All cultural formations and ethical commitments are, of course, in motion, undergoing transformation, and yet many technological worlds, such as free software, undergo relentless change. What is written in the forthcoming pages will provide a discrete snapshot of F/OSS largely between 1998 and 2005. Much of this book will still ring true at the time of its publication, while other elements have come and gone, surely to have left a trace or set of influences, but no longer in full force. And despite my inability to provide a warranty for this archival ethnography, I hope such an account will be useful in some way.

PART I

HISTORIES

ᴄᴆᎧᏳᴌ

While we read history we make history.
—George William Curtis, *The Call of Freedom*

The next two chapters are general in their scope, meant to introduce readers to the world of free software, and do so from two related although distinct vantage points, both historically informed. Chapter 1, as mentioned above, describes a typical life history compiled from over fifty in-person interviews along with twenty email and/or Internet Relay Chat (IRC) interviews. It portrays everyday life and historical transformation as many experience it: in a mundane register, and without the awareness that we are making or are part of history. What it seeks to show is how hackers become hackers slowly over time and through a range of varied activities. This process, though experienced in quotidian ways, is ultimately a historical affair, for the hackers of yesteryear are not quite the same as those of today, despite crucial continuities. The first chapter tracks some of the changes within free software and also provides basic sociological data about free software developers: where they learned to program, where they work, and how they interact with other developers.

Chapter 2 turns away from personal accounts to tell a more global story. It traces two distinct but overlapping legal trajectories and their eventual clash. During the same period in which intellectual property law assumed tremendous and global regulatory power, free software also rose to prominence, eventually providing one of the most robust challenges ever to intellectual property laws. The legal alternatives made and supported by free software did not always follow from politically motivated action, but rather from the experiences involved in the production of free software. These experiences were formative, leading a generation of hackers to become astute legal thinkers and producers—knowledge that was in turn eventually marshaled for political protest against the current intellectual property regime.

Before turning to these two chapters, it is worth highlighting how historical representation is a delicate play of fabrications, or stated a little more eloquently by Voltaire in his short story "Jeannot et Colin, "fables agreed upon." By fable, I don't mean false, yet it is imperative to acknowledge the constructed nature of the accounts. Choices have to be made about what to include, what to exclude, and most important, *how* to include them. For the life history chapter, I have chosen stories, elements, and events that I hope faithfully capture the zeitgeist of becoming a free software hacker, ending with one of the most memorable hacker events: the hacker conference. The subsequent chapter, by examining the dual character of our age, whereby we are subject to an omnipresent legal system and also have at our disposal a vibrant set of legal alternatives, is meant to inspire a paradoxical degree of hope and despair, thereby contributing, in its reading, to the making of history.

CHAPTER 1

The Life of a Free Software Hacker

ೊ⊚ഌ

> One may say that true life begins where the tiny bit begins—where
> what seems to us minute and infinitely small alterations take place.
> True life is not lived where great external changes take place—
> where people move about, clash, fight and slay one another—it is
> lived only where these tiny, tiny infinitesimal changes occur.
> —Leo Tolstoy, "Why Do Men Stupefy Themselves?"

THE BASIC "SPECS" OF A LIFEWORLD

A life history, by definition, belongs uniquely to one person, textured by innumerable details, instances, events, idiosyncrasies, and happenings.[1] As such, the writing of a "typical" life history is an impossible, quixotic task, seeking to standardize and represent what evades such a neat distillation. Nonetheless, to the best of my ability, here I provide some fairly typical experiences derived primarily from seventy interviews and other sources, such as blogs, conversations, and autobiographical tales.

Although the exact details vary, many hackers reminisced about their technological lives using a relatively standard script that traces how their inborn affinity for technology transformed, over time and through experience, into an intense familiarity. A hacker may say he (and I use "he," because most hackers are male) first hacked as an unsuspecting toddler when he took apart every electric appliance in the kitchen (much to his mother's horror). By the age of six or seven, his actions ripened, becoming volitional. He taught himself how to program in BASIC, and the parental unit expressed joyous approval with aplomb ("look, look our little Fred is sooo smart"). When a little older, perhaps during adolescence, he may have sequestered himself in his bedroom, where he read every computer manual he could get his hands on and—if he was lucky enough to own a modem—connected to a bulletin board system (BBS). Thanks to the holy trinity of a computer, modem, and phone line, he began to dabble in a wider networked world where there was a real strange brew of information and software to ingest.

He could not resist. He began to drink himself silly with information on UFOs, bomb building, conspiracies, and other oddities, downloading different categories of software, shareware, sometimes warez (pirated software), and eventually free software.[2] Initially he spent so much time chatting he would "pass out on his keyboard, multiple times." The parents, confusing locked doors and nocturnal living with preteen angst and isolation, wondered whether they should send their son to a psychologist.

Once he met like-minded peers in high school, college, or online, the boy's intellectual curiosity ballooned. He initiated a quest to master all the ins and outs of a technical architecture like the Linux OS, one or two computer languages, and the topographical terrain and protocols of a really cool new virtual place called the Internet. He soon discovered he could never really master all of this, and that he actually exists in an asymptotic relationship to technology. Nonetheless, he grew to adore the never-ending, never-finished nature of technological production, and eventually fell, almost entirely by accident, into a technical movement.

That movement, the free software movement, seemed to describe his personal experiences with technology in a sophisticated yet accessible language. It said that sharing was good for the community, and that access to source code is not only handy but also the basis by which technology grows and improves. Eventually, he understood himself to be connected to a translocal community of hackers and grew increasingly peeved at their stereotyped representation in the media. As he grew older and more financially independent (thanks to lucrative information technology jobs as a programmer or system administrator that gave him the financial freedom, the "free time," to code for volunteer projects, or alternatively paid him explicitly to work on free software), he consistently interacted with other geeks at work, over IRC, on a dozen (or more) mailing lists, on free software projects, and less occasionally, at exhausting and superintense hacker conferences that left him feeling simultaneously elated and depressed (because they invariably have to come to an end).

Over time, and without realizing when it all happened, he didn't just know how to hack in Perl, C, C ++, Java, Scheme, LISP, Fortran, and Python but also came to learn arcane legal knowledge. His knowledge about technology had become encyclopedic, but ironically he was still wholly dependent on the help of his peers to get just about anything done. He firmly came to believe that knowledge access and transactions of sharing facilitate production, that most types of software should be open source, and that the world would be a better place if we were just given choices for software licensing. Although not exactly motivated to engage in F/OSS production to fulfill a political mandate, he understood the political dimension of coding in an entirely new light. In fact, since reading Lawrence Lessig's *Code and Other Laws of Cyberspace*, and through his daily reading of Slashdot and Boing Boing, popular Web sites reporting technology news and geek esoterica, he came to understand that code is law; code regulates behavior. But so do the copyright industries, which are using everything in their arsenal to fundamentally shape legal policy and even behavior. They suck.

ꙮ

This chapter expands the narrative introduced above to present some consistent features of the hacker lifeworld by visiting the sites, practices, events, and technical architectures through which hackers make as well as remake themselves individually and collectively. Drawing on a rich set of sources, I typify common life experiences of many F/OSS developers. I have attempted to include the sense of excitement, humor, and sensuality that I witnessed as hackers told me about their adventures in hacking.

Following the anthropologist Michael Jackson (1996, 7–8), I understand a lifeworld as "that domain of everyday, immediate social existence and practical activities with all of its habituality, its crises, its vernacular and idiomatic character, its biographical particularities, its decisive events, and indecisive strategies." The account I present of the hacker lifeworld might be better described as a tempo-historical phenomenology. My concern is not to privilege one of its elements (such as a detailed description of the experience of administering a server, programming, or hacking with peers) but instead to paint a panoramic picture of hacking over a fairly large swath of time. Through this, it will be clear that hackers make and remake themselves in a slow, piecemeal rhythm as they engage in diverse activities (coding, debating, reading, gaming, playing, and socializing) in equally diverse settings and institutions (the Internet, conferences, development projects, places of work, and at home).

Although the following life history uses the first-person point of view of phenomenology, I follow Alfred Schutz (1967, 1970) and Maurice Merleau-Ponty (1962) in maintaining that experience is intersubjective. Personal experience is frequently rooted in collective and practical activities whose nature is stable, coherent, and patterned, although constantly, if minutely, in flux. Even if transformations are rarely detectable to those immersed in the everyday flux of living, an existing lifeworld, says Merleau-Ponty (ibid., 453), is "never completely constituted," for action and reaction occur in shifting contexts, and thus "we are open to an infinite number of possibilities." While lifeworlds are most often experienced as free of contradiction and ambiguity (in contrast to the large-scale events and tribulations usually thought to make up the stuff of history, which I visit in the next chapter), they are invariably stamped by particular events, material conditions, and time.

There is one event, however, which is generally experienced as startlingly unique and special—the hacker conference, which I cover in detail at the end of the chapter. The conference is culturally significant because it allows hackers to collectively enact, make visible, and subsequently celebrate many elements of their quotidian technological lifeworld. Whether it is by laying down cable, setting up a server, giving talks about technology, or hacking up some new source code, these actions at the hacker conference unfold in an emotionally charged setting. What the conference foremost allows for is a "condition of heightened intersubjectivity" (Collins 2004, 35) where copious instances of hacking are brought into being and social bonds between participants are made manifest, and thus felt acutely. Taking what is normally experienced prosaically over the course of months, hackers collectively condense their lifeworld in an environment where bodies, celebration, food, and drink exist in excess.

Even if most of the chapter affirms Tolstoy's maxim cited above, the hacker conference allows participants to celebrate this very quotidian life in more exceptional terms. In short, for a brief moment in time, the ordinary character of the hackers' social world is ritually encased, engendering a profound appreciation and awareness of their labor, friendships, events, and objects that often go unnoticed due to their piecemeal, mundane nature.

The Thousand-Mile Journey Starts with a Personal Computer

Most F/OSS developers got their start with technology at a fairly young age, usually around seven or eight, although sometimes as young as four or five. When asked in formal interviews about when they first used computers, F/OSS developers would almost without fail volunteer the name and model number of the specific device (Atari 130xe, Radio Shack Tandy 1000 286, Apple IIe, Commodore 64, and the Sinclair Spectrum). As they spoke of these early computers that commanded so much of their youthful attention, it was unmistakable that they held a deep fondness for the anchor—the computer—that pulls hackers together as a collective.

Many would use and eventually colonize a computer purchased by their parents. Those who came from working-class families used a school, library, or friend's computer. Later on, some would attribute their ability to climb up the class ladder because of capacities and skills acquired through computer use—a climb that many claimed they were not intentionally seeking. Rather, the climb was a by-product of economically valuable knowledge gained by following their personal passion for computing. They wrote their first programs often by using some source code they copied from a manual or from one of the early electronic magazines, such as *Nibble*, *Popular Computing*, *Byte*, or *Dr. Dobbs*. Retrospectively, they came to understand this as their first act of sharing code. Those who started to hack in the late 1970s or 1980s did most of their learning through magazines or friends, by "memorizing" manuals they borrowed from teachers, or later on, at the workplace.[3]

Nearly all of the developers I interviewed learned some of the basics of programming, many with the computer language BASIC, by writing software for some of the first mass-marketed, relatively affordable personal computers. While some only dabbled with BASIC, others became quite proficient in it. Child programmers would often write short programs from scratch, or modify some existing piece of software to enhance its power and features. Johan explained that "by sixth grade, I had pretty much reached my peak with the Atari, writing controller software for the joysticks and trackball, using trickery like character set redefinition to make games at a higher resolution than any of its graphics mode supported."[4] During this period, many hackers spent much of their time learning about computers by themselves, coding small bits of software mostly for fun, excitement, learning, or self-use. Some hackers alternated between coding and playing games, and they frequently coded games or traded more sophisticated game software with friends at school. Many recalled enjoying programming because it provided "immediate gratification" or was "instantly rewarding"—features that many still find seductive.

Although many of their childhood experiences with programming were personal and noncommercial, a surprising number of geeks, by the time they reached high school (sometimes as early as late elementary school), wrote software that was used or purchased by peers or superiors. Whether via informal uses (a teacher using a student's program to randomize the homeroom seating arrangements, for example) or more formal ones (a local public library purchasing a child's math program), many child programmers witnessed their creative outputs being used in the real world. They experienced early on that programming was not just personally gratifying but also that it held a form of social utility and/or economic power that solved real-world problems.

As kids, many programmers had already started to collaborate. Some of these youthful collaborations became the basis of close friendships that entailed playful public contests. Bill told me that in high school, "there were two or three folks who I really developed long-lasting relationships and friendships with. [. . .] We would stay after school and mess with the computer for hours. It was just an intense number of hours playing with systems and goading each other on." Others went to math camp, where they found like-minded technical companions. Or as explained by Doug, it was not uncommon to "emulate" a friend's software by writing one's own version (which he told me with pride ran "more efficiently").[5] Thus young programmers engaged in a practice of "mimesis" (Benjamin [1933] 1999) that combined competitiveness with at least a practical (if not yet ethical) acknowledgment that one is bound to peers, often friends, through coproduction. Later on, they would encounter a social movement that brought intelligibility to these early childhood experiences.

By the time programmers reached high school, many of them came to adopt the identity of hacker or programmer—an identity now acquired at progressively younger ages because of access to the Internet, where discussion about the cultural and technical facets of hacking is common. Many hackers did not awaken to a consciousness of their "hacker nature" in a moment of joyful epiphany but instead acquired it imperceptibly. In some cases, certain books, texts, movies, and places of interaction sparked this association. Some came to identify their personal relationship to computers as hacking by, for example, watching a movie (*War Games*), reading a book (*Hackers*) or manifesto ("The GNU Manifesto"), or during interactions with other people who also called themselves hackers in various locations such as a user group meeting, conference, math camp, or most especially a BBS where hackers congregated in droves during the 1980s and early 1990s.

MEETING OTHER HACKERS ON BBSS

A BBS is a computerized meeting and announcement system where users can upload and download files, make announcements, play games, and have discussions. Many were run and frequented by hackers, and hence discourses and texts about hacking were ubiquitous (Scott 2005; Sterling 1992; Thomas 2003).[6] While the Internet existed in the 1980s, and its architecture was open, practically speaking it operated under a lock, with the keys available only to a select number of hackers, engineers, administrators, and scientists gainfully employed at research labs, universities, and government agencies (Abbate 1999). Given this, BBSs played an important role in hacker history because they were the basis for one of the first expansions of hacking through which hackers could interact autonomously, anonymously, and independently of official institutions.[7] Although this networked expansion entailed a movement outward and beyond institutions (such as the workplace and university), the use of the BBS on a personal computer also represented an inverse move in the other direction, into the privacy of the home. Prior to the 1970s and even for much of the early 1980s, most computing occurred at work or the university.

So long as they could pay the phone bill and temporarily bracket off basic biological needs like sun and sleep, hackers could explore BBSs to their heart's delight, with each BBS independent like a virtual pond. BBSs were not networked until FidoNet came along, creating a first taste of global networking for those who did not have Internet access.[8] BBSs were exciting, for they were informal bazaars where one could access and trade rare as well as sometimes-seedy information. Files traded there spanned low-brow conspiracy theory, hard-hitting political news, playful nonsense, low-grade and more rarely high-octane noir, voyeurism, personal gossip, and one of the most important cultural goods among hackers, software (including shareware, warez, and eventually free software). Before free software was widely known, many young programmers acquired their software primarily on BBSs, and many used this medium to release their own software into the world, usually as shareware.

Since BBSs were unconnected to each other until FidoNet, and long-distance phone bills were expensive (especially for kids and teenagers), many boards were quite rooted in place, with users living in the same city, suburb, region, or local calling area (within which calls didn't incur intra-state long-distance charges). The location of many BBSs was clear, as much of the online information was about local politics, news, and so forth. Many hackers recall BBSs as places of audacious social interactions that readily spilled into the real world during "BBS meet ups," when participants would get together at someone's home or "the local Denny's at 3 in the morning" to continue doing what they did online: talk and trade software. Many BBS members became close friends. It is not farfetched to describe some areas has having a dynamic, complex BBS scene in which hackers, as one of them told me, would "haunt the multiliners and knew most everyone in the scene in the LA area."

At some meetings, hackers would erect a small-scale informal market to barter software and games, with such marketplace transactions cementing hackers together. As portrayed by one hacker in an email message, "My friends and I had shoebox after shoebox of games and utilities. [. . .] We'd trade over BBSs, at BBS meets (since they were all regional, it wasn't uncommon to have meets once every couple months)."

Despite its locally rooted nature and limited network capacity, a BBS, much like the Internet now, was technologically multifaceted, allowing for private and public interactions. Some BBSs were home to more subversive, harder-to-access underground hacker groups, which gained media notoriety in the late 1980s and early 1990s after a string of raids and arrests due to their actions, including some computer break-ins. Largely operating from within private BBS bunkers, these groups operated on an invite-only basis (Sterling 1992). Other BBSs and groups existed more publicly with phone access numbers listed in local computer magazines or posted on other BBSs, thereby attracting many nontechnical users who shared information on this platform.

The mid- to late 1990s heralded the end of the BBS era—a passing that hackers would not let slip away without due commemoration and celebration. In 1993, to bid adieu to this artifact, hackers organized the first Defcon in Las Vegas. Meant as a onetime event, its popularity overrode its original intent, and Defcon remains one of the largest celebrations of hacking. The fact that the BBS period is now over indicates that much of the hacker life-world is constituted through technological infrastructures with their own features and histories, and as subject to birth, growth, and decay as any other social formation.

While many younger hackers have never used a BBS, older geeks (which can mean a still-young thirty years of age, though there are certainly much older ones) in the presence of their younger counterparts will, at times, fondly reminisce about life and hacking on BBSs. For example, once when I asked about BBSing on an IRC channel, all the geeks started to share memories of this vanished era. One programmer humorously and with some retroactive embellishment explained his passion for BBSing with this short account:

> \<hacim\> you call
> \<hacim\> it is busy
> \<hacim\> you set your modem on redial
> \<hacim\> you wait
> \<hacim\> your mom yells at you to get off the phone
> \<hacim\> you stop redial
> \<keg\> haha
> \<hacim\> she talks with whoever while you impatiently wait
> \<keg\> you finally learn *70, and life changes forever [*70 stops call wait-
> ing, which if activated, would boot you off the modem when someone
> else calls]
> \<hacim\> you hide behind her door listening to her talk so you know ex-
> actly when she has hung up
> \<keg\> or 1170 on rotary :) [the code for disabling call waiting on rotary]
> \<hacim\> while sighing really loud so she can hear
> \<hacim\> then you can call!
> \<hacim\> sweeeeet!
> \<hacim\> you run upstairs
> \<hacim\> anyways, you manage to call, you get the REALLY
> SATISFYING modem noise
> \<hacim\> you login
> \<hacim\> and then you go the message boards
> \<hacim\> you crawl them
> \<hacim\> and you see what the last person posted on each subject board
> \<hacim\> sometimes it was the last person to call; that felt really cool
> \<hacim\> the thing was, you had these message boards, where you talked
> about specific subjects
> \<hacim\> and people really got into exploring them
> \<hacim\> and everyone KEPT up on them

The Internet

As these lower-tech ponds for virtual communication dried up, a roaring ocean replaced them: the Internet. If the BBS felt like a small, cramped, and overpriced studio (although retroactively recalled as special because of its intimacy), the Internet was more like an outlandishly spacious penthouse apartment with many luxurious features—and a much more affordable one with each passing year.

With its array of complementary communication tools, email, file transfer protocols (FTP), and IRC, hackers naturally flocked to this technological oasis to continue to do what they did with unwavering passion on BBSs: access information, talk, collaborate, trade files, and make friends as well as some enemies. Geeks started to productively mine mailing list archives for technical data, and eventually Web browsers facilitated the search and discovery process. IRC, created in 1988 by a student in Finland, largely replaced the BBS for real-time communication. In a short period, an astounding number of IRC networks and individual channels spanning the globe appeared.[9]

By virtue of the knowledge gained from these early experiences, geeks began to land gainful employment in then-nascent Internet-related industries (what we think of as the public Internet in certain respects began in 1992, when the US government opened it up to commerce). Some geeks operated one-person consulting shops, working from home-building database back ends for e-commerce Web sites. Others joined forces, dropping out of college to start a local or national Internet service provider or other small-scale technology firm. Hackers living in Silicon Valley would work ridiculously long hours for handsome benefits and inflated stock options at hip, smallish dot-coms, or more traditional tech firms like Oracle, Apple, and Adobe.

FREE SOFTWARE

During the years of early technological spelunking on the Internet, many hackers also came to learn about a new category of software—free software. Like the Internet, its full potential and meaning became apparent primarily through assiduous excavation, use, technological extension, and endless discussion with peers. During interviews, many developers could date their first rendezvous with free software—less in reference to calendar time, but usually with mention of the release version number of a piece of software ("I first discovered Linux in v0.9") and the place of discovery (such as at work or school).

Whatever the location or time, most programmers who learned about free software anywhere between 1985 and 1996 greeted it as if they had stumbled onto a hidden treasure trove of jewels, with the gems being Unix-based software and its precious underlying source code. The experience of discovering that there existed an (almost) fully working Unix system (Linux is a flavor of Unix, and there are dozens of flavors) for a personal computer with available source code was, as one developer put it, "jaw-dropping." Another hacker described it as "almost kinda like a hippie dream thing." Excited but bewildered, the hackers I interviewed dove into this new and small technological cove, never to look back.

For much of the 1990s, but especially in the early part of the decade, the channels through which hackers learned about free software were informal, primarily by word of mouth (in person or online) at school or work, or perhaps through one of the early print journals. As one South African developer now living in the Netherlands recounted during an interview:

> It was a friend in that big [college] residence who came along with a floppy, and because of his typical, very dramatic personality, he just put the floppy in my computer and switched it on, and up came Linux 0.9, and it was the end of 1993 and that was the end for me as well, or at least the beginning. All these flashing lines coming by [. . .] just immediately appealed to me.

The "ah-ahhh," "oh my gosh," "this is so cool," "oh my god" factor of discovering free software depended on a myriad of intersecting elements. For some hackers, free software meant they could finally have a workable Unix operating system for their personal computer (previously, Unix ran primarily on larger, more expensive machines). Gone were the days of having to trudge through snowy streets to access a beloved Unix machine in the computer science department.

Prior to Linux, there were few workable Unix systems that ran on personal computers and were nonproprietary. The production of Linux thus represented a general liberation of the Unix architecture, and also inaugurated its individualization, decentralization, and proliferation. Unhitched from the sole province of the university, corporation, and stringent rules of conventional intellectual property law, Linux was released as a public good and was also produced in public fashion through a volunteer association.[10] Most significantly, hackers were able to run Linux on mass-produced personal computers at home, spending more quality one-on-one time than before with an architecture that even now, still demands an active and dedicated partner. One programmer explained his early excitement as "finally" having "a workshop with all the most powerful tools to hack on real stuff at home." Most young hackers, however, were thrilled, and many were downright "floored," at the newfound unlimited access to source code.

Yet the real adventure of free software came *after* its discovery. In the early days, when Linux distributions were only available off the Net, one had to download the system from a slow connection, usually a modem—a technical feat in and of itself. Taking at least a week to accomplish, the connection would undoubtedly crash, multiple times (but fortunately the download protocols allowed resuming from where it crashed), and a number of the floppies would invariably be corrupt. Once completed, Linux would often occupy around "forty floppy disks."[11] With a stack of floppies, some hackers would immediately begin installation, and then had to hack at the system to make it actually work. Others first had to fend off accusations of piracy from what some developers intimated was some pesky, ignorant, low-level computer lab administrator. The annoyed but excited hacker could offer the administrator only an ambiguous defense, because at this time most hackers lacked the vocabulary with which to describe the

meaning and purpose of free software. They might have said it was shareware, to use a term that probably would have been understood, even if it
was technically incorrect. Without the intimacy that is born from time and
discussion about the nature of objects with peers, free software and Linux
in the early 1990s existed for many hackers as an unconceptualized "thing"
in the ways theorized by Martin Heidegger ([1927] 2008), whose meaning had yet to be actualized, naturalized, or solidified as a social "object"
known collectively by many.

Once the download was complete and the suspicious administrator was
sufficiently placated, hackers would then proceed to the next phase of the
adventure: the death match of installation. Uninstalled, the OS was an un-
ruly creature that had to be transformed into an obedient object so that it
could be used for other acts of creative production. Until at least around
1998 (and arguably still so with many distributions, depending on the user's
experience and skills), Linux installation was nothing short of a weeklong
grueling ritual of esoteric initiation into an arcane technical world that
tested skills, patience, and a geek's deepest resolve to conquer the seemingly
unconquerable. Just to configure basic components of a system like X windows (the graphical user interface) required technical wizardry and diligent
work. The install was so precarious in the 1990s that, as a hacker told me,
"you could risk destroying your monitor."[12] Some geeks described installation as an example of the "larval stage" of hacking—

> [a] period of monomaniacal concentration on coding apparently passed
> through by all fledgling hackers. Common symptoms include the perpe-
> tration of more than one 36-hour hacking run in a given week; neglect
> of all other activities including usual basics like food, sleep, and per-
> sonal hygiene; and a chronic case of advanced bleary-eye. Can last from
> 6 months to 2 years, the apparent median being around 18 months. A
> few so afflicted never resume a more "normal" life, but the ordeal seems
> to be necessary to produce really wizardly (as opposed to merely com-
> petent) programmers. See also wannabee. A less protracted and intense
> version of larval stage (typically lasting about a month) may recur when
> one is learning a new OS or programming language.[13]

Through this quest, many hackers who had never laid their eyes or hands
on a Unix system came out the other side, transformed as excited disciples
of an existing technical religion that goes back to the early 1970s: that of
the Unix "command line." If hackers conceive of computers as the general-
purpose machine that allows them the unfettered ability to create infinite
numbers of minimachines (pieces of software), then Unix is the modus operandi of choice. For example, a hacker named Mark explained that Linux is
"where I started liking the [Unix] paradigm, the whole way of doing things."
For many it unlocked the hood of their previously locked OS. Many hackers had used Microsoft Windows 3.1 and had often programmed in it. As
further elaborated by one Unix devotee during an interview:

But that only offered you so much. [. . .] You had to operate within the constraints that the Windows environment allowed, but when you ran Linux you got all the tools and all the pieces, and the hood opened wide. The constraints were no longer arbitrary; they were limited by your technical abilities, knowledge, desire to push deeper.

UNIX AS "OUR GILGAMESH EPIC"

For those uninitiated in the religion of the command line, it is helpful to compare Linux/Unix to the most commonly used desktop OS, Microsoft Windows (which many F/OSS hackers love to loathe). This will provide a better sense of why Unix is adored as a tinkerer's paradise, and why it holds a kindred aesthetic spirit to F/OSS's philosophy of freedom and sharing. For those who take the time to learn its intricacies, Unix offers a more interactive relationship between user and OS than Microsoft Windows does. Unix is architecturally transparent; every part of the system is a "file" that can be seen, altered, and customized. It gives users the ability to "go behind the scenes" to individually configure the system for specific needs and operates along a similar logic to that of open source. Customization may mean something as seemingly insignificant as setting your own keyboard shortcuts (which in fact is crucial if you are typing most of the day, seven days a week) or rewriting any configuration file to optimize your hardware.

In addition, Unix is equipped with a developer environment of tools and applications called into being not by clicking an icon but instead by a command written as text. These commands can be used to perform programming or administrative tasks, which can in turn be strung together in innovative ways to create new functionalities. Just as programmers might admire elegant code, programmers and system administrators also admire as well as share clever Unix uses and configurations. Given that it is considered a flexible partner, Unix is loved by hackers: "You can make it work exactly as you want [it to]. [. . .] There is always some kind of program that does that little thing different from the one that makes it easier or better for your own personal plan." Like coding, a Unix environment works well as one in which hackers can fashion and cultivate their technical self.

If hackers value Linux/Unix for its ability to be customized, its architecture is nonetheless held in place as a stable object by a coherent logic of aesthetic features, technical philosophy, cultural lore, a complicated legal history, and a peculiar brand of humor, embodied in its very name. Indeed, like so many hacker naming conventions, the name Unix is a clever historical referent—in this case, indexing its conditions of birth. Unix derives from another related OS, the much larger Multics, originally developed in AT&T's Bell Labs. In 1969 Bell Labs canceled funding for Multics; its authors, Ken Thomson and Denis Ritchie, salvaged (and many would say improved) Multics by parsing it down to a much smaller system, which they renamed Unix. Once Unix was "cut down," its creators renamed Multics to "eunuchs" to capture the idea that some really significant "things" had been cut from its body, but what was created was something forever eternally beautiful. Eventually, its creators kept the phonetic instantiation of eunuchs (Unix) to commemorate and signal its conditions of birth as an essentially castrated version of Multics.

The cultural depth of Unix far exceeds naming conventions. Unix has been described as "our Gilgamesh epic" (Stephenson 1999), and its status is that of a living, adored, and complex artifact. Its epic nature is an outgrowth of its morphing flavors, always under development, that nevertheless adhere to a set of well-articulated standards and protocols: flexibility, design simplicity, clean interfaces, openness, communicability, transparency, and efficiency (Gancarz 1995; Stephenson 1999). "Unix is known, loved, understood by so many hackers," explains sci-fi writer Neal Stephenson (1999, 69), also a fan, "that it can be re-created from scratch whenever someone needs it."

Due to its many layers and evolving state, learning the full capabilities of Unix is a lifelong pursuit, and it is generally accepted that most users cannot ever learn its full capabilities. In the words of one programmer who helped me (a novice user) fix a problem on my Linux machine, "Unix is not a thing, it is an adventure." As such, for hackers, the processes of working on or learning about technology, while riddled with kinks and problems, is an activity defined in terms of exploratory, blissful quests. It is often experienced as a convergence of sensual pleasure, logical rigor, and grounds for intellectual pedagogy.

Matching its variations is a great storehouse of ancillary knowledge archived in texts, books, manuals, and especially stories and conversations about Unix. Dissected in great detail, the endless storytelling (over Unix's history, uses, legal battles, problems, and variations) is one important vehicle by which hackers extend themselves into objects, also linking past generations with current ones. These objects become a material token that allows hackers to intersubjectively connect with each other. Unix is but one of the many technical lingua francas (others being programming languages, text editors, and other tools) by which hackers, system administrators, and computer users communicate and forge a shared sense of technical common stock, of sense "know-how," that mixes technological lore with arcane, esoteric humor.

"SOMEONE MUST BREW THE BEER"

While most hackers first became interested in free software on technical grounds, and were thrilled at having access to a robust OS, some were immediately impressed by Stallman's (considered to be the father of free software) philosophy, codified in "The GNU Manifesto" included with many programs, or by reading the first free software license, the GNU GPL. The moral message of software freedom instantly resounded with this minority of the developers I interviewed. Stallman's project to ensure software freedom "just made immediate sense," one of them told me. Others, however, were repelled by the message, saying it sounded "too socialistic or ideological," even though Stallman actually steered clear of any strong language of traditional Left/Right (anticapitalism, for example) politics, and instead used plain and simple language, emphasizing, say, the good that comes from sharing with your neighbors.

The majority of developers I interviewed, though, were not initially swayed in either direction, neither especially repelled nor attracted. Many hackers' understandings of the morality and legality of free software were quite rudimentary. Although the technical implications of unhampered access to code were usually quite clear, few developers understood this access in relation to the GPL in particular or legality in general. Largely unaware of the complicated moral-legal issues surrounding freedom and intellectual property law (much of which was then still defined only through basic terms and a few documents, later to grow as a body of theory on F/OSS projects), hackers saw free software as equivalent to "free beer." This is especially ironic, since most programmers now adamantly insist that the free in free software is precisely about "speech, not beer."

In fact, the very expression "free as in speech" was nearly nonexistent or at best uncommon until at least the mid-1990s. Although the message of freedom was circulating along with free software, many hackers initially grasped this new technological wonder and its moral qualities using the language of money and consumerism. During an interview, Sharkie, now a free software activist, remarked that he learned about copyright through copyleft—another commonly used name for the GPL—and elaborated, "I had no understanding about copyright before this. I knew it was free beer from the beginning and I thought that was very cool." Matthew, another developer, expressed a similar sentiment when he told me "the first draw was, I don't have to pay for this— awesome!" Sharkie's and Matthew's accounts were typical of developers who first learned about free software in the 1980s and early to mid-1990s, especially those who were young or students, without a steady income to pay for expensive software like compilers (a tool that transforms source code, written in a programming language, into machine readable binary code).

Early in their relationship with this technology, most hackers developed a strong pragmatic and utilitarian commitment to free software. But the underlying philosophy underwent change as more developers started to attach and make their own meanings. Access to source code and the model of open development represented by Linux, they said, was a superior technical methodology. Many likened it to the scientific method as an ideal. They saw it as under assault, corrupted by abuse of intellectual property law by corporations and, worse, universities that had started to patent inventions liberally in the 1980s. Others emphasized the pedagogical freedom that F/OSS provided them. "I realized," a developer named Wolfgang wrote me over email, "that I could delve through that code and learn things that I could never learn from a high school teacher. It's one of the reasons why I feel so strongly about the GPL'd software now; it allows anyone to learn and participate."

Some developers who first only used free software later developed it and eventually took the next step: releasing their software under a F/OSS license: "For free beer to flow," Devon, another developer, realized, "someone must brew the beer." (This developer is quite aware that it is more common to say that free software is "free as in speech, not beer," especially since developers are not barred from selling free software. Yet even if one sells free software, one cannot close off the source code, and thus there is some sort of free beer always available, too.) With this line of reasoning, Devon started to release his own software under the GPL, and soon after, participated in a community project. Many began to feel that releasing their own software under the GPL was just the "right thing to do," and that it made unarguable pragmatic sense, because software is a nonscarce resource that benefits from continuous contributions and modifications.

Matthew, quoted above, described his changing attitudes about free software when he told me, "Later [I realized], you know, though I was Joe Schmoe, I can still make this better. I can do what I want with this. And if I don't like it, I can change it, and if I make changes, I can make it available to other people and [. . .] I am just a regular guy. That is a really powerful concept." The experience of using, making, and distributing free software rendered the language of price largely obsolete, while language about the "freedom to tinker" and improve the software for oneself as well as for others gained more ground.

Soon Linux and other popular pieces of free software became more common in the geek and engineering communities, and as a result, much of the fundamental Internet infrastructure was being handled by important F/OSS applications. Apache, started in 1995, was powering Web servers; Sendmail, a program used by servers to transfer email, composed the lion's share of mail transfer nodes; Perl was becoming the language of choice for Web site development; and BIND, a critical piece of the network infrastructure providing name-to-address translations, was increasingly popular among system administrators. If many developers first thought of free software as a set of tools that transformed personal computers into powerful Unix workstations, they quickly learned that it was also the force powering much of the Internet and hence a socially validated type of software. This is more remarkable given how many people, such as Silicon Valley businesspeople and managers, knew little about its existence. The growing ubiquity of F/OSS confirmed developers' sense that free software, while lacking an official warranty, marketing, and glossy packaging, was the real deal, equivalent or even superior to proprietary software. This added to a growing conviction about the technical superiority of the F/OSS method of development, with its requirement of continual access to information.

FREE SOFTWARE IN THE WORKPLACE

Before the widespread corporate acceptance of free software, some developers stealthy smuggled free software into work. In the early to mid-1990s at some of the larger companies, a few of the most enlightened managers "could be convinced" to switch their servers to Linux, but for the most part, use had to be kept to a minimum or under the radar. Some claimed this was not so hard to do because most (nontechnical) managers were "clueless," as *The Hacker Jargon File* definition of "suit" makes sardonically clear:

> n. 1. Ugly and uncomfortable "business clothing" often worn by non-hackers. Invariably worn with a "tie," a strangulation device that partially cuts off the blood supply to the brain. It is thought that this explains much about the behavior of suit-wearers. Compare droid. 2. A person who habitually wears suits, as distinct from a techie or hacker. See loser, burble, management, Stupids, SNAFU principle, and brain-damaged. English, by the way, is relatively kind; our Moscow correspondent informs us that the corresponding idiom in Russian hacker jargon is "sovok," lit. a tool for grabbing garbage.[14]

Developers who were self-employed or working in a small tech company that had few or no managers powered everything on free software, crediting the success of the company to solid technology as well as the money saved on software. As free software became acceptable in the corporate sphere, geeks no longer had to hide their use of this software. A few told me during interviews that they "started to put my Debian work on my resume."

As these examples illustrate, for most developers (with the exception of anticapitalist activist-geeks), acceptance of free software rarely led to a wholesale political opposition to corporate producers of proprietary software. Instead, developers used their experiences with free software to develop a critical eye toward proprietary software firms, targeting their complaints at specific practices, such as abuse of intellectual property law and the tendency to hide problems from customers. As one developer put it starkly, "free software encourages active participation. Corporate software encourages consumption." Another one told me that he only realized the extent to which corporations hid software problems from their customers when he confronted the transparency of free software's bug reporting:

One of the things that you see with commercial, proprietary software is that vendors don't want to talk about bugs. They are pretty closed mouth about it. It is hard to find out about it. They don't want to acknowledge it. When I started using Unix and started reading the man pages, I was astounded. All these main pages had bug sections in them, and where they explained the major bugs, it was an epiphany. People would acknowledge and even explain their bugs.

Probably the single most important difference flagged in interviews was that F/OSS software never could be "wrongfully" jailed under the deadweight of nondisclosure agreements and intellectual property law, never to see the light of day—the tragic fate of much proprietary software if a project is canceled. This closure violates the meritocratic tradition of recursively feeding knowledge back to the community—something that is necessary to secure ongoing technical production. Unlike proprietary software, F/OSS always has a chance to live free "even if abandoned by the original author." As hacker Jeremiah explained in greater detail:

> The important difference for me is whether I come away feeling that I have created something of lasting intrinsic value or not. I've sometimes come away from corporate development with that feeling, but it is a lot more common with free software. I honestly don't feel like there are vast differences in areas like enjoyment gained in the programming, stress level, levels of collaboration, and stuff like that. But most often when I am done with corporate software, it's dead, and when I am done with free software, it is alive.

FREE SOFTWARE SPREADS

A nascent, circumscribed political sensibility that differentiated proprietary software from F/OSS was fertilized by everyday geek news on Web-based periodicals like *Linux Weekly News* and Web sites such as Slashdot, which presented moral and political analyses alongside mainstream news features as well as prolific analyses about life as a coder. "Programmers started writing personally, intently, voluminously," observes journalist Scott Rosenberg (2007, 301), "pouring out their inspirations and frustrations, their insights and tips and fears and dreams on Web sites and in blogs. It has been the basis of if not a canon of great works of software, at least an informal literature around the day-to-day practice of programming."

By the late 1990s, a number of academic lawyers had arrived on this scene, specifying the issues in a legal though accessible language that reinforced the ones hackers were themselves formulating. The works and opinions of these lawyers (whether derived from books, blogs, articles, or speeches) have been particularly influential, especially those of Lessig (who I will give more attention to in the conclusion). As a small token of this "lawyer effect," I quote part of an email-based letter from a Debian developer who wrote Lessig to express dismay over a legal ruling (and its coverage), give his thanks, and explain his current contribution to the politics of information freedom:

> As a brief aside, two days ago I finished reading *The Future of Ideas*.
>
> I was already familiar with much of the factual material in the book (at least in broad strokes), but I have seldom put down a book so inflamed with rage. Rage at the copyright and telecommunications cartels, not the author, of course. This evening I attended the Indiana Civil Liberties Union's holiday party, and the President offered to put me on the ICLU's special committee on "Civil Rights in the Information Age." In some small way I hope that I can contribute to averting the bleak future you outline in your book.
>
> I wanted to take this opportunity to thank you for authoring an extremely interesting book, and ask you or a colleague of yours to rebut Prof. Hamilton's *FindLaw* article.[15]

Lessig wrote back, encouraging him to pour his energies into fighting those who take a conservative and protective view of intellectual property law: "I like your rage. Focus it. And direct it well and rightly against people who think the only truth is in what our framers may have said. There is more. There is what we say, now."[16]

While many geeks were surprised to learn that high-quality software was available with source code and began to refine their legal vocabulary, many were as intrigued to find out that there was an identifiable community of geeks who programmed not for the sake of profit but rather for the sake of technology. One developer explained how through free software, he discovered the existence of other like-minded geeks:

> What really grabbed me was the community. That was what really grabbed me, and you have to understand at the time, it was a completely foreign notion. [. . .] I had stumbled on this group of people that were interested in the same things that I was interested in that had, basically for no particular reason, built this thing, this operating system, and it actually worked, and I could do my work in it and I had not paid a dime for it; they did not ask anything of me when I downloaded it or used it.

No longer confined to their local area code and guided by a provocative real-world example in Linux, hackers joined forces, cobbling various communication and collaboration tools into rudimentary but highly effective virtual guildlike workshops on the Internet. There they coded software applications as well as the tools that could facilitate their work. Developers congregated on IRC for the daily pulse of interaction, mailing lists were teeming with vibrant and at times contentious debates, while code repositories (where developers checked in and checked out source code plus tracked changes) and bug-tracking software became the crucial back-end architecture, allowing developers to manage and organize the complexity of long-distance collaboration (Yuill 2008).

Specifically, the Linux kernel project, led by a Finnish programmer and college student named Linus Torvalds, and initiated in 1991, was a tsunami of inspiration, causing hackers and developers to follow suit. In 1993, Ian Murdock, dissatisfied with the available Linux distributions, emulated the Linux kernel development model to start Debian, a distribution made "by developers and for developers."[17] During an informal discussion at Debconf, Murdock described the idea behind it:

> [It] was to get more than one person involved. And the inspiration for that was the Linux kernel. And for some reason the Linux kernel development model seemed to work. You have one guy, Linus, coordinating things, and random people would come and go and send patches and test things, and it seemed to work, and I figured, what the hell, let's give it a try and perhaps we can apply the same idea to this distribution.

He announced the Debian project in August 1993 on the Linux kernel newsgroup, comp.os.linux. Immediately a handful of volunteers offered their time, attention, and labor. By the end of the following year, the number of volunteers grew to a couple of dozen. As Murdock designed the technical architecture to standardize a software package management system, he took it on himself to theorize and conceptualize the nature of this labor (like many other geeks who initiated virtual projects). Along with his initial announcement, Murdock also published "The Debian Manifesto," where he extended and reformulated ideals in Stallman's "GNU Manifesto," addressing the pragmatic importance of transparency and distributed collaboration:

> The Debian design process is open to ensure that the system is of the highest quality and that it reflects the needs of the user community. By involving others with a wide range of abilities and backgrounds, Debian is able to be developed in a modular fashion. Its components are of high quality because those with expertise in a certain area are given the opportunity to construct or maintain the individual components of Debian involving that area. Involving others also ensures that valuable suggestions for improvement can be incorporated into the distribution during its development; thus, a distribution is created based on the needs and wants of the users rather than the needs and wants of the constructor. It is very difficult for one individual or small group to anticipate these needs and wants in advance without direct input from others.[18]

On their project Web pages, which act as the initial portal to these projects, most large-scale F/OSS projects (Gnome, Apache, KDE, Perl, Python, etc.) showcased similar documents, articulating the virtues of collaboration and transparency, and the pragmatic advantages of open-source development. Even projects like Apache, which ideologically distance themselves from the morality of free software, justifying openness in primarily utilitarian terms, have detailed documents that explain the "open-source way."[19]

By contributing to a project, hackers came into closer contact with this discourse on the nature of their labor and the moral implications of licenses—a vocabulary that they themselves helped to create and transform. The growing unification of technical experience and its representation became notable on project news Web sites, mailing lists, blogs, books, and articles; these texts provided developers with a rich set of ideas about creativity, expression, and individuality. Equipped with this language of freedom and creativity, hackers brought coherence to the technical act of coding, frequently conceptualizing it as an act of individual expression, as we see here with Matthew:

> Code is a form of expression. And for some people, well it is very hard for a nontechie to think that way. [. . .] It is hard to teach the everyman the value of free. [We] need to teach [that] free is a product of the creativity of the programmer. They sat down and they put creativity into it, and they put thought into it.

Programmers deliberately placed source code in the realm of freedom—a space often closely linked to public and rational communication. "I think this open communication," Michael added, "is based on the freedom of the source code. Members of the community are free to discuss the intricate details of a program without fear of breaking any agreements."

While developers enunciate a sophisticated language of freedom that makes individual experiences of creation intelligible, their language also elaborates on ideals that are more collectivist and populist in their orientation—such as cooperation, community, and solidarity. While many geeks have come to value free software as an avenue for self-expression or because it can secure technical independence (as they can rely on themselves to code an application just as they see fit), F/OSS is valued for providing a communal space where people with shared interests can band together to produce as they collectively see fit. When asked about the nature of this sort of collaboration, Jeremiah responded that while it is "at times frustrating and maddening," it is "most often rewarding. You learn really quickly that there are a lot of really smart people in the project and that an idea is always, always improved after they've all beat on it some."

The effects of any public discourse are multiple and profound, as theorists of publics have long maintained (Taylor 2004; Warner 2002). On one level, the discourse of F/OSS works to represent and confirm experience (for after all, F/OSS development seems to work as well or, in some cases, better than proprietary development), but on another level, by concretizing experience into a rich and accessible format, it alters the nature of experience itself. With a set of "typifications" (Berger and Luckmann 1967, 31) over the philosophical meaning of source code in place, hackers draw on them to give meaning to their own actions, although these typifications can and do change over time.

Public discourse is a vehicle through which hackers' immediate experiences with technology along with their virtual and nonvirtual interactions with one another are culturally generalized. Their interactions are conceptualized in terms of expression, transparency, efficiency, and freedom. Hackers don't solely derive meaning either through virtual interaction, though, or by making, accessing, and extending public discourse. In-person interaction is also a pervasive feature of their lifeworld, working to confirm the validity of circulating discourse. The single most important site of in-person sociality is the hacker conference, the final topic of this chapter (see figure 1.1).

Much has been made of the fact that hacking and F/OSS development unfold in the ethereal space of bits and bytes. "Indeed, serious hackers," writes Manuel Castells (2001, 50), "primarily exist as hackers on-line." The substantial academic attention given to the virtual ways that hackers produce technology is undoubtedly warranted and rich, and has advanced our sociological understanding of labor and virtuality. But what this literature fails to substantially address (and sometimes even barely acknowledge) is the existence of face-to-face interactions among these geeks, hackers, and developers.

Perhaps this is so because much of this interaction seems utterly unremarkable—the ordinary stuff of work and friendships. Many hackers, for example, see each other with remarkable consistency, usually every day at work, where they may share office space and regularly eat lunch together.

FIGURE 1.1. Debconf1, Bourdeaux, France
Public domain, https://gallery.debconf.org/v/debconf1/roland/aap.jpg.html
(accessed July 29, 2011). Photo: Roland Bauerschmidt.

During downtime they will "geek out," perhaps delving deep in conversations about technology, hacking on some code, or patching and recompiling their Linux kernel just to try something out. On a given day, they might dissect the latest round of the Recording Industry Association of America lawsuits launched against person-to-person file sharers and bemoan the discovery of a particularly obnoxious security hole in the Linux kernel. If they live in a location with a high density of geeks, generally big cities with a thriving technology sector (for instance, Amsterdam, Montreal, Munich, Bangalore, Boston, São Paulo, San Francisco, Austin, New York City, and Sydney), face-to-face interactions are more common, especially since geeks are often roommates, or interact through informal hacker associations, collectives, and hackers spaces, now quite common in cities across Europe and North America.[20]

We should not treat networked hacking as a displacement of or replacement for physical interaction. These two modes silently but powerfully reinforce each other. Reading the latest technical, legal, or social news about F/OSS on a Web news portal every morning, then posting the article link on a mailing list (perhaps with a brief analysis), and discussing this news with friends over lunch all bolster the validity as well as importance of such public discourse. Public discourse grabs attention effectively not only because it circulates pervasively but also because of the ways developers consistently talk about and reflect on this discourse with each other in person.

Admittedly, hackers may not think of this type of daily or weekly in-person interaction among friends and workmates as the locus of the community commonly referred to when speaking of computer hacking or F/OSS. For many hackers, the locus of sociality is, as much of the literature argues, networked and translocal. Composed of a vast, dispersed conglomeration of people—close friends, acquaintances, and strangers—they see themselves united by a fervent interest in and commitment to technology. They are connected via the applications of the Internet that allow them to communicate and build technologies.

Even if hackers have come to situate themselves in a vast global communications network, and imagine themselves in terms of networks and virtuality, they also have increasingly done so by celebrating their translocality in person. More than ever, hackers participate in and rely on a physical space common to many types of social groups (such as academics, professionals, hobbyists, activists, and consumers): the conference, which in hacker lingo is usually designated by its shorthand: the con. Coming in multiple formats, the number of hacker cons is astonishingly high, although it must be emphasized that their emergence is quite recent. Nonexistent before the early 1980s, the semiautonomously organized hacker con has proliferated most dramatically during the last fifteen years, keeping pace with the seismic expansions of networked hacking and undeniably made possible by changing economies of air travel.[21]

To adequately grapple with the nature of hacker sociality, whether virtual or in person, we must also give due attention to these events, which constitute an extraordinary dimension and, for some hackers, deeply meaningful aspect of their lifeworld. Taking what is normally experienced prosaically over the course of months or years, hackers collectively condense their lifeworld in an environment where bodies, celebration, food, and drink exist in excess. Interweaving hacking with bountiful play and constant consumption, the con's atmosphere is one of festive interactivity. As if making up for the normal lack of collective copresence, physical contiguity reaches a high-pitched point.[22] For a brief moment in time, the ordinary character of the hackers' social world is ritually encased, engendering a profound appreciation as well as awareness of their labor, friendships, events, and objects that often go unnoticed due to their piecemeal, quotidian nature.

Evidence of this appreciation and awareness is everywhere marked, especially at the end of a conference, when participants say their good-byes and find time to reflect on the con:

> My first Debconf was probably the best single week of my entire life. Yeah, it was that awesome. [. . .] I won't talk about all the stuff that happened, because that would just take too long. The most important thing was that I got to see a number of old friends again and spend more time with them in one run than ever before. That alone was really enormous for me. On top of that was the pleasure of finally meeting so many people in person. I met a few XSF members finally, including Julien Cristau, my partner in crime. [. . .] There was staying up until 5 in the morning and stumbling back to the hostel in the dawn to try to get some sleep before running back to the conference. The most delightful thing about all this was that so many people I already knew and loved were there, and everyone who I hadn't met in person turned out to be even better in real life. It was like a week of the purest joy.[23]

These types of intense, pleasurable emotional experiences and expressions are abundant. They are deeply felt and often freely expressed, which brings hackers not only a new appreciation of their world but also a new way of actually experiencing their lifeworld.

THE HACKER CON AS LIFEWORLD

Hacker cons occur infrequently but consistently. They reconfigure the relationship between time, space, and persons, allow for a series of personal transformations; and perhaps most significantly, reinforce group solidarity. All of these aspects of conferences make them ritual-like affairs (Collins 2004). While experiential disorder, license, intense bonding, and abandon are common to them, cons tend to lack the types of reversals or inversions found in traditionally identified forms of ritual, which feature carnivalesque play, rites of passages, resolution of social contradictions, or periods of seclusion (Bakhtin 1984; Gluckman 1963; Turner 1967).

Instead, hacker conferences are rituals of confirmation, liberation, celebration, and especially reenchantment, where the quotidian affairs of life, work, labor, and social interactions are ritualized, and thus experienced on fundamentally different terms. Through a celebratory condensation, hackers imbue their actions with new, revitalized, or ethically charged meanings. Lifting life "out of its routine" (Bakhtin 1984, 273), hackers erect a semistructured but highly flexible environment, in which the kinetic energy is nothing short of irresistible and the interactivity is corporeal. These are profound moments of cultural reenchantment whereby participants build and share a heightened experience of each other.

Since there are "only hosts for there are no guests, no spectators, only participants" (Bakhtin 1984, 249), most everyone arrives on an equal footing, ready to contribute their part to what can only be characterized as a dizzying range of activities.[24] These include formal talks, informal gatherings usually called "birds of a feather" (BOF) sessions, copious eating and drinking, maybe dancing, hacking, gaming, sightseeing, and nonstop conversations.[25] A little bit like a summer camp but without the rules, curfews, and annoying counselors, many hacker cons are the quintessential hacker vacation—one that often involves furiously exhausting work, a lack of sleep, and the need to take a real break afterwards.

Though organizers spend many months of hard work planning these conferences, the participants tend to experience them as evanescent. Because very little beyond talks and a few planned events can be foreshadowed or predicted in advance, the social atmosphere is pregnant with possibility. Time takes on new qualities. Most especially, time in the ordinary and often annoying sense of having to keep it is unimportant, as are many other demands of day-to-day living. Participants can change the outcome of the con itself by self-organizing, announcing new sessions, planning events, or buying a lot of alcohol, which when drunk, inadvertently derails other plans. The con's temporal potency resides in its sheer intensity, a feverish pace of life in which freedom of expression, action, interactivity, and laughter are let loose, and often channeled into securing the bonds behind the "intense comradeship" (Turner 1969, 95) undoubtedly felt by many. Reflexivity and reflection are put on momentary hold, in favor of visceral experience. Attention is given to the present moment, so much so that the totality of the conference is usually recalled as startlingly unique, with its subsequent representation—whether in text, photos, or video—a mere shadow lacking the granularity and depth of what actually transpired.

But while its power seems to reside entirely in its temporal singularity, its effects are multiple, far outlasting the actual con itself. By the end, due to sleep deprivation, overconsumption, and interacting with peers, the hackers' bodies and minds are usually left worn out, torn, and entirely devitalized. Nonetheless, by witnessing others who share one's passions and especially by freely partaking in those passions, the hacking spirit is actually revitalized in the long run, after the postcon recovery needed to return to normal life. Participants come to think of their relation to hacking or a particular project in a different light. Above all, any doubts about one's real connection to virtual projects and relationships are replaced by an invigorated faith in and commitment to this world.

It is clear that these events are significant for hackers, who are able to celebrate and appreciate their social world. For academics interested in the relationships between virtual and nonvirtual domains, the con can be used to pose important questions about how social actors like hackers, who are routinely immersed in networked digital media, might indigenously conceive of the relationship between the screen and the physical space where bodies meet. While hackers as a group rarely collectively theorize the nature of virtual interactivity, as academics are prone to do, the immense value these hackers place on these face-to-face encounters points to how they imagine the nature of and even limits to virtual interactivity. The hacker conference is not only a social drama that produces feelings of unity, as I will demonstrate below, but can also be fruitfully approached as ethical and social commentary—a native critique—that speaks to how hackers themselves imagine interaction. By emphasizing so strongly the human interactivity of the conferences, hackers are implicitly agreeing with the idea that virtuality, however meaningful, cannot ever fully replace or mimic face-to-face sociality.

The Social Metabolism of a Typical Developer Con

After hours of travel, hackers who tend to come from western Europe, Australia, New Zealand, Latin America, the United States, and Canada (and a handful from Asia) trickle in throughout the first day and night to the venue.[26] The Debian developer conference, for example, is held every year in a new location for over a week and brings together around four hundred developers who work on maintaining this Linux distribution. Veteran attendees traveling significant distances arrive exhausted but enthusiastic, knowing what lies ahead. For first timers, the anticipation may be a little more amorphous yet no less significant. The prospect of finally meeting (actually in person) people you often interact with, although typically only through the two-dimensional medium of text, is thrilling. Many participants, unable to contain their excitement, skip the first (and maybe second) night of sleep, spending it instead in the company of peers, friends, alcohol, and of course computers.

No respectable hacker/developer con could be called such without the ample presence of a robust network and hundreds of computers—the material collagen indisputably connecting hackers together. Thin laptops,

FIGURE 1.2. Debconf10, New York
Photo: E. Gabriella Coleman.

chunky personal computers, reams of cable, fancy digital cameras, and other assorted electronics equipment adorn the physical environment. Animated by fingers swiftly tapping away at the keyboards, computers return the favor, animating faces in a pale blue hue. Most cons now host a hacklab, a room filled with long tables, nearly every inch occupied by computers networked together, available for experimentation, testing, playing, demonstrating, and so on. In the first few days, much of the technological chatter centers on the difficulties and solutions behind setting up the network, which in the case of the Debconfs is usually commemorated in detail in the final report:

> The building itself had to be wired from the 2nd floor to the basement, and we ended up stringing approximately a kilometer of cable for the network backbone. [. . .] Every room was interconnected with redundant links. This turned out to be fortunate: we did have wiring failures, but no one except the admins noticed and work continued uninterrupted.[27]

Virtually communicating with participants as well as those unable to attend, hackers continue to give due attention to their work and networked interactivity even while in the presence of others, as we see in the picture (figure 1.3).

Since coordinating the hundreds, sometimes thousands, of hackers at a con can be a bit challenging, geeks naturally turn to technology for help. Even before the start of a conference, organizers erect an IRC channel, mailing list, Web page, and wiki. Many geeks, who are coming from out of town, change their cell plans, rent a cell phone, or get a new chip for their cell phone to provide them with cellular service at the local rate. Some of the

FIGURE 1.3. HackNY, New York
Attribution-ShareAlike 2.0 Generic (CC BY-SA 2.0), https://secure.flickr.com/photos/
hackny/5684846071/ (accessed October 23, 2011). Photo: Elena Olivo.

many technical discussions are, naturally, about the latest mobile technologies and local mobile network. These tools are prolifically used to locate people, spontaneously coordinate new events, collect all sorts of information, post slides, compile lists of where people are from, and find out where to do laundry, along with other coordination tasks.

During talks, IRC becomes the high-tech peanut gallery. Hackers unabashedly discuss the presentations as they unfold, giving those not there in person, but online, an often-humorous textual play-by-play. At the con, these networked and virtual technologies exist in much the same way they ordinarily do. Rarely used in isolation or to replace the "meat world," they augment interactivity (Hakken 1999; Miller and Slater 2001; Taylor 2006). And hackers have grown adept at fluidly moving between them, cultivating a peculiar incorporated competence—a *hexis*, or "durable manner of standing, speaking and thereby of feeling and thinking" (Bourdieu 1977, 93) used to negotiate this movement. Even while typing away furiously, eyes scan various open windows on the computer, but ears are usually perked up, listening to the chatter and ready to contribute to the conversations unfolding in the room. Here and there, material and virtual, bodies sit at an intersection, processing bits and bytes as well as other physical bodies, who do the same.

Cons offer ample opportunity for individuals to present their own work or new, fledging ideas to a larger audience. After laboring either in isolation or with a handful of others in person, developers feel a rush of pride and honor in presenting their work to a roomful of collaborators and peers who are keen to learn more or lend a helping hand. Despite the fact that many participants stay up until the crack of dawn, many still manage to put aside biological imperatives to stay awake to attend the talks. Though many talks are on technical matters, they usually span multiple topics, such as technology, law, politics, and cooperative sociality, among many others.

While the experience of a con may ostensibly evade representation (or strike participants as entirely fleeting), they are nonetheless important historical conduits—perhaps one of the most significant places for simultaneously experiencing the past, present, and future of a project. During cons, participants make crucial decisions that may alter the character and future course of the developer project. For example, at Debconf4, the few women attending, spearheaded by the efforts of Erinn Clark, used the time and energy afforded by an in-person meeting to initiate and organize Debian Women Project, a Web site portal and IRC mailing list to encourage female participation by visibly demonstrating the presence of women in the largely male project.

Following the conference, one of the female Debian developers, Amaya Rodrigo, posted a bug report calling for a Debian Women's mailing list, explaining the rationale in the following way:

> **From:** Amaya Rodrigo Sastre <amaya@debian.org>
> **To:** Debian Bug Tracking System <submit@bugs.debian.org>
> **Subject:** Please create debian-women mailing list
> **Date:** Tue, 01 Jun 2004 22:12:30 +0200
> Package:lists.debian.org
>
> Severity: normal
>
> Out of a Debconf4 workshop the need has arisen for a mailing list
> oriented to debating and coordinating the different ways to get a larger
> female userbase. Thanks for your time :-).[28]

While decisions, such as the creation of Debian Women, address present conditions to alter the future history of a project, cons also imbue projects with a sense of history. Different generations of hackers intermix; older ones recollect times past, letting the younger hackers know that things were once quite different. At Debconf4, younger developers added their own stories about how they ended up working on Debian.[29] Though information may strike outsiders as mundane, for those involved in the project, learning how its social organization radically differed ("the New Maintainer Process [NMP] for me was emailing Bruce Perens") or finding out where key Debian servers were once housed ("under x's desk in his Michigan dorm room") is nothing short of delectable and engaging. Murdock, who attended his first Debconf in Porto Alegre, explained to a captivated audience, for instance, how he came to start the project—a treat for those who knew little or nothing about Debian's birth. Over days of conversation, younger developers become acquainted with their project's history, which grows increasingly complicated each passing year. Younger developers, in return, respond to stories of the past, adding their own accounts of how they became involved in the project and what role they may have played in changing its procedures. This back-and-forth storytelling, especially when based on personal memories and project history, provides an apt example of the "second-order stories" that Paul Ricoeur identifies as part of an intersubjective process of "exchange of memories." These, he writes, "are themselves intersections between numerous stories," the effect of which is a more pronounced form of entanglement through narrative (Ricoeur 1996, 6). Other conversations center on more somber matters, such as sharing stories over one of the many lunches, dinners, and bar visits about a developer who has since passed on, like Joel "Espy" Klecker of the Debian project, who died at the all-too-young age of twenty-one after fighting an illness that left him bedridden for many years.

For some developers, the awareness of a shared social commonwealth takes on a decidedly moral character, leading some developers to reappraise their virtual interactions and behavior with fellow developers. Take, say, this memorable email sent during Debconf4, titled "Here at DebConf4," where one longtime developer, Texan Ean Schuessler, known for his argumentative tone on emails, offered the following collective apology to the entire project:

> Well folks, I'm here at Debconf4 and I've had some firm feedback that I am not as funny as I think I am. I knew this was the case in advance but the irritation some people feel with the brand of my comedy has given me pause.
>
> I've argued that since I'm a volunteer that you all have to put up with my attitude. I realized that attitude sucks. It sucks up your valuable volunteer time reading the insulting, acidic emails I throw off when I am frustrated with people. [. . .]
>
> So I'm going to do something unprecedented. [. . .]
>
> I would like to apologize, without reservation, for the accounting flamewar I started on spi/debian-private [a private email list for Debian developers].[30]

Some developers who collaborate on a piece of software take the opportunity to sequester themselves for a couple of days and overcome some particularly stubborn technical hurdle, thus accomplishing more in two days than they had during the previous two months. To nonhackers, the value of this in-person collaboration may seem odd when the collaborators tend to work pretty much as they do at home—that is, alone on their computers. This is a consequence of the single-user design and function of computers. While at a con, collaborators might physically sit next to the person they work with online (and so never see), and will frequently stop and talk with them, or hammer out a problem over a meal, the actual act

FIGURE 1.4. Debconf7, Edinburgh
Attribution 2.0 Generic (CC BY 2.0), http://www.flickr.com/photos/aigarius/569656268/
in/set-72157600344678016/ (accessed August 2, 2011). Photo: Aigars Mahinovs.

of "working" on a project is determined by the object-necessitated state: in a state of interacting with their computer, more often than not, alone. This is occasionally mitigated by the shoulder-surfing and "check this out" stuff that brings people together to look at the same screen, but typically for any substantial work to get done, only one person can operate the machine at a time. The time spent looking at someone else typing, making mistakes that one wouldn't make, solving a problem in a way that seems inefficient, or bumbling around unable to fix something makes people quickly gravitate back to being in control of their own machine in a state of mental isolation. The operative object necessities of a computer are particularly interesting at a con, because the con fundamentally challenges yet never overcomes completely these necessities.

What makes the shared sociality of projects so interesting is that people do end up working together—in fact relying on each other—even though their instrument usually demands only one operator. Take, for example, the following developer, Martin Kraft, who wrote about running into "a wall" when working on his software package, but was rescued by two developers who "dedicated their time to listen to my design and the problems and helped me clear the mess up."[31] Or Tom Marble, who highlighted on his blog "why attending these conferences is great," for he got to "spend some time discussing the future of Xorg with Debian's maintainer, David Nusinow.

FIGURE 1.5. Hackers on Planet Earth, New York
Attribution 2.0 Generic (CC BY 2.0), https://secure.flickr.com/photos/
ioerror/196443446/in/set-72157594211715252 (accessed August 2,
2011). Photo: Jacob Appelbaum.

We talked about how to work around the infamous XCB bug with Java and
also about the future of X including OpenGL support."[32]

Other hackers, who had hoped to get a significant amount of work done,
entirely fail to do so, perhaps because socializing, sightseeing, nightclubs,
and the occasional impromptu concert (after fixing an old church organ)
prove a greater draw than late-night hacking.

Most hackers, however, intermix play with hacking, giving themselves ample opportunity to see the sights, dance the dances, play the games, eat the
local cuisine, hit the parks and beaches, and stay put with computers on
their laps, hacking away next to others doing the same, generally into the
early morning.

During hacker cons, there is a semiotic play of profound sameness and
difference. Signs of sameness are everywhere. Most people are attached to
their computers, and share a common language of code, servers, protocols,
computer languages, architectures, LANs, wireless, kernels, man pages,
motherboards, network layer, file sharing, stdout and stderr, Debian, and the
FSF. Many hackers wear geeky T-shirts. With each passing day, the semiotics
of sameness are enlivened, brought to a boiling point, as participants increasingly become aware of the importance of these personal relations, this
form of labor, and F/OSS—in short, the totality of this technical lifeworld.

Within this sea of sameness, eddies and tides of difference are sculpted by
individual personalities, the unique existence of physical bodies in proximate
space, and political and cultural differences. Mixtures of different thick ac-
cents cascade over endless conversations. The melodic Italian competes with

FIGURE 1.6. Debconf3, Oslo
Public domain, https://gallery.debconf.org/v/debconf3/wolfgangklier/amk.jpg.html
(accessed August 2, 2011). Photo: Wolfgang Klier.

the enchanting Portuguese. The German "Jaaaaaa" always carries a more
weighty affirmation than the American English "yeah." Everyone adopts
the basics ("please," "yes," "no," and "thank you") in the native language
of the home country hosting the event. Italian anarchists work alongside
US liberal democrats. Bodies sleeping, eating, and interacting make themselves known without asking, with the peculiar corporeal details—green
hair, a wheelchair, gray beards, red-flushed cheeks, a large toothless smile,
the Texan drawl, a freckled face, and the paucity of females—all making a
lasting imprint, and captured in the thousands of photos that are taken and
posted on the Debconf gallery.[33]

By the end, the play of sameness and difference no longer can make their
mark, for bodies exist deflated, slightly corpselike. Unable to process signs
of life or even binary, some hackers experience a personal systems crash.

At the airport, awake but often a little dazed, participants engage in one
final conversation on technology, usually mixed with revisiting the notable
events that transpired at the con. Before the final boarding call is made, some
voice their commitment to return to next year's Debconf, which is usually
already being planned by excited participants who want to ensure another
great (possibly better) event: "I'll be back in Argentina unless something
goes seriously wrong," one developer wrote on his blog after Debconf4.[34]
Another mentioned that "I look forward to attending additional DebConfs
in the future and encourage everyone to experience DebConf—they won't
regret it!"[35] For those who return annually, the hacker con takes on the particular ritual quality of a pilgrimage.

If immediacy and immersion set the tone of the con experience, as soon
as one leaves, a new experiential metabolism takes its place: one of heightened reflexivity. As noted by Victor Turner (1986, 2; see also Turner 1967,
105), ritual allows for an acute form of apprehension in which social actors
reflect "upon themselves, upon the relations, actions, symbols, meanings,

codes, roles, statuses, social structures, ethical and legal rules, and other sociocultural components which make up their public 'selves.'" After the sheer
intensity of action recedes and a feeling of nostalgia kicks in, hackers start
to reflect on the importance and meaning of the conference.

Small bits of this process are openly shared on mailing lists and blogs,
especially by con neophytes:

> It was the first Debconf for me and it was very exciting and brought
> many different views on software development and deployments, even
> though I'm now hacking for over 12 years. [. . .][36]
>   I don't think I could ever have had a better first debconf experience.
> I think it was as close to perfect as possible, everyone was friendly and
> that was the most important thing. [. . .] There is only one thing that
> I am sorry about and that is that I had to leave so soon.[37]
>   The best moment of the whole event was the formal dinner with the
> rain, the mariachi, the mole, and the animations. I could never have
> been so happy. That's the way I see Debian: alive.[38]

For weeks afterward, the IRC channel remains highly active as people
who spent the week together reach out over virtual channels to try to re-
gain the social interactivity they have lost. Conversations detailing particular events work as inscription devices (Latour and Woolgar 1979), making
sure that such events are transformed into collective memories in order to
outlast the place and time of their occurrence. The duller (and for some, op-
pressive) atmosphere of the office makes the con more wondrous, bringing
into sharper relief its creative, open potentials and fueling the strong desire
to return, yet again.

If cons cement group solidarity, they also usher in personal transformations. Liberated "from the prevailing point of view of the world [. . .] and
established truths, from cliches, from all that is humdrum and universally
accepted" (Bakhtin 1984, 24), people embark on decisions and actions that
they probably would not have considered otherwise. Some hackers decide
to formally apply to become a Debian developer, while longtime developers
decide not to quit the project—just yet. Others may tone down their mailing
list flaming after meeting the developers in person. Some fall in love during
the con, sometimes with another participant, and at other times with a local.
A few may quit their jobs working on proprietary software, feeling that if others can make a living from free software, they ought to be able do so as well.

CONCLUSION

The hacker con is a condensed, weeklong performance of a lifeworld that
hackers usually build over decades of experiences and interactions connected to various media, institutions, and objects. And as long as a hacker
continues to connect to others via IRC, submits patches to open-source

FIGURE 1.7. Debconf7, Group photo, Edinburgh
Attribution-NonCommercial-ShareAlike 2.0 Generic (CC BY-NC-SA 2.0), https://
secure.flickr.com/photos/aigarius/591734159/in/set-72157600344678016/
(accessed August 2, 2011). Photo: Aigars Mahinovs.

projects, reads about their technical interests on Web sites, argues with their
buddies over the best-damn text editor in the world (Emacs), layers of experiential sedimentation are added to their lifeworld. Like a large geologic
rock formation, a lifeworld has detectable repetitions, but it clearly exhibits
patterns of change. In one era, hackers connected with others through BBSs;
now they have transitioned into a larger space of interactivity, tweaking
the Internet technology that, as Chris Kelty (2005, 2008) has argued, is the
regular basis for their association.

In the last decade, the participants in and content of the hacker public
have dramatically expanded and diversified (Jordan 2008; Coleman and
Golub 2008). Over blogs and at conferences, many geeks engage in a discussion with lawyers and media activists about a range of legal as well as technical topics concerning the future of net neutrality, the digital commons, and
the expansion of copyright into new domains of production. A day rarely
passes without hackers creating or reading the publicly circulating discourse
that, in text, represents this lifeworld, otherwise experienced in embodied
interactions, maniacal sprints of coding, and laughter poured over the latest Dilbert, xkcd cartoon, or Strongbad video at work. Insignificant as each
of these moments may be, taken together, they become the remarkable and
powerful undercurrent that sustains a shared world.

There are lines of continuity and discontinuity with times past. Hackers today are still tweaking and building technology like they did as children on their first beloved computer (the Apple IIe, Sinclair, or Atari), but now they are equipped with more technical know-how, their computer's cpu is vastly more powerful, their online interactions are more frequent and variegated, and they have created and are always creating new lingo. Even though their technical lives have become more public, given that so many mailing list discussions are accessible to all after a simple search query, hackers' social and technical production happens in the domestic and private space of the home. Publicity in this case is often matched by the privacy of the room or office, where hackers labor during the day, in the evening, on the weekend, and for some, all of these times. A lifeworld is situated within its historical times, even if rarely experienced as anything other than prosaic time, except during rare moments like the con.

All conferences, despite their many differences, might be theoretically approached as the ritual underside of modern publics, in the sense theorized by Michael Warner (2002) and Taylor (2004). While theorists of publics have always noted that face-to-face interactions, such as meetings in salons, are part of the architecture of the public sphere and publics (Habermas 1989), there has been little detailed attention given to the ways that physical copresence might sustain and expand discursive forms of mediation. Perhaps the circulation of discourse captivates people so strongly, and across time and space, in part because of rare but socially profound and ritualistic occasions, such as conferences, when members of some publics meet and interact. Approaching the conference in terms of its ritual characteristics may also demonstrate how social enchantment and moral solidarity, usually thought to play only a marginal role in the march of secular and liberal modernity, is in fact central to its unfolding.

The relations between the conference and the public have affective, moral, technical, economic, and political dimensions. Transportation technologies, trains in times past and planes in times present, are as much a part of the (often-unacknowledged) architecture of publics as are newspapers and the Internet, for they transport bodies, normally connected by discourse, to interact in an intense atmosphere for a short burst of time. It requires a significant amount of labor and money to both organize and attend these events. The contexts of labor and organization—Is it affordable? Should it be held in a downtown hotel or a small forest outside of Eugene, Oregon? How is the conference advertised? Is it open to all or based on invitation? What is the environmental impact of far-flung global travel?—shape their moral and political valence. Given that most conferences, even those that are consciously made affordable, usually require long-distance travel, the economics of conferences make them significantly less accessible to certain populations. The poor, the unemployed (or the overly employed who cannot get time off to attend these events), the young, the chronically ill, and those with disabilities often cannot attend. A political economy of the conference can illuminate how members of a public are poised differentially to each other because of their ability or inability to meet in person.

Just as a public has different instantiations, the same can be said of the conference. If some publics, as Warner (2002, 119) perceptively argues, are counterpublics that maintain "at some level, conscious or not, an awareness of [their] subordinate status," similar typologies might help us understand the social power and political force of a conference. While most conferences, at some level, share similar features (presentations, talks, and dinners), there are notable differences, especially as it concerns things like sleeping and eating. The differences between the American Psychiatric Association annual meetings, where doctors are dressed in suits and mill about during the day at San Francisco's Moscone Center, retiring individually in the evening to a luxury San Francisco high-rise hotel after a nice dinner, and the outdoor festival held by European hackers, where bodies are clothed in T-shirts and shorts (if that), and many participants can be found sleeping together under the stars, are difficult to deny. Although many hackers find themselves in well-paid jobs (like doctors), they are cognizant of the controversial politics surrounding the term hacker—a name many take on willingly. The cultural ethos and class of a group is inscribed in where they are willing to meet, what they are willing to do with their bodies, what they are willing to do with each other, and what they are willing to express during and after these conferences.

Despite the differences in their moral economy, conferences tend to be the basis for intense social solidarity that sustain relationships among people who are otherwise scattered across vast distances. For hackers, given the fierce celebration of some of their cons, these gatherings feel entropic. They experience a cathartic release of laughter and pleasure, in which the daily rhythms and trouble of life can be set aside. Yet these events work against entropy, sustaining unity while also engendering new possibilities.

Sometimes, as one sits at their computer, coding feverishly for a project, thousands of miles away from some of their closest friends and interlocutors, one has to wonder, "Does this matter to others in the same way as it does to me? In what ways does this matter?" And more than any other event, the hacker conference answers such questions with lucidity and clarity. During the con, hackers see themselves. They are collectively performing a world that is an outgrowth of their practices, quotidian daily life, and deepest passions. The con powerfully states that this world, which is usually felt in unremarkable terms, is as important to others as it is to each hacker—a clear affirmation of the intersubjective basis by which we can conceptually posit any sort of lifeworld.

CHAPTER 2

A Tale of Two Legal Regimes

ᴄ✇ᴆ

It was the best of times, it was the worst of times; it was the age of
wisdom, it was the age of foolishness; [. . .] it was the season of
Light, it was the season of Darkness; it was the spring of hope, it
was the winter of despair.
—Charles Dickens, *A Tale of Two Cities*

In 1981, journalist Tracy Kidder published *The Soul of a New Machine*,
which earned a Pulitzer Prize for its incisive commentary on the heightened commercial turn in computing during the late 1970s and early 1980s.
The book ends pessimistically with a programmer lamenting how managers
at large computer firms robbed the "soul" of computing away from their
makers: "It was a different game now. Clearly, the machine no longer be-
longed to its makers" (Kidder 1981, 291).

In 1984, a few years after the *Soul of a New Machine* hit bookstores,
Stallman also spoke of the soulless state of computing when he lamented
the tragic end to hacking in starkly cultural terms: "I am the last survivor
of a dead culture. And I don't really belong in the world anymore. And in
some ways I feel like I ought to be dead," Stallman said (quoted in Levy
1984, 427). Just when a handful of scholars and journalists first began to
document the cultural mores of this subculture (Kidder 1981; Levy 1984;
Turkle 1984; Weizenbaum 1976), Stallman declared its death, blaming it on
the cloistering of source code.

While Stallman and others may have accurately described some of the
economic and legal conditions transforming programming and hacking in
the 1980s, hacking never actually died. Contrary to Stallman's predictions,
but in part because of his actions, hacking did not simply survive; it flour-
ished, experiencing what we might even portray as a cultural renaissance
whose defining feature is the control over the hackers' means of production:
software and source code. Between Stallman's dramatic declaration of the

death of hacking and its current worldwide vibrancy thus lies a palpable irony about the unexpected outcomes that mark social life, political action, and broader historical transformations.

The fact that these dire speculations and predictions turned out to be spectacularly false is more remarkable given what has transpired in the realm of intellectual property law in the last thirty years. Free software hackers and enthusiasts have successfully secured a domain of legal autonomy for software production during an era of such unprecedented transformations in intellectual property law that critics have described it in ominous terms like "information feudalism" (Drahos and Braithwaite 2002). Never before has a single legal regime of copyrights and patents reigned supreme across the globe, and yet never before in the short history of intellectual property law have we been graced with such powerful alternatives and possibilities, best represented by free software and the host of projects that have followed directly in its wake.

This chapter, foremost meant to familiarize readers with the historical rise of free software, will present the constitution of two competing legal regimes, conceptualized here as two distinct trajectories that once existed independently but have come into direct conflict, especially over the last decade. The first trajectory pertains to free software's maturity into a global technolegal movement. The second trajectory covers the globalization of intellectual property provisions so famously critiqued in the works of numerous scholars (Benkler 2006; Boyle 1996; Coombe 1998; Lessig 1999, 2001a; Litman 2001; Vaidhyanathan 2001). These partly independent trajectories intersected to become inseparable histories, with their horns locked in a battle over the future of the very technologies (the Internet and personal computer) that have enabled and facilitated the existence of both proprietary software firms and the free software movement.

What follows is not a comprehensive history.[1] Instead, this chapter starts by discussing what is at stake in representing the conflicts between two legal regimes and then considers them in tandem. In so doing, I will emphasize various unexpected and ironic outcomes as I elaborate a single development that will continue to receive considerable treatment in the conclusion: the cultivation, among hackers, of a well-developed legal consciousness.

A POLITICS OF HOPE

In 1997, when I first learned about free software and the GPL, I found myself excited (and puzzled) by the legal alternative it provided. Although I ultimately became more interested in how the free software movement changes the way we think about computer hacking, legal statutes, and property rights, I remained invested in the politics of access, and vociferously read works on this topic.[2] But as time passed, I also grew dissatisfied with many of the political analyses of free software, open access, and digital media, largely for either being too broad or limited in their assessments. Take, for instance, Andrew Ross's critique of free software. He quite correctly characterizes free software as "artisanal":

> For the most part, labor-consciousness among FLOSS communities [. . .] seems to rest on the confidence of members that their expertise will keep them on the upside of the technology curve that protects the best and brightest from proletarianization. There is little to distinguish this form of consciousness from the guild labor mentality of yore that sought security in the protection of craft knowledge. (Ross 2006, 747)

He deems this insufficient, however, poetically stating: "Voices proclaiming freedom in every direction, but justice in none" (ibid., 748). If Ross faults free software for its supposed political myopia, others shine a more revolutionary light on free software and related digital formations, treating them as crucial nodes in a more democratic informational economy (Benkler 2006), and as allowing for novel forms of group association and production (Shirky 2008). If one position demands purity and a broader political consciousness from free software developers, the other position veers in the opposite direction: it has free software perform too much work, categorizing it and other digital media as part of a second coming of democracy, shifting in fundamental ways the social and economic fabric of society.

Analyses that either call for more political orientation or assume fundamental, widespread democratic effects tend to paper over the empirical dynamics animating the political rise of free software. What follows is a more nuanced account of not only the importance of free software but also its historical constitution. While many free software hackers are driven by the pleasures of hacking—chiefly motivated by a desire to ensure their productive freedom (and not by some commitment to justice, as Ross has correctly identified)—the social element of this movement inadvertently offers an education in relevant laws and statutes. It has produced a generation of hackers that function as an army of amateur legal scholars. Over the last number of years, many developers, armed with this legal consciousness, have questioned or directly protested the so-called harmonization (i.e., tightening) of intellectual property law. To rephrase labor historian E. P. Thompson (1963, 712), hackers have "learned to see their own lives as part of a general history of conflict"—a consciousness not always steeped primarily in class struggle, as was the case with the early industrialists/workers described by Thompson, but instead tied to legal battles. Given the significance of the law in shaping and guiding political transformations, especially in the transnational arena, this form of political consciousness far exceeds the narrow ethics of craft that people like Ross stress. Legal consciousness and especially legal knowledge are integral elements of almost any present-day political program.

Despite the legal alternatives provided by free software, there is no sign that the copyright industries have curtailed their demands for additional restrictions. Yet as the domain of free software has grown and matured, it has without doubt shifted the axis of intellectual property law, providing a model that has inspired others to build similar endeavors in various fields stretching from journalism to science. Thus, one of the most profound political effects of free software has been to weaken the hegemonic status of intellectual property law; copyright and patents now have company.

Nevertheless, the existence of free software (and the related though distinct digital practices, such as crowdsourcing) should not be mobilized to make overblown assessments of the role of digital media formations in changing the more general political makeup of society. No simple connection between democracy and social media can be sustained (Ginsburg 2008; Hindman 2008; Lovink 2007; Morozov 2011; Rossiter 2007), nor is that what I am advancing here.[3] Instead, we should recognize the viable alternatives in a moment when intellectual property law is itself undergoing rapid transformation. When it comes to the politics of access, these are the best *and* worst of times. Examining existing political possibilities, such as free software, flags the insight of Antonio Gramsci (1971, 175) about the nature of radical critique: at its most powerful, it should be "armed with pessimism of the intellect and optimism of the will." One way to light the "spark of hope in the past," in the memorable words of Walter Benjamin (1969, 255), is to bring into plain view the forms of conflict, alternatives, and struggles not only of our past but also those in our midst. Now let us see how free software came to provide an alternative to copyrights and patents.

1970–1984: THE COMMODIFICATION OF SOFTWARE

During the 1960s, and for some of the 1970s, most computer firms sold hardware with software accompanying it, while legislators and courts had yet to grant either patent or copyright protection for software. Prior to the personal computer's development, a few firms started to sell stand-alone software products, such as Informatics' Mark IV, a pricey (thirty thousand dollars) but popular file management system that enabled businesses to computerize their operations (Campbell-Kelly 2003). In 1969, the nascent software industry received an inadvertent boost when the International Business Machines Corporation (IBM) started to sell some software independently of its hardware—a strategic move to avert an impending government antitrust suit over bundling (Swedin and Ferro 2005).

Given the lack of legal restrictions on software, hackers and programmers in various university labs routinely read and modified the computer source code of software produced by others. Prior to the 1970s, most hackers and programmers accessed computers—usually large mainframes—within universities, businesses, or the military, but this predicament would change soon after an enthusiastic community of computer hobbyists mushroomed. Throughout most of the 1970s, computers were a far cry from being mass-produced or accessible, yet hobbyists, many of them clustered in high-tech areas, followed the latest developments in computing and electronic technologies by regularly meeting in person at gatherings (Akera 2001; Ceruzzi 1998; Freiberger and Swaine 2000). The hobbyists of Silicon Valley's Homebrew Computer Club, in particular, played an important role in popularizing what was the first commercially available home computer in the United States, the Altair (Friedman 2005). A kit composed of a "big, empty box with a CPU card and 256 bytes of memory" (Freiberger and Swaine 2000, 52), the Altair was manufactured by MITS, a two-person Albuquerque-based company, which sold the bare-bones kit as a mail-order product. Though the Altair lacked what we now see as the indispensable components of a personal computer, notably the keyboard and video terminal, the hundreds of Homebrew hobbyists first using it were thrilled that *anything* of this technological sophistication was commercially available for individual, personal use.

Also originally lacking any software, the Altair eventually included new features, added by MITS, such as an interpreter of the BASIC computer language written by two young programmers, Bill Gates and Paul Allen, who dropped out of college to found "Micro-Soft" [*sic*]. When the pair got wind of the fact that hobbyists had freely distributed copies of their BASIC interpreter at one of the Homebrew meetings, they were infuriated. In 1976, just as companies first consistently began to assert copyrights over software, Gates wrote a letter to the Homebrew hobbyists chastising them for, as he saw it, stealing his software. As Gates (1976; emphasis added) maintained:

> To me, the most critical thing in the hobby market right now is the lack of good software courses, books and software itself. Without good software and an owner who understands programming, a hobby computer is wasted. Will quality software be written for the hobby market? [. . .]The feedback we have gotten from the hundreds of people who say they are using BASIC has all been positive. Two surprising things are apparent, however, 1) Most of these "users" never bought BASIC (less than 10% of all Altair owners have bought BASIC), and 2) The amount of royalties we have received from sales to hobbyists makes the time spent on Altair BASIC worth less than $2 an hour.
>
> Why is this? As the majority of hobbyists must be aware, most of you steal your software. Hardware must be paid for, but software is something to share. Who cares if the people who worked on it get paid?
>
> Is this fair? One thing you don't do by stealing software is get back at MITS for some problem you may have had. MITS doesn't make money selling software. The royalty paid to us, the manual, the tape

and the overhead make it a break-even operation. *One thing you do is prevent good software from being written.*

Although at the time Gates and Allen could not have foreseen just how important copyrights and patents would become to secure their company's financial success, they were already justifying their position with one of the most common utilitarian rationales for intellectual property law. For "good software" to be written, they insisted, authors must be given a financial incentive in the form of copyrights, and therefore be given tight control over the reproduction of software.

What started as a vibrant though niche hobbyist phenomenon had by 1977 turned into a "gold rush" personal computer business craze (Campbell-Kelly 2003). As Gates built the most profitable software firm in the world, securing profits through the deft application of intellectual property law and other business tactics, he would not have to worry much about "obsessive" hobbyists for another twenty-two years. At the time, the threat from these amateurs quickly receded as a handful of the Silicon Valley Homebrew hobbyists became capital-seeking business entrepreneurs, starting a few of the nearly two dozen small desktop-computing companies.

As the US software, personal computing, and telecommunications industries came to dominate national as well as international markets in the late 1970s and early 1980s, Japan surpassed the United States in the global automobile and steel markets, and did so in the context of a US economy suffering from high trade deficits and the outsourcing of manufacturing. Amid fears of losing ground to foreigners in a flagging economy, US legislators launched an aggressive campaign to develop and fund the high-tech and knowledge economic sector (Dickson 1988; Mowery 1999; Sell 2003). In addition, under US president Ronald Reagan, the glimmerings of what is now known as neoliberalism—an ideology of enlightened selfishness marshaled by a government catering to big business in the name of laissez-faire economics—flickered brightly within the US political and economic landscape.

In this climate, legislators encountered little friction, much less outright opposition, when proposing changes in intellectual property law and other corporate-friendly policies. These initiatives included new laws that facilitated collaborations between private industry and educational institutions (most famously through the Bayh-Dole Act), encouraged the industrial support of scientific research, and preserved defense funding for applied science and technology (Boyle 1996; Dickson 1988; Jaffe 1999).

Changes in intellectual property law boosted the nascent software industry into a state of high profitability. Given the ease and extremely low cost of software replication, changes in intellectual property law proved crucial to protect source code, the "crown jewels" of the software industry.[4] In 1974, the Commission on New Technological Uses of Copyrighted

Works (CONTU) deemed "computer programs, to the extent that they embody an author's original creation [. . .] [the] proper subject matter of copyright."[5]

Legislators took CONTUs recommendations and modified the copyright statute in 1976 to include provisions for new technologies, prompting computer-related companies to routinely assert copyrights over software. The changes to the 1976 copyright statute were significant on various fronts. As noted by legal scholar Jessica Litman (2001, 54–63), it was a statute of "broad rights and narrow exceptions."[6] By 1980, legislators amended the statute to officially include software, making statutory what CONTU had recommended. Copyright applies to the "expressive" implementations of a software application, and covers the program code along with any graphic images and documentation.

In the late 1970s, patents were still off-limits. Courts considered software algorithms (the underlying recipes or formulas that specify how parts of a program do their job) to be mathematical processes, not machines or mechanical devices, and thus unfit for patent protection. You could copyright the program's source code, but you couldn't patent what the code did. According to Adam Jaffe, before 1980 the US Department of Justice, Federal Trade Commission, and the US federal courts were far more reluctant than they are today to uphold disputed patents in court. Interpreting patents through antitrust law, courts and regulators often ruled against them, concluding they were anticompetitive. This stance was "essentially reversed in 1980" (Jaffe 1999, 3; see also Drahos and Braithwaite 2002; Sell 2003) and culminated in a "historically unprecedented surge in patenting by U.S. inventors" (Jaffe 1999, 1).[7] By the mid-1980s, courts ruled that new objects were eligible for patent protection. For example, starting in the 1980s, courts deemed new materials, like modified bacteria, genes, algorithms, and eventually business methods, as suitable for patents. In the 1990s, judges redefined software as a technical invention akin to physical machines (Jaffe and Lerner 2004). Patents and copyrights, used together, now offer the software industry multiple points of control over distinct components of individual software programs.[8]

1984–1991: HACKING AND ITS DISCONTENTS

The rise of an independent and soon to be enormously profitable software industry based on the pervasive use of copyrights and, eventually, patents came to reshape the social organization of hacking within the MIT artificial intelligence lab (as well as other similar communities) where Stallman landed in 1971. Starting in the late 1970s, but becoming more common in the 1980s, corporations started to deny university-based hackers access to the source code to their corporate software, even if the hackers only intended to use it for personal or noncommercial use. With this decrease in access came a dramatic increase in business and professional opportunities as countless firms sought to hire talented programmers. In the particular case of the MIT lab where Stallman worked, a number of computer companies hired away a cohort of his peers, ultimately creating a rift between the few who remained and those who left. These hackers working at new software firms were barred from collaborating on projects they had previously created together.

As these changes were under way, many hackers were unaware of—one might even say oblivious to—the intricacies of copyright or patent law, as the work of Kelty (2008) has keenly demonstrated. Many hackers, and Stallman in particular, nonetheless viewed these transformations and new legal barriers as a personal affront as well as significant cultural threat. Stallman fundamentally viewed the sharing of source code as the bedrock supporting the hacker practices of inquisitive tinkering and collaboration, and thus for Stallman, the end of sharing amounted to the end of hacking.

The evisceration of his community drove Stallman into a fit of depressive rage, leaving him "downtrodden and resigned," as he described it in a documentary film (Florin 1986). His first response was maniacal retaliation, and his fury was launched against the specific corporation he felt was personally responsible for splintering his beloved hacker community: Symbolics. In 1982, Stallman sequestered himself in near isolation; for the next two years, he adopted the persona of a revenge programmer. He re-created the changes made to the LISP OS by Symbolics, and then offered the altered version to its competitor, Lisp Machine Incorporated.[9] Stallman's incarnation as a revenge programmer, during which time he matched "the work of over a dozen world-class hackers" (Levy 1984, 426), is now recognized as legendary—indeed, nothing short of one of the greatest feats in programming history.

In 1984, Stallman radically switched strategies. Devising a more personally sustainable response with a far broader scope than revenge, he focused on the politics of cultural survival (Coleman 1999). He resigned from the MIT lab (in order to prevent MIT from claiming any proprietary rights over his work) and began developing what he called "free software," which for a couple of years was not attached to any alternative licensing.

In 1985, Stallman founded the nonprofit FSF, and along with a handful of volunteers, concentrated on developing important technical tools and assembling the components of a free OS. He chose to model it on the design of Unix, which at the time was the most portable OS, meaning it could run on the widest range of hardware. Stallman named his version of Unix GNU—a recursive acronym for "GNU's Not Unix." This acronym cleverly designates the difference between the FSF version and Unix, the popular AT&T proprietary version. Unix was growing increasingly popular among geeks all over the world, and as Kelty (2008) has shown, was already binding geeks together in what he identifies as a recursive public—a public formed by discussion, debate, and the ability to modify the conditions of its formation, which in this case entailed creating and modifying software.

Stallman (1985, 30) formulated and presented his politics of resistance along with his philosophical vision in "The GNU Manifesto," originally published in the then-popular electronics magazine *Dr. Dobb's Journal*:

> I consider that the golden rule requires that if I like a program I must share it with other people who like it. Software sellers want to divide the users and conquer them, making each user agree not to share with others. I refuse to break solidarity with other users in this way. I cannot in good conscience sign a nondisclosure agreement or a software license agreement. For years I worked within the Artificial Intelligence Lab to resist such tendencies and other inhospitalities, but eventually they had gone too far: I could not remain in an institution where such things are done for me against my will. So that I can continue to use computers without dishonor, I have decided to put together a sufficient body of free software so that I will be able to get along without any software that is not free.

During this period, Stallman and the FSF stayed financially afloat by selling FSF/GNU software on tape as well as informal in-kind support from the MIT artificial intelligence lab. Unlike proprietary software, the FSF gave its software users the permission to share, modify, and redistribute its source code (the FSF also often sold applications at cheaper prices than its proprietary competitors), but this was based on an informal agreement instead of a formal legal code. For Stallman, an early pressing concern was how to release software in a way that future, modified versions of FSF software (that is, modified from the original piece of software) would remain open and accessible—a guarantee not necessarily provided by releasing software into the public domain. It would take a major dispute over copyright and his Emacs program (a text editor) for Stallman to actually turn to the law for a solution.

Due to a fairly complicated multiyear controversy unfolding between 1983 and 1985 (whose details need not concern us here, but in which Stallman was accused of illegally copying source code into the version of Emacs he was working on), the legal issues concerning patents, copyrights, and public domain first and palpably became clear to software developers.[10] Catalyzed by this controversy, Stallman started to use more formal legal language in 1985 to protect free software, and by 1989, had crafted a clear legal framework for free software in order to prevent the type of controversy that had erupted over his Emacs work from recurring plus add a layer of protection for free software and, crucially, user freedoms.

Stallman approached the law much like a hacker treats technology: as a system that by virtue of being systemic and logical, is hackable. In other words, he relied on the hacker technical tactic of clever reuse to imaginatively hack the law by creating the GNU GPL, a near inversion of copyright law. The GPL is a license that while built on top of copyright law, reverses traditional copyright principles.[11] Instead of granting the owner the right to restrict copies, the owner of a copyright grants the *users* the right to copy and share programs. And the GPL goes further, projecting into future versions: it behaves like a legal firewall against the threat of future private enclosure. Future versions of a distributed software program licensed under the GNU GPL must remain under the same license, and hence can also be used, shared, modified, and distributed by other users. (This differs from putting software in the public domain, since material released this way can be subsequently incorporated into a new piece of work, which in turn can be copyrighted).

By grafting his license on top of an already-existing system, Stallman dramatically increased the chances that the GPL would be legally binding. It is an instance of an ironic response to a system of powerful constraint, and one directed with unmistakable (and creative) intention—and whose irony is emphasized by its common descriptor, copyleft, signaling its relationship to the very artifact, copyright, that it seeks to displace.

While Stallman felt that open access to knowledge would lead to more efficiency in programming, his primary goal was freedom: he wanted to engineer a legal structure to secure freedom, as he explained to Glyn Moody (2001, 28), one of the early chroniclers of the free software movement:

> The overall purpose [of the GPL] is to give the users freedom by giving them free software they can use and to extend the boundaries of what you can do with entirely free software as far as possible. Because the idea of GNU is to make possible for people to do things with their computers without accepting [the] domination of someone else. Without letting some owners of software say, "I won't let you understand how this works; I'm going to keep you helplessly dependent on me and if you share with your friends, I will call you a pirate and put you in jail."

The creation of the FSF and especially the copyleft were intentional acts of political resistance to halt the increasing proprietization of information. Yet Stallman did not launch a radical politics against capitalism or frame his vision in terms of social justice. Rather, he circumscribed his political aims, limiting them to securing a space for the technocultural values of his passion and lifeworld—computer hacking.

Many hackers and developers learned about the ethical and legal message of free software early in its history, via the GPL or "GNU Manifesto," both of which circulated on Usenet message boards and often accompanied pieces of free software. At the same time, many first-generation hackers who used free software were frequently unaware, unmoved, or even downright repelled by the ethical arguments presented by Stallman and his dramatic manifesto. During interviews, for example, many spoke of their negative or puzzled reaction to Stallman's "quacky" and "strange" ideas. One developer explained his ambivalent posture by saying, "I was a little confused. To me it ["The GNU Manifesto"] sounded socialistic and ideological, a bit like [the] Jehovah's Witness, something which will never come to pass. At the time I disregarded it as a mad man's dream. But I did continue to use Emacs and GCC."

Indeed, many of the early adopters were attracted to free software simply because the applications were cheap and robust. Even better, the license agreement granted permission to read the source code and modify it. The majority of the hackers I interviewed, in other words, came to free software at first merely for the sake of affordable, better-built technology and had little knowledge about the existence, much less the workings, of intellectual property law.

The year that Stallman resigned from MIT to write free software in his battle to secure software freedom, 1984, proved to be a milestone for the globalization of intellectual property laws as well. This was also the year when various industries formed a slew of new trade associations, notably the Intellectual Property Committee, International Intellectual Property Alliance, and Software Publishers Association, which sought to tighten intellectual property laws domestically and export them internationally. Acting largely as an umbrella group for other similar organizations, the International Intellectual Property Alliance in particular would come to play an indispensable role as one of the most powerful copyright lobbyist organizations in the world. By the end of the 1980s, its membership included the following eight trade associations: the Association of American Publishers, American Film Marketing Association, Business Software Alliance (BSA), Computer and Business Equipment Manufacturers Association, Information Technology Association of America, Motion Picture Association of America (MPAA), National Music Publishers Association, and Recording Industry Association of America.

Throughout that year, these and other trade organizations lobbied on Capitol Hill for amendments to a key US trade treaty, the General System of Preferences. The treaty granted member countries the right to export certain commodities tariff free to the United States, and these trade organizations successfully pushed for General System of Preferences status to be contingent on recognition of US intellectual property law and protection of the goods covered under those laws. Concurrent with these changes, legislators amended Section 301 of the US Trade Act, giving the president the power to withdraw other trade benefits if the Office of the United States Trade Representative decided that a country was not providing "adequate and effective" protection for US intellectual property (Drahos and Braithwaite 2002, 89).

1991–1998: Silent Revolutions

If two opposing legal trends emerged between 1984 and 1991, then the years between 1991 and 1998 represent their global consolidation, which

occurred largely beneath the radar of public awareness and scrutiny. The
expanding use of desktop computers and networking at home, especially for
business purposes, guaranteed steady profits for the software industry, and
transformed small firms like Microsoft, Oracle, Novell, Cisco, and Adobe
into some of the most influential as well as profitable corporations worldwide. In the early 1990s, even with healthy profits, a lucrative market, and
well-established intellectual property regulations, the trade associations representing the software industry and other sectors of the knowledge economy
were unsatisfied with the legal state of affairs. Trade groups intensified their
efforts to secure more changes in intellectual property law largely through
international treaties to better serve the interests of the corporations they
represented.

To achieve this, they integrated four new approaches into their arsenal:
they worked with federal law enforcement agencies to strike against "pi-
rates"; they pursued civil court remedies against copyright infringers; they
launched moral education campaigns about the evils of piracy (Gillespie
2009); and finally, they pushed aggressively for the inclusion of intellectual
property provisions in the multilateral trade treaties of the 1990s, notably
the Trade-Related Aspects of Intellectual Property Rights (TRIPS).

In the United States, these tactics were assisted by new legislation signed
into law by President George Bush in October of 1992 that redefined a
class of copyright infringement cases in the United States as felonies. Before 1992, copyright infringers could face only civil suits and criminal
misdemeanor charges, but after the changes made to Title 18 of the US
Crimes and Criminal Procedure Code, a person who made more than ten
copies of a software program could receive up to two years in jail and
a $250,000 fine.[12] In making a class of copyright infringement a felony,
policymakers and intellectual property association representatives could
then argue for more inclusion of law enforcement agencies in the global
fight against piracy.

On the international front, in 1994, after years of intense US-led lobby-
ing efforts, TRIPS became incorporated within the General Agreement on
Tariffs and Trade (GATT), and in 1995, was passed off to GATT's more
robust replacement, the World Trade Organization. At the time, this treaty
represented a sweeping global change to intellectual property law, as it required all member nations to eventually adopt a single legal standard deriving largely from US legal principles. Among other provisions, some of the
most significant were the following: patents had to ultimately be open to all
technological fields (including software), the copyright term was modeled
on the US 1976 copyright statute, and nations could only grant narrowly
defined exemptions to copyright and patents. Along with accepting these
provisions, signatory nations had to commit to building the infrastructure
(patent and copyright offices along with criminal units) needed to uphold
and monitor intellectual property protection—a substantial financial invest-
ment for many developing nations.[13]

These extensive legal changes, mandated by global regulatory institutions, are an example of one of the central contradictions in the neoliberal instantiation of free trade. Neoliberalism champions the rights of individuals, deems monopolies regressive, and relishes establishing a world free of government regulation, so that goods, and especially capital, can cross national boundaries with little or no friction (Ong 2006). In practice, however, the actual instantiation of neoliberal free trade requires active state intervention, regulation, and monopolies (Harvey 2005; Klein 2008). And the global regulation of intellectual property law is perhaps one of the clearest instances of the contradictory underpinnings of neoliberal practice—a monopoly mandated by trade associations as a global precondition for so-called free trade.

On the national front, many changes were also afoot. In 1995, the Clinton administration released a white paper, developed under Bruce Lehman, the assistant secretary of commerce and commissioner of patents and trademarks, which agreed with the assessment made by the copyright industries that their intellectual property holdings were under dire threat by new technologies. The ease of duplication and circulation enabled by new information technologies, the copyright industries insisted, would prevent them from releasing content digitally, thus retarding the Clinton administration's goal of creating a commercially robust national information superhighway. Echoing Gate's earlier admonishments against the Homebrew hobbyists, the administration's rationale was that the information superhighway "will not be realized if the education, information, and entertainment protected by intellectual property law are not protected effectively. Creators and other owners of intellectual property rights will not be willing to put their interests at risk."[14] Although Congress did not pass the maximalist copyright recommendations proposed in this white paper, it would implement similar ones a few years later with the DMCA's passage.

In this neoliberal climate, the message, politics, and artifacts produced by Stallman were barely audible, as media theorist Thomas Streeter (2011, 156; emphasis added) has aptly observed: "In a neoliberal world that was both in love with high technology and that seemed completely stuck in the assumption that innovation only sprung from the unfettered pursuit of profit, Stallman's approach *was so different as to be almost invisible*." However muted Stallman's approach was in the early 1990s, free software would soon experience massive growth, breaking away from its geeky enclave to instigate a radical and fundamental rethinking of the assumptions that in the 1990s still worked to marginalize Stallman's "crazy" ideals.

While the increasing personal and business use of desktop computers along with the commercialization of the Internet contributed to a diverse, steady market for proprietary software firms, cheaper desktops and more affordable Internet access also lubricated the emergence of a novel form of network hacking in ways that altered the public face and future direction of free software. Indeed, in 1991, just a year before President Bush signed legislation to reclassify a class of copyright infringement as felonies, Torvalds kicked off the development of the Linux kernel—a kernel being the liaison between the hardware and software of a computer, and therefore the core of the computer's OS. At the time, Torvalds had no intention of developing a project that would eventually help form the nucleus of a fully operational and powerful OS—Linux—that could compete in the market with propriety products. Nor was he motivated by a politics of resistance or cultural survival, as was clearly Stallman's impetus. Torvalds was simply trying to get some help with a personal project that had captivated his attention.

Concurrent with the ongoing development of GNU applications, but independent of the FSF, Torvalds began to develop a basic kernel. He released the source code on an Internet newsgroup, comp.os.minix, with the hope of coaxing feedback from others and to allow other programmers to "play" with it. His first posting to the minix newsgroup on August 25, 1991, when he announced his project, reflects his initially humble intentions (which he contrasted with the FSF GNU project): "I'm doing a (free) operating system (just a hobby, won't be big and professional like gnu). This has been brewing since april, and is starting to get ready. I'd like any feedback on things people like/dislike in minix, as my OS resembles it somewhat." At the end of this message, he predicts, incorrectly, that the OS "probably never will support anything other than AT-harddisks, as that's all I have :)."[15] Given just how common Linux is today, Torvalds's statement is famous among F/OSS developers for its historical irony.

Yet a kernel, on its own, is a far cry from a functional OS. Since Stallman's GNU project had already made many components required for an OS, but had not yet developed a fully operational kernel, Torvalds decided to integrate GNU's copylefted software applications and components with his kernel. This decision would prove crucial; it required Torvalds to license Linux under the GNU GPL, and assured that the Linux source code would remain accessible throughout its many future modifications and versions. In a 1994 interview, Torvalds remarked that choosing the GPL license was "one of the very best design decisions I ever did, along with accepting code that was copyrighted by other holders (under the same copyright conditions, of course)."[16] Pairing the GNU project with Linux was also a marriage between the purely technical motivations of Torvalds and the philosophical, political motivations of Stallman—a marriage that would come to see some tense moments in the future.

Indeed, Stallman was not known for his deft leadership skills, while Torvalds's was to become well known for his open and effective style of leadership. Stallman was foremost a political crusader, attempting to salvage what he saw as the withering away of a culture; Torvalds was a fierce technical pragmatist, embodying a no-frills sensibility commonly championed by many hackers. In marked contrast to Stallman, who tightly controlled the development of FSF software, Torvalds was keen to receive any feedback from peers through newsgroups, where programmers could contribute bug fixes and improvements that, if deemed worthwhile by Torvalds (who became known as the project's "benevolent dictator"), would be incorporated into new versions of the Linux kernel. Unlike earlier generations of hackers, Torvalds could now do a significant amount of work from the comforts of home (thanks to the personal computer and an Internet connection), and in the process of developing the new kernel, he became a skillful leader, coordinating the contributions of geographically dispersed developers over the Internet.

The Linux kernel development project helped usher in a new era of networked hacking, in which project leadership validates its status as much through its ability to evaluate and coordinate contributions from others as through the leaders' own technical prowess. This mature form of networked hacking differed in at least three respects from previous instances of hacker collaboration: production was not affiliated solely with a single institution; production occurred largely independent of market pressures and conditions; and contributions, from previously unknown third parties, were encouraged and, if deemed technically helpful, accepted. Through this experimentation, hackers would ultimately produce software applications robust enough to compete with proprietary software in the market, although few knew this at the time.

Before the advent of Linux, the idea that complicated software systems could be produced by geographically dispersed hackers was largely disparaged (Raymond 1999). While it would be an exaggeration to claim that long-distance collaboration between programmers was nonexistent prior to the Linux project, its pace was slow, its scale was contained, and its effects were often piecemeal, especially since such collective laboring had required sending tapes over postal mail.[17] In this period, the FSF had already released a number of widely used and technically respected software tools and applications, based on the integrated work of many programmers.

Linux was, even if not entirely novel, certainly game changing, paving the way for others. In the ensuing decade, some of the biggest names in free software—Apache, GNOME, and KDE—got their start functioning and operating not in the style of the FSF but instead following the example set by Torvalds. Linux initiated a global network of associations composed of hackers who, over time, came to not only identify and alter the principles of freedom first enshrined by Stallman but also shift the material practice of collaborative hacking. The pragmatic and ethical hallmarks of hacking— innovation, creativity, collaboration, a commitment to openness, and imaginative problem solving—that Stallman established as a bulwark against proprietization became the basis of long-distance free software development.

This emergence was not consciously engineered by Torvalds but rather was realized through the open vicissitudes of practical experimentation and action. "It is in the nature of beginning that something new is started," writes Hannah Arendt (1998, 157), "which cannot be expected from whatever may have happened before. This character of startling unexpectedness is inherent in all beginnings." What Arendt conveys is that because at some level the present is always in the process of becoming, we live in a temporal state with some degree of elasticity and underdetermination that allows for an experimental engagement with the world. Much of the early history of free software existed in just such a temporal state of flexibility, demanding a certain level of skeptical and open experimentation on the part of developers and hackers. Stallman's intentional politics of resistance, however crucial to the viability of software freedom as a mode of legal production, was incomplete without the participation of social actors also willing to openly experiment with new possibilities whose future success was up in the air.

Legal and technical groundwork were of course central to this experimentation. Notably the GPL, commonly referred to as the "Constitution" of free software, and similar licenses ensured that source code would always remain available. The availability of the personal computer, networking, and other key technologies materially enabled a sustainable form of virtual collaboration.

An additional element fueling the early development of free software as a collaborative practice was the technical fact that most applications were centered on the Unix OS architecture. Unix is considered one of the most technically influential OSs of all time because of its philosophical elegance and flexible functionality. Since its release in 1969 by Bell Laboratories, it has elicited a dedicated and passionate following among geeks around the world, especially at universities, where it was and still is used for teaching purposes (Kelty 2008; Salus 1994). Until the arrival of Linux, hackers were usually confined to using Unix at work or a university, because most versions rarely ran on desktop personal computers and the cost of most Unix licenses ran high. Just as the hardware hobbyists of the 1970s were thrilled at the arrival of the Altair for bringing computing one step closer to home, hackers of the 1990s were excited that Linux brought their beloved Unix architecture into the private sanctuary of their personal computer. Again, domestic production helped fuel a public practice.

All of these elements—material objects, legal agreements, leadership styles, and human practical experimentation—were significant agents and actors (Latour 1988) in the constitution of a robust sociotechnical movement. Although collaboration had previously existed in the university hacker community, it reached a new depth, breadth, and salience through networked hacking, in the process reconfiguring the environment within which free software development could take place.

Despite this global turn, at this juncture in the early 1990s, the commercial elements of free software were yet in their infancy. It was still the grassroots period of free software, and the mood among developers was akin to festive bewilderment. Although programmers and developers were glad to have access to Unix-compatible free software for home use, many

were surprised that hackers working virtually through a volunteer association could produce reliable and stable software applications. Enthusiasts
and programmers spread the news about this "new wonder" on mailing
lists and IRC. Face-to-face encounters also steadily grew in importance. The
first Linux user group was established in Silicon Valley in 1995, the same
year that the first Linux-specific trade show and conference was launched by
an unincorporated student organization at North Carolina State University.

Starting in this grassroots period, entrepreneurs and geeks founded small
companies, like Red Hat, providing support services for free software applications, while professional print magazines, like *Linux Journal*, were published for a diversifying technical community. Despite this initial turn to the
market, the mainstream press barely noticed this new mode of technological
production, while most managers at corporate firms were either unaware
of the existence of free software or wholly uninterested in migrating to or
developing free software. Free software enthusiasts nevertheless sometimes
made the move themselves by installing free software applications at work,
but hiding this from "clueless" managers. As noted by Jon "maddog" Hall
(2000, 118), an early free software evangelist, most managers at various
technology companies would always respond "no" when asked if they used
Linux, while many of the technical people would respond "yes"—adding,
"but don't tell our managers."

Many developers confirmed this dual life during my research interviews.
One Debian developer described it as living a bipolar, "Jekyll and Hyde"
existence. Although privately preferring free software, he was always a little
afraid that his boss might find out that multimillion-dollar deals were being transacted on software with no corporate backing or warranty. No one
knew at the time that in a mere few years, the commercial sector would
jubilantly embrace free software, even if a few things had to change, including its name.

1998–2004: Triumph of Open Source and Ominous DMCA

By 1998, the Silicon Valley tech boom was truly booming. Technology entrepreneurs were amassing millions in stock options from inflated initial public
offerings fueled in part by techno-utopic articles in *Wired* and the *New York
Times*.[18] Internet companies like DoubleClick, Star Media, and Ivillage, all
fledgling star Silicon Valley firms, were awash in venture capital funding and
feverish stock market investments. In the context of one of Silicon Valley's
most pronounced tech booms, geeks continued to install free software servers and other applications in universities and, more than ever, companies,
including many Silicon Valley start-ups. Thus by 1997, the grassroots en-
thusiasm of free software had grown material roots in the corporate sphere.
Multiple Linux distributions—most famously Slackware, Debian, and Red

Hat—were under vigorous development, and newer software applications, like Apache, were gaining significant visibility and being used by high-profile dot-coms like Amazon. Many of the backbone technologies of the Internet were by this time powered by free software (BIND for the domain name system, Sendmail for email, and Apache and Perl for the Web, for example).

The LinuxWorld trade show had grown considerably in size, while users around the world were forming Linux user groups (and other free software groups) in new locations. Geek news sites like the Web site Slashdot and online periodical *Linux Weekly News* acted as virtual glue for an emerging public, publishing general-interest pieces on free software, along with detailed discussions on the host of new legal questions prompted by the new technologies. More and more developers found jobs that hired them to write or maintain free software.

In August 1997, Linux finally made the front cover of *Wired*. Torvalds had garnered enough fame from his hobby to be hired by a Silicon Valley hardware firm (Transmeta). In 1998, a couple of computer science graduate students at Stanford University released Google, a search engine powered entirely by Linux. All this activity signaled that although free software was still expanding through grassroots energy, hackers were clearly moving it much closer into the orbit of high-tech capitalist entrepreneurialism. Amid this trajectory, the last-ditch effort of one famous company, Netscape, at economic survival and a name change would bring free software from the geek underground out into the open, in full public view, and even on to the trading floor of the New York Stock Exchange.

In 1998, Netscape, one of the early great successes of the dot-com era, was battling severe financial losses due to competition posed by Microsoft's Internet Explorer. In January 1998, the company announced a loss of $88.3 million and cut three hundred jobs (Kawamoto 1998). As part of an attempt to remain in business, Netscape released the source code of its popular browser under an open-source license, causing waves in the mainstream press for its breach of corporate intellectual property norms. Netscape thus brought this new concept of intellectual property law—free software—into the public limelight. To justify its heretical choice to shareholders and the public, Netscape offered the following rationale: "This aggressive move will enable Netscape to harness the creative power of thousands of programmers on the Internet by incorporating their best enhancements into future versions of Netscape's software."[19] The announcement introduced the idea that perhaps free software could offer economic advantages to corporate America, with the allure of free, "creative" labor constituting the support for the argument.

During the same months when Netscape technology workers convinced their management that a radical change in the company's intellectual property model might stave off economic demise, another group of geeks organized by an influential tech industry publisher, Tim O'Reilly, was planning to alter free software's public image so that other corporations could follow in

Netscape's footsteps. The group wanted to present free software as a safe and irresistible business opportunity, and felt that the name free software got in the way. This collection of free software geeks, Silicon Valley entrepreneurs, and enthusiasts met in April 1998 in Palo Alto, California, at the Freeware Summit to discuss the future of free software. They were primarily interested in its business potential. The summit conspicuously lacked Stallman.

In intentionally excluding Stallman from this semi-secret get-together, certain participants were trying to sever the message of free software from its intellectual progenitor. Though by this time the public, developers, and hackers identified free software beyond the efforts of a single individual, Stallman was nevertheless still seen as its ideological mouthpiece, and his message remained focused on software freedom. Some participants at the Freeware Summit were concerned that Stallman's personal idiosyncrasies, uncompromising radicalism, and constant use of the terms free and freedom might send the corporate world a message of anticommercialism—or worse, some variant of communism or socialism. Even though free software licenses do not bar one from selling free software, the summit organizers felt that Stallman's conceptualization of free might deter investors. They also pointed out that the term free software was confusing to the public—a sentiment expressed even by many ideological supporters of free software, since it so strongly suggests issues of price and not freedom.

The group solved this problem through a process of linguistic reframing (Lakoff 2004), replacing the term free software with open source. They wanted the word open to override the ethical messages and designate what they were touting simply as a more efficient development methodology. They knew, however, that creating a new image for open source would "require marketing techniques (spin, image building, and re-branding)" (Raymond 1999, 211)—a branding effort that some of the participants were more than willing to undertake. Eric Raymond, who had recently written what would become an influential article on free software, "The Cathedral and the Bazaar," took it on himself to become the mouthpiece and icon for this new open-source marketing strategy.

Although Raymond's goal was to bring free software into the business world, like Stallman, he was also deeply engaged in the politics of cultural revaluation (Coleman 1999). While Stallman felt that a certain type of commercial incursion (in the form of intellectual property law) threatened the values of hacker culture, Raymond wanted to bring open source to the market to improve the hacker cultural experience. If hackers could gain a respectable foothold among Fortune 500 companies, he argued, it would allow them to reap enough social capital so that they could escape a cultural ghetto of marginalized nerdiness. While Raymond (1999, 211) described the ghetto as "fairly comfortable [. . .] full of interesting friends," it was still "walled in by a vast and intangible barrier of prejudice inscribed 'ONLY FLAKES LIVE HERE.'" For Raymond, aligning hacking with the capitalist spirit would allow hackers to accrue socially respectable forms of prestige.

Solely judging from the amount of media attention it received, the open-source marketing campaign was a success. Mainstream journalists complemented their ensemble of sensationalist articles on the Silicon Valley miracle with tales about the wonders of open source. Engineers and geeks working in corporations had actually accomplished much of the silent grunt work that could, in certain respects, back up parts of these stories. Learning the technical, legal, and social ropes of free and open software, these technology workers taught their corporate managers (whose interest in this novel concept had been piqued by the articles in *Forbes* and *Wired*) about this enigmatic sociotechnical world or revealed the fact they were already using this software. Geeks were more than happy to finally be public about their secret work life and explain to their perplexed bosses why free software, which often came with no warranty and no corporate technical support, was superior to the business default, Microsoft. These moments are recollected with great pride as an early triumph of F/OSS.

Gates, who had already dealt with "pesky" hobbyists in his youth, had to respond to the product and messages of these impassioned volunteers. Early in 1998, Gates publicly stated that Linux posed no competitive threat to Microsoft. In an interview, he confidently asserted that "popular newcomers such as Linux pose no threat to Windows. Like a lot of products that are free, you get a loyal following even though it's small. I have never had a customer mention Linux to me" (quoted in Lea 1999).

Despite Gates's proclamations, top-level managers were writing anxious internal memos about the threat posed by open source—memos that were eventually leaked online by a Microsoft employee. They revealed that the Redmond, California, giant was in fact eminently concerned by the "loyal following":

OSS poses a direct, short-term revenue platform threat to Microsoft, particularly in server space. Additionally, the intrinsic parallelism and free idea exchange in OSS has benefits that are not replicable with our current licensing model and therefore present a long-term developer mindshare threat.[20]

Referring to them as the "Halloween Documents" to commemorate the day of their unauthorized release, Raymond provided extensive commentary on the memos, which circulated on the Internet like wildfire. In the short history of F/OSS, this soap opera has become one of the most memorable and influential incidents, and has been received as one of the ultimate historical ironies that many geeks savored. Since Gates's famous 1976 letter to hobbyists is part of hacker cultural lore, it was doubly ironic to have his admonishment against the Homebrew hobbyists— "One thing you do is prevent good software from being written"—historically nullified twenty-two years later due to the action taken by hobbyists.

While Netscape's announcement provided a dose of credibility to an informal hacker practice and its concomitant legal arrangements, everyone knew Netscape was releasing the source code as a last-ditch effort to halt further financial hemorrhaging. Netscape's move was an experiment whose outcome and effect on the future of open source was entirely uncertain. But having Microsoft, one of the largest, most financially secure, and certainly most influential software firms in the world, acknowledge the viability of F/OSS (as both a method and product) sent the clearest possible message to the public: open source was to be taken seriously.

For the Freeware Summit participants who had recently launched an open-source marketing campaign to bring commercial legitimacy to this fringe practice, the leak's timing was a blessing. The surprising yet sweetly vindicating Halloween documents sealed the idea that open source was nothing short of "the real thing" and could make waves in the market. The era of festive bewilderment was over, and it was replaced by a period of revelry as the dot-com boom also fueled the newfound discovery and celebration of the open-source phenomenon.

Although Microsoft stated in its internal memos that it would not lead a campaign of fear, uncertainty, and doubt against open-source products, it feverishly implemented the well-worn corporate tactic of disinformation, using everything in the company's powerful marketing arsenal to discredit the reliability of Linux. Launching a direct attack against the bulwark of F/OSS, the GPL, Microsoft representatives described this legal agreement with three of the most feared words in the United States: cancer, communism, and un-American. In 2001 during a media interview, Microsoft's CEO, Steve Ballmer, stated unabashedly, "Linux is a cancer that attaches itself in an intellectual property sense to everything it touches" (quoted in Greene 2001). Even amid various advertising campaigns, none of these words ever stuck.

Microsoft's early assaults against Linux only fueled an existing anti-Microsoft sentiment among developers. Yet not everyone in the trenches of the free software community was enthused by the newfound commercial popularity of open-source software. Not surprisingly, Stallman was deeply concerned and felt that he had lost control over the crucial message of freedom—a sentiment he expressed in a 1998 interview with a sympathetic Bay Area reporter. Stallman remarked that "certain people are trying to rewrite history," concluding that he might be denied his "place in the movement" (quoted in Leonard 1998). He was afraid that the GNU project's message of freedom and sharing would get forever squashed, buried under the commercial prospecting characteristic of the dot-com boom.

By early 1999, not a month passed without some well-known company—Dell, IBM, Sun, or Oracle—issuing a press release about its involvement in or support of open source. By 2000, corporations released these statements weekly. Instead of community-run free software projects, commercial ventures became the most visible players at the Linux trade shows, and began to hire some of the most active developers from leading projects like the Linux kernel and Apache. Even though much of free software (from compilers to Web servers) was stable, mature, and usable before the commercial incursion, the support and services provided by corporate dollars significantly accelerated development and improved the quality of certain products.

Although Stallman was not opposed to the presence of the market in free software (he repeatedly stated that he hoped programmers would be paid for their labor), he was concerned that as Linux became a high-profile commercial product, the FSF's contributions would become barely audible, marginalizing the ethical message of free software. While arguing with other developers on the Linux kernel mailing list about the need to include the name GNU within Linux (since the OS, after all, included many pieces of GNU software), Stallman again offered a dire prognosis about the future of free software: "If this thread is annoying, please imagine what it is like to see an idealistic project stymied and made ineffective, because people don't usually give it the credit for what it has done. If you're an idealist like me, that can ruin your whole decade."[21]

At this time, it truly did seem as if the idealism of free software was perhaps a thing of the past. The corporate discourse of technical efficiency and market power was growing to be a Goliath in comparison to the eccentric "David" (Stallman) who initiated the idea and politics of free software. I myself wondered how the message coming out of a small nonprofit in Cambridge, Massachusetts, could ever compete with corporate behemoths like IBM that had million-dollar advertising campaigns at their disposal. Many people were coming to learn about open source through slick advertising campaigns (in the form of print ads, television commercials, and even spray-painted images on city streets) that only corporate giants could afford.

The corporate acceptance of Linux and open source, however, did not completely eliminate the idealistic elements of free software production. In fact, the popularity of Linux among hackers, the ability of hundreds and eventually thousands of programmers to contribute to it (and other software projects), and its success in the commercial sphere had the effect of rendering visible the underlying ethics of free software to a much larger audience than the FSF and Stallman had ever reached.[22] By turning Linux and open source into household names, many more people learned about not just open source but also the ethical foundations—sharing, freedom, and collaboration—of free software production. In other words, historical outcomes proved to be more unpredictable, complex, and ultimately ironic than anyone could have ever imagined.

As Linux and open source gained more visibility in the public sphere, corporations were not the only entities and actors to learn about as well as embrace F/OSS. Influential academic lawyers like James Boyle, Yochai Benkler, and Lawrence Lessig, who were all concerned with diminishing public access to knowledge, were studying the dynamics of F/OSS, and using them as the prime example to argue persuasively for alternatives and moderation in intellectual property law. Debian, the free software project with the largest number of members, had by this time committed to the idea of *free* software, a morality enshrined in its Social Contract (a list of promises to the F/OSS community) and Debian Free Software Guidelines (DFSG, clarifying the legal meaning of freedom for the project). By 1998, people inspired by the GPL had created similar licenses for other forms of content. Lessig institutionalized this expansion in 2002 in Creative Commons, a media-savvy and well-respected nonprofit that now provides a collection of alternative copyright licenses. More and more grassroots F/OSS projects, most of them small (one to five developers) and unfunded, were appearing. By 2000, there were over twelve thousand documented F/OSS projects hosted on Source-Forge, a widely used central repository for F/OSS programs.

Outside the sphere of F/OSS production, other Net enthusiasts and users were also deeply enmeshed in techniques of collaboration enabled by the Internet and cheap computers. For example, seasoned political activists who were part of the Independent Media Centers (IMC) first established in 1999, during the heat of the counterglobalization protests raging at the time in many European and US cities, were posting news and photos on Web sites powered by free software. Aware of the social and political implications of free software, some of these IMC organizers ideologically aligned the meaning of free software with a radical political outlook (B. Coleman 2005; Pickard 2006; Milberry 2009). Among netizens, new tools like wikis and blogs, many written as F/OSS, fueled the production of noncorporate-controlled content during an unprecedented commercial intrusion into the Internet—a trend that continues today, most famously with projects like Wikipedia (Benkler 2006; Reagle 2010; Shirky 2008).

In short, F/OSS production was only one instance of a broader set of changes taking place on the Internet, propped up by the idea that information access is, if not a fundamental right, a noteworthy social good, and the best conduit by which to foster collaboration and creativity. Free software production was at this time the most dynamic, ethically coherent, and vibrant example of the new social phenomena, for it had developed into a full-fledged movement composed of a technical methodology, legal agreements, and a sophisticated ethical philosophy. Open source, as Steven Weber (2004, 7) claims, is "one of the most prominent indigenous political statements of the digital world." As such, F/OSS has attained a robust sociopolitical life outside the digital world as a touchstone for like-minded projects in art, law, and journalism—some notable illustrations being MIT's OpenCourseWare Project, School Forge, and the BBC's decision to open its archives under a Creative Commons license.

Still, all parties did not celebrate the forms of information access, open content, and collaboration facilitated by new information technologies. Major corporate copyright owners were aghast at the promiscuous file sharing enabled by a broadband connection, a home desktop computer, and peer-to-peer systems. As these technologies became more accessible, the copyright owners feared file sharing and piracy would become a routine part of everyday life, thereby cutting into their profit margins—although these fears were curiously at times conceptualized not solely in economic terms but also in cultural and moral ones. The following statement made at the turn of the twenty-first century by Richard Parsons, at the time the president of Time Warner, became a well-known declaration about the cultural threat posed by weak intellectual property protections:

> This is a profound moment historically. This isn't just about a bunch of kids stealing music. It's about an assault on everything that constitutes the cultural expression of our society. If we fail to protect and preserve our intellectual property system, *the culture will atrophy*. And corporations won't be the only ones hurt. Artists will have no incentive to create. Worst-case scenario: The country will end up in a sort of cultural Dark Ages.[23]

The copyright industries told Congress that their economic future in the new millennium utterly depended on a drastic revision of copyright law (Vaidhyanathan 2001). Congress listened. These industries successfully pushed for a bill—the DMCA—that fundamentally rewrote intellectual property law by granting copyright owners *technological control* over digitized copyright material. The main thrust of the act, with a few narrowly defined exceptions, is that it prohibits the circumvention of access and copy control measures that publishers place on copyrighted work.

Exceeding the mandates in the 1996 World Intellectual Property Organization treaty on copyrights, the DMCA imposes severe criminal penalties (a single offense can involve up to five years in prison and a $25,000 fine) against those who circumvent access control measures protecting copyrighted material. The act steps even further into unprecedented legal territory: the DMCA also outlaws the distribution, trafficking, and circulation of *any device* with the potential to decrypt an access or copy control, even if the device can be used for an entirely lawful purpose. Thus, along with making the act of circumvention per se illegal, it bans any technology that can potentially be used to circumvent an access control method. As noted perceptively by one media scholar, the DMCA's circumvention clause actually makes the "Digital Millennium Copyright Act" a misnomer; it is an "Anticopyright act" (Vaidhyanathan 2004, 85), since the DMCA grants copyright holders the right to "circumvent" the few restrictions built into copyright law such as expiration terms, first sale, and fair use.

Hence, just as a swath of volunteers and a segment of the corporate world embraced the open-source credo of access and openness, other corporate players were relieved when President Bill Clinton signed maximalist copyright principles into law with the DMCA on October 28, 1998. The DMCA, signed only a week after the Sonny Bono Copyright Term Extension

Act (which retroactively extended copyright an additional twenty years), signaled a new era in which copyright owners would wield tremendous influence over legislation.

The DMCA passed without much public awareness, much less any controversy. Trade associations working on behalf of the entertainment and copyright industries backed the act. During hearings, these associations consistently claimed that unless copyright owners were given total control, they would never digitize content. Without the said protections, economic growth would halt. The BSA was armed with unverifiable statistics to buoy its stance, reporting that the eradication of piracy would add 430,000 jobs in the United States, worth five billion dollars in wages (Benkler 1999, 423).

In 1999, after hackers released DeCSS (a short program used by Linux enthusiasts to circumvent DVD access control), the MPAA sued various programmers and publishers for publishing this program. In Norway, one of its authors, Jon Johansen, was arrested—although not under the DMCA (this is described in greater detail in chapter 5). These events, and others that followed, mark the moment when two legal trajectories finally clashed.

In 2001, at Adobe's urging, the FBI made its first arrest under the DMCA—as mentioned earlier, the Russian programmer Sklyarov. Sklyarov was arrested as he was leaving Defcon, where he had presented a paper on a software application he helped code for his Russian firm. It was a piece of software deemed illegal under the DMCA. The US Office of the Attorney General charged Sklyarov with violating the DMCA for his role in developing the Advanced eBook Processor. As Sklyarov was whisked off to prison, the FBI's first arrest under the DMCA sent a chilling message to the other five thousand hackers who attended Defcon in the heat of Las Vegas. The industry was more than ready to follow through with extreme measures to control the production of technology, which also meant controlling what hackers did on their personal computers in the privacy of their homes. For many hackers, this meant controlling thought itself.

Soon after the Sklyarov indictment, the BSA, satisfied at a job well done, released the following statement:

> US prosecutors have now obtained the first indictment under the Digital Millennium Copyright Act, involving Elcomsoft, and its employee, Dimitry Skylarov [sic]. This indictment under the DMCA is consistent with the plain reading of the law and with Congress's intention when the law was drafted and enacted in 1998. Law enforcement actions are critical to the BSA's anti-piracy efforts, which resulted in over $11 billion in losses to the industry alone. The BSA has a productive history working with the Department of Justice on anti-piracy measures and educating the public about software piracy. We look forward to continuing efforts in this area.[24]

The copyright industry clearly found great comfort in using a law that granted it a generous degree of technological control over digitized content while outlawing a certain class of technologies. But the BSA and its peer associations were in for a shock, as an unforeseeable series of events erupted soon after the corporation persuaded the US attorney's office to bring legal actions using the DMCA: hackers, in the face of such new restrictions, responded to the arrest and lawsuits with a series of protests, during which they affirmed their free speech right to write and circulate source code. Hackers and programmers took to the streets following the arrests of Johansen and Sklyarov. They received the arrest and other threats doled out under the DMCA as a crisis for their community, and responded with potent expressions of dissent. These protests further cemented the pragmatic and political associations that many US and European F/OSS programmers had been forging between free speech and source code—a link they now use liberally to argue against the incursion of intellectual property restrictions in software production.

Thus, under the DMCA banner (and the lawsuits and arrests doled out under its jurisdiction), free and open-source licensing along with conventional intellectual property law, both now part of a liberal legal tradition, came into furious conflict. As noted by legal scholar Dan Hunter (2005, 1113), "these statutes [the DMCA and the Sonny Bono act] motivated a number of public interest groups in a way that had never occurred before. Up until the passing of this legislation, corporate interests lobbied for IP expansion without much, if any public comment." In particular, the DMCA's application to halt the dissemination of software led to some of the most powerful expressions of protest among hackers and aligned various groups (academics, librarians, and hackers) in their fight against various trends in intellectual property law. Sklyarov's arrest proved a greater boon to the consolidation of the anti-DMCA movement than to the suppression of so-called piracy.

During the 1990s, when trade associations began in earnest to expand and strengthen the global reach of intellectual property laws while linking them with trade issues, free software production acted informally as a training ground for an army of amateur legal scholars, critical of the new intellectual property legislation. Free software hackers came to deeply value a legal morality other than the neoliberal credo spun by copyright industries. As part of this informal education process, hackers collectively learned a great deal about the law of copyrights, patents, trademarks, and the DMCA—a regime that many of them choose to resist, seeing it as a limitation on the pursuit of hacking.

If most geeks and hackers were unaware of intellectual property law in one era, in a subsequent period they had grown intimate with its inner workings. To get an initial taste of the depth of legal consciousness among hackers, take, for example, the IRC below among a handful of Debian developers, who are simultaneously judging a piece of technology and its copyright notice. This form of legal exegesis, which we will see in much greater detail in the conclusion, is today simply a part of the routine landscape of many free software projects. In this case, a developer named "vilinger" is posting the copyright terms of a piece of software. Vilinger's fellow developers are critical of not only the software but its license as well, observing that it is a "real crappy copyright statement" due to its vague language:

<vilinger> * Copyright © 1998–1999 by [. . .]
<vilinger> * License: Free for any use with your own risk [. . .]
<vilinger> that doesn't allow redistribution, does it
<wondele> vilinger: that's a really crappy copyright statement.
<wondele> vilinger: it can mean almost anything [. . .]
<muffield> vilinger: doesn't allow anything. effectively no license
<muffield> another license written by an idiot who didn't comprehend
    what copyright is
<muffield> (it's a reasonably accurate description of the default, unli-
    censed state of a work)
<lisa> My next copyright is going to just contain "Ask muffield"

Over ten years of active development and use of free software, a critical mass of hackers had inculcated not simply a commitment to their craft but also a well-developed ethos for information freedom and sharing that ran aground against developments in intellectual property law.

Although much of the work of so-called intellectual property harmonization has been completed, it is too early to declare it a thing of the past, a completed history; its future is still open. In fact, despite the fact that harmonization is so often used to describe the creation of a single global standard of intellectual property law, the marked conflict over intellectual property law that resulted is far from harmonious. To take one prominent illustration, in 2005 the European Parliament overwhelmingly rejected a proposed software patent directive that was under consideration for a number of years. This decision came after pressure from a grassroots movement that engaged in years of demonstrations, many of them organized and attended by F/OSS developers (Karanovic 2010). The directive sought to establish and fully harmonize the criteria for software patentability, since each national patent office still follows a slightly different set of principles. The European Commission over the last few years has aggressively tried to pass patent measures that outline principles for adoption throughout the European Union—criteria that, like the US system, overwhelmingly favor private enclosure over public access.

Not surprisingly, the intellectual property associations, once oblivious to the legal alternatives provided by free software, are now not only aware of open source but also actively attempting to halt the spread of this rival legal regime. The International Intellectual Property Alliance, for instance, issued the Special 301 Report about Brazil (recommending that Brazil remain on the watch list due to numerous violations), and included the following suggestions about open source: "Avoid legislation on the mandatory use of open source software by government agencies and government controlled companies," as though open source itself were an example of piracy.[25] If free software developers are actively fighting the harmonization of intellectual property law, the intellectual property associations are actively fighting not only copyright infringement but more remarkable, the global spread of open-source software too.

CONCLUSION

In the late 1970s and early 1980s, a tidal wave of commercialization transformed software from a technical object into a commodity, to be bought and sold in the open market under the alleged protection of intellectual property law. At least for a period of time, the soul of the machine seemed to retreat from public view, leaving certain people, like Stallman, deeply perturbed by these trends. And it was in part because of the political actions that Stallman took—notably by chartering the FSF, writing free software, and most crucially, coming up with a legal hack to protect it—that hacking as a craft based on the open exchange of knowledge continued to exist, although it would be radically transformed.

Nevertheless, and this is key to emphasize, while Stallman's political actions were pivotal, they were not enough. In the ensuing years, his actions even sat in tension with the apolitical pursuit of hacking that also contributed to the vibrant explosion of free software. Even though Stallman injected an important spirit of resistance and a legal basis by which to practically secure a zone of partial autonomy, when free software enlarged into a global movement, conscious resistance or political intention figured less prominently. During the subsequent years (1991–98), free software grew into a much larger technical and social movement in which geeks all over the world participated in the day-to-day development of free software while learning a new vocabulary by which to comprehend its cultural, technical, and political significance. It was a period of open experimentation and festive bewilderment, when developers slowly but surely started to inhabit a new ethical terrain.

Critical to this enlargement was the widespread availability in the early 1990s of mass-produced technologies, like the personal computer, which hackers used to connect to a "novel" global network, the Internet. On computers, on the Internet, they could do what they found great pleasure in doing: tinkering, experimenting, and building software together. During this era, hackers developed new technologies and social mechanisms for working together virtually when not physically together. This brought hackers' long-standing ideals and practices for collaborating to unforeseen heights, and accidentally shifted where and how hacking could occur.

If F/OSS grew into a discernible technical movement that was global in scope between 1991 and 1998, then subsequent years (1998–2004) witnessed its diversification. It gained credibility and visibility across vast sectors of society, though in ways that sometimes conflicted. For example, while a linguistic name change from free software to open source made this arena "open" for business, at the same time, and in a different direction, free software inspired radical political activists to create free software to run technology collectives and grassroots media publishing Web sites. It was also during this period that hackers formed a more acute consciousness of the legal implications of F/OSS work and labor along with the laws and trends, such as those of the DMCA, threatening their productive autonomy. During the years that trade associations like the BSA pushed even more aggressively for the expansion of the existing global intellectual property regime, the social movement behind free software cohered, in many unexpected ways, to become a potent *legal counterpower*—one composed of legal agreements, free software, volunteer associations, conferences, journals, Web sites, and a worldwide group of hackers now ethically committed to the idea of F/OSS.

In telling this history, I shared part of the story of what is frequently referred to as the second enclosure movement (Boyle 2003). These developments, especially the early ones concerning software, were part of the broader neoliberal context that helped engender free software in the first place. Indeed, the early application of copyrights and patents on software was the grain of sand that initiated the growth of the resulting pearl that is free software. And yet at that time, although Stallman (and most other hackers) were at some level cognizant of the impact of intellectual property on their productive autonomy, they barely understood the particular workings of copyright or patent law. The trade association representatives, of course, were completely unaware of what was brewing within a particularly esoteric and geeky enclave. Those hackers would, within twenty years, leave this enclave to throw monkey wrenches into the project of harmonization, sometimes intentionally, and at other times often unintentionally.

By the late 1990s, this landscape of consciousness had undergone a massive and historically significant transformation. Both hackers and the spokespeople for these trade associations were not only aware of each other; many hackers also spoke a sophisticated legal language about the workings of intellectual property and free software law that ran into direct opposition to the dominant legal trends in intellectual property law. Two independent legal trends, once worlds apart, now stand together in a state of direct conflict.

PART II

CODES OF VALUE

⤜❦⤛

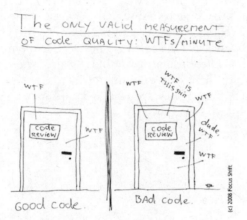

The only valid measurement of code quality: WTFs/minute

WTF

WTF   WTF is this shit   WTF

code review   WTF   code review   dude, WTF

WTF

(c) 2008 Focus Shift

Good code.   Bad code.

FIGURE 3.1. WTFs/minute
Credit: Thom Holwerda.

Anthropologists often focus on cultural value—those ethical, aesthetic, and political attributes of social life that a group has come to deem important, and that ultimately help define it as distinct from other groups. The next two chapters tackle the question of cultural value as a starting point to address a host of questions about hacker technical and cultural production along with the tensions that mark hackers' social dynamics, collaborative practices, and organizational forms.

Although we might be able to identify some indisputable commitments among hackers, such as meritocracy and the form of individualism it entails, the foundation of value among hackers is never without dispute and friction. Indeed, hacking, like all social domains, is shot through with a series of notable tensions. These oscillate between individualism and collectivism, elitism and humility, and frustration and deep pleasure, among others. There are various codes—informal and formal—by which hackers negotiate the tensions that characterize their productive landscape.

The next two chapters attend to what hackers value as well as the tensions that are part and parcel of hacking, and the social codes by which these tensions are partially resolved. Chapter 3 will examine the pragmatic and aesthetic demands of writing code. Humor figures prominently since it mirrors the formal/pragmatic and poetic/aesthetic dimensions of coding, and gets us closer to the most palpable tension in the hacker world—that between individualism and collectivism, which is necessary to grasp notions of creativity and authorship.

Chapter 4 steps away from the craft and aesthetics of hacking toward the workshop where hacking now unfolds—the free software project. Focusing on the Debian project, I continue to give attention to the central contradictions that mark hacking, notably that between elitism and populism. A new thread concerning ethical commitments to information freedom and free speech also appears. Free software projects, while most famous as the place where technical coordination unfolds, is also where significant ethical work transpires. It is here where commitments to free speech are inculcated, thorny issues of meritocracies are resolved, and hackers embody and live out a dense ethical practice.

CHAPTER 3

The Craft and Craftiness of Hacking

✑ↂᕲ

I have nothing to declare but my genius.
—Oscar Wilde

I, for the first time, gave its proper place among the prime necessities of human well-being, to the internal culture of the individual.
—John Stuart Mill, *Autobiography*

Hackers value cleverness, ingenuity, and wit. These attributes arise not only when joking among friends or when hackers give talks but also during the process of making technology and writing smart pieces of code. Take, for example, this short snippet of what many hackers would consider exceptionally clever code written in the computer language Perl:

```
#count the number of stars in the sky
$cnt = $sky =~ tr/*/*/;
```

This line of Perl is a hacker homage to cleverness; it is a double enten-
dre of semantic ingenuity and technical wittiness. To fully appreciate the semantic playfulness presented here, we must look at the finer points of a particular set of the developer population, the Perl hacker. Perl is a computer language in which terse but technically powerful expressions can be formed (in comparison to other programming languages). Many Perl coders take pride in condensing long segments of code into short and sometimes intentionally confusing (what coders often call "obfuscated") one-liners (Mon-
fort 2008). If this above line of code were to be "expanded" into something more traditional and accessible to Perl novices, it might read something like:

```
$cnt = 0;
$i = 0;
$skylen = length($sky)
while ($i < $skylen) {
```

```
    $sky = substr($sky,0, $i) . '*' . substr($sky, $i+1,
    length($skylen));
    $i++;
}
$cnt = length($sky);
```

We see that the Perl programmer has taken six lines of code and reduced them to a single line by taking advantage of certain side effects found in the constructs of the Perl language, and the very act of exploiting these side effects is a great example of a hack. With this transformation of "prose" into terse "poetry," the developer displays a mastery of the technical aspect of the language. This mastery is topped on the semantic level by a quip. The programmer has named the variable $sky, and the star is the asterisk (*) character.[1] The counting function in this program counts any appearance of the asterisk symbol—hence, "counting the number of stars in the sky." This code has a technical function, but within a community of peers, its performance is also a declaration and demonstration of the author's savvy.

Hackers will publicly acknowledge such acts of "genius" and are thus fiercely meritocratic—in ideology and practice. Yet given that so much of hacker production is collective, a fact increasingly acknowledged and even celebrated in the ethical philosophy of F/OSS, a commitment to individuality, meritocracy, and independence is potentially subverted by the reality of as well as desire to recognize their fundamental interdependence. The belief in the value of individuality coupled with the constant need for the help of other hackers points to a subtle paradox that textures their social world. The tension between individualism and collectivism, in particular, is negotiated through the extremely well-developed and common penchant that hackers have for performing cleverness, whether through technological production or humor. Hackers do not treat all forms of expression, technology, and production as original and worthy expressions of selfhood. Instead, one must constantly manifest, in the face of one's peers, a discriminating and inventive mind by performing its existence through exceptionally ingenious and clever acts. By contributing a shining, awe-inspiring sliver of their creative self in a domain otherwise characterized by a common stock of knowledge and techniques, hacker utilize humor or clever code to perform their craftiness, and thus momentarily differentiate themselves from the greater collective of hackers.

While this chapter describes the ethnographic expression of humor and cleverness among hackers (which might be valuable and interesting in its own right), it does so at the service of other, analytic goals. Examining humor and cleverness will allow me to more richly demonstrate how tensions (say, between individualism and collectivism) arise through the course of technological practice, and how hackers partially resolve them. Taking a close look at these frictions takes us a long way toward understanding the social context under which these hackers labor and why free speech ideals—in contrast to those of intellectual property instruments—resonate with their experiences. The friction between individualism and collectivism (and its articulation in meritocratic discussions) helps, for one, underwrite a dynamic social environment in which hackers labor. Second, this tension speaks directly to issues of authorship, selfhood, creativity, and intellectual property in a way that extends, contrasts, and critiques the dominant intellectual property regime.

The analysis opens by examining the pragmatics and aesthetics of hacking, by which I mean the constraints and properties of their technological activities, and contrasting the writings of two hackers, Espe and Da Mystik Homeboy (DMH). Understanding the pragmatics of hacking is necessary to grasp the contradictions/tensions that mark hacking along with what I call the poetics of hacking: the extreme value hackers place on ingenuity, craftiness, and cleverness. I will explore these largely through the angle of humor. The final section revisits the tension between individualism and collectivism. Hackers assert a form of individualism that valorizes self-expression and development among peers engaged in similar acts of technological production, while tightly entangled with each other through constant collaboration.

Hacker Pragmatics

Python: Reaching a Transcendental Space

I remember when I found python, back in the 1.52 days [1.52 refers to a version number].[2] I was an unemployed slacker living in a student co-op. I'd sit in a (since disappeared) cafe in Berkeley and write reams of more or less useless code, simply for the joy of it. I'd reach some sort of transcendental state fueled by relevant whitespace, clear syntax, and pints of awfully strong, black coffee. In those days I first felt the pure abstract joy of programming in a powerful way—the ability to conjure these giant structures, manipulate them at will, have them contain and be contained by one another. I think I learned more in those couple of months, thanks to Google and a free ricochet connection, than in my previous years in CS [computer science].

Eventually, however, it became clear I had to get a real job. Flaky freelance contracts which never paid sucked so hard. So, I hemmed and hawed and was conflicted and finally got a job, and it involved perl. It was, perhaps, a worst-case perl scenario. A very rapidly growing website, a few developers with vastly different styles, a lack of real communication, and a pronounced lack of appreciation for namespaces. From my high tower of control and purity, I'd been thrown into a bubbling pool of vaguery and confusion. Cryptic variables would pop out of the aether, make an appearance in a 2000 line CGI [Common Gateway Interface], and never be heard from again. Combating naming schemes would meet where different spheres of developer influence overlapped—$postingTitle and $PostingTitle doing battle in the same subroutine. Scripts almost—but not quite—deprecated. The situation is quite a bit more under control now, 3 years later.

— *Espe*

PERL: HACKING IN THE BIG BALL OF MUD

Perl has been derided by many people as an ugly, difficult to learn language that enforces bad habits. I generally do not advocate perl to people who are attempting to learn programming, or even mention it's existence. However, perl, for better or worse, is a culmination of decades of culture. Perl is a Unix Gematria—an arcane relation of symbols evolved in a manner similar to Jewish Qabbalistic numerology. Many other languages, such as python or Java, attempt to enforce a strict framework and rule set of contracts, interfaces, strong typing, and private methods to delineate functionality. While much of this stems from noble traditions of SmallTalk and ML [they are computer languages], much of it also fails to realize the point of these ancestral languages: categorization (such as through strict typing and object models) is itself a form of computation. When this fact is not respected, you wind up with a bastardized language that is [. . .] Anal.

Perl was designed by a linguist, and realizes that people have different things to say in different contexts, and your language is defined by the environment and not vice versa. As Paul Graham said, both the world and programming is a "Big Ball of Mud," which perl has evolved around. The implicit variables, the open object model, the terse expressions all contribute to hacking on the Big Ball of Mud.

Finally, there is a very pragmatic reason to like perl: It will save your ass. Those who are fluent enough in the culture to realize that "this problem has been solved before," will be able to invoke forces through perl. Again, similar to the numerologists, with a few arcane symbols that are undecipherable to the outside world, great acts of magik can be accomplished.

— *Da Mystik Homeboy*

Espe is a San Francisco hacker who is clearly fond of Python, an open-source computer language. Originally created by a Dutch programmer as a teaching language, Python is now a thriving open-source project. The language's distinguishing feature (both aesthetic and technical) is its strict technical parameters that require bold syntactic clarity. For example,

Python is unusual among programming languages in that the amount of space used to indent a line of code actually affects the code's meaning. On his blog (excerpted above), Espe explains how he was able to hack to his heart's delight for no other reason than to experience "the joy of programming." His stance toward Python is reverent, rooted in deep pleasure. He obviously adores both the formal structure—Python—and the substance— coffee—that have enabled him to hack for his own enjoyment and self-development. In this instance, Espe constructs programming as a pleasing, unencumbered exercise of ample creativity. He seeks in hacking to reach the elusive quality of perfection.

By the next paragraph, however, his register shifts to one of dismayed irreverence toward another programming language, Perl, considered by many to be the antithesis of Python, and therefore a source of antipathy for many Python fanatics. Eventually forced to hack for money (a problem itself for this programmer), he was handed "a worst-case scenario." Poorly coded Perl transformed programming from an activity of boundless satisfaction into a nightmarish ordeal. Espe describes this unfavorable turn of events as being plucked from his "high tower of control and purity," only to be "thrown into a bubbling pool of vaguery and confusion." In having to read and parse other people's codes, programmers routinely encounter what has been depicted aptly as a "twisting maze of corridors, a bottomless pit" (Ullman 2003, 262).

In the second extract, we have DMH, also a San Francisco hacker, but unlike Espe, a self-styled Perl alchemist. Perl's creator, a linguist and programmer named Larry Wall, intended the code to embody the flexible and often-irrational properties of a natural language. As noted by DMH, Perl's aesthetic and technical features are opaqueness, complexity, and flexibility. Also run as an open-source project, Perl is incorporated into the identity of many of its supporters, who call themselves Perl Monks, underscoring the single-minded dedication they have for what is considered a language that can produce poetic (or highly unreadable code) that is creatively displayed during obfuscated code contests, which are usually held for Perl, C, and C++.[3]

While DMH respects Perl for what it is most famous for—its cryptic nature and poetic elegance—he is drawn to Perl for pragmatic reasons. Its "implicit variables, the open object model, the terse expressions," DMH says, allow him to hack on the "Big Ball of Mud"—that is, the world of thick, unmanageable problems and constraints. For DMH, Perl's appeal lies in its extensive common stock of shared solutions and architectural flexibility, which he contrasts to Python, a language so "anal" it is unable to accomplish "great acts of magik." By this he means what is known among Perl geeks as the Perl's motto: "TIMTOWTDI" (There's more than one way to do it).

Digital computers allow for the creation and use of *mini-machines* (aka software) written by programmers using any number of computer languages.

Instead of having to build a piece of hardware for every type of desired function (like a calculator, music recorder, or word processor), the computer is a general-purpose machine that once animated by software programs, can potentially behave as all those functional objects. Espe captures the expansive technical capability of software when he defines coding as "the ability to conjure these giant structures, manipulate them at will, have them contain and be contained by one another." This is computing in its dimension of unfettered freedom.

If at one level hackers adroitly exploit the expansive technical capabilities of the computer, they are also significantly limited by a powerful force field of constraint—the Big Ball of Mud that DMH refers to in his tract on Perl. Constraints are constant and of a nearly infinite variety, such as hardware specifications and failures, computer language syntax, "clueless" managers, inherited "crufty" or vague code, spam, incompatible file formats, "dumb" patent laws, misguided customers, technical specifications, and manager-dictated deadlines. Problems are so central to software that some have even portrayed "glitches" as the "manifestation of genuine software aesthetic" (Goriunova and Shulgin 2008, 111).

Programming thus entails an expansive form of exploration and production that unfolds into a labyrinthine landscape of intricate barriers and problems. Julian Dibbell (2006, 104; see also Ensmenger 2010, 3) depicts the nature of computing, quite poetically, as an "endlessly repeatable collusion of freedom and determinism—the warp and woof of fixed rules and free play, of running code and variable input." Because of constraints and the complexity of coding, to hack up solutions effectively, as Michael Fischer (1999, 261) notes, requires "a constant need for translation, interfacing, sharing, and updating."

As part of this practical capacity, the very nature of hacking—turning a system against itself—is the process of using existing code, comments, and technology for more than what their original authors intended. This is the paradox of constraint. Since many technical objects are simultaneously bound by certain limits yet exhibit potential excesses (Star and Griesemer 1998), during the course of their existence, they can be exploited and redirected toward new paths of functionality by acts of hacking. Hackers are thus attuned not simply to the workings of technology but also seek such an intimate understanding of technology's capabilities and constraints that they are positioned to redirect it to some new, largely unforeseen plane. They collectively and individually derive pleasure in outwitting constraint. In essence, while hacking follows a craftlike practice, it is predicated on a stance of craftiness to move the craft forward. Hacking is where craft and craftiness converge.

Programming and similar technical activities require extremely rigorous logical skills, an unwavering sensitivity to detail (a single wrong character can render a program useless), and such an intimate command of a system that one can, if need be, exceed the conventional or intended constraints of the system. It requires, in the words of programmer Ellen Ullman (2003, 177), a "relentless formalism." Given the accelerated pace of technological change, hackers also have to perpetually learn new technologies as old ones are phased out due to obsolescence, in order to remain competitive in a marketplace.

· Out of this routine form of technical activity hackers have constituted an expansive pragmatic practice of instrumental yet playful experimentation and production. In these activities the lines between play, exploration, pedagogy, and work are rarely rigidly drawn. Sometimes hackers will be motivated by a work-oriented goal, as is/was the case with DMH. At other times, they are motivated to hack for the sheer pleasure of doing so, as Espe emphasized. In either case, frustration *and* pleasure are fundamental to hacking.

A lifetime of creative and pleasurable technical production that often depends on computers also blurs the line between selves and objects. As famously phrased by Sherry Turkle (1984), computers are a hacker's "second self." The hacker relationship to computers and software, though, rarely exists in a steady state in which the self unproblematically melds with this object to catapult hackers into a posthuman, postmodern state of being. The hacker relationship with the computer is a far more finicky, prickly, and interesting affair in which computers themselves constantly misbehave and break down (as do the hackers, at times, when they burn out from such an intense and demanding craft). Hackers sometimes confront their computers as an unproblematic and beloved "object," and at other times view them as an independent and recalcitrant "thing"—a differentiation posed by Heidegger ([1927] 2008) in his famous exploration of things and objects.

In Heidegger's cartography, an object strikes its users as familiar and beyond the scope of critical awareness. Its social meaning is held in place through regular patterns of use and circulation. But when we misuse an object (a spoon used as a knife or a can opener utilized as a hammer) or when an object malfunctions, its thingness is laid bare in the sense that its material characteristic becomes evident. As noted by scholar of things and stuff Bill Brown (2001, 4), "the story of objects asserting themselves as things is the story of how the thing really names less an object than a particular subject-object relation."

In order to appreciate the hacker relationship to computers, this subtle differentiation between an object and a thing is crucial. Hacker technical practices never enact a singular subject-object relation, but instead one that shifts depending on the context and activity. There are times when hackers *work with* computers, and in other cases they *work on* them. Much of hacker technical practice can be described as an attempt to contain the thingness of computers that arises through constant problems and constraints by transforming it back into a pacified, peaceful object that then becomes an ideal vehicle for technical production as well as creative expression. At times, their labor is characterized by grinding effort, and in other instances, it involves far more pleasurable streams of seemingly friction-free work. The "Python versus Perl Wars" above articulates the metapragmatic understandings of hacker labor that makes it possible to enter into this relational oscillation in the first place.

HACKER CLEVERNESS

Humor can be dissected, as a frog can, but the thing dies in the process and the innards are discouraging to any but the pure scientific mind.
—E. B. White, *A Subtreasury of American Humor*

As the examples provided by Espe and DMH display, hacker technical practice is rooted in a playful, analytic, and especially reflective stance toward form that switches between reverence and irreverence depending on individual preferences as well as the context of activity. Hackers routinely engage in a lively oscillation of respect and disrespect for form, often expressed in arguments over the technical idiosyncrasies, strengths, and weaknesses of a programming language, OS, or text editor. These disagreements are the subject of a range of humorously formulated "holy wars," such as Perl versus Python (which we just got a glimpse of), vi versus Emacs (text editors), and Berkeley Software Distribution versus Linux (different Unix-based OS). Despite this, hackers otherwise share an ideal about how labor and production should proceed: with remarkable craftiness and wit.

One important vehicle for expressing wit is humor. As Mary Douglas (1975, 96) famously theorized, joking brings together "disparate elements in such a way that one accepted pattern is challenged by the appearance of another," and can be generally defined as "play upon form." Before expanding on the role of humor among hackers, it is key to highlight that hackers are able to joke with such facility because of the habituated dispositions (Bourdieu 1977) of thought along with tacit knowledge (Polanyi 1966) acquired through a lifelong and routine practice of logic-oriented problem solving. Hackers liberally enjoy hacking almost anything, and because their cultivated technical practice requires an awareness and rearrangement of form, they are able to easily transfer embodied mental dispositions into other arenas. To put it bluntly, because hackers have spent years, possibly decades, working to outsmart various technical constraints, they are also good at joking. Humor requires a similarly irreverent, frequently ironic stance toward language, social conventions, and stereotypes (Douglas 1975).

The mastery and craft of hacking, however, do not fully account for the *craftiness of hackers*.[4] Many of the engineering arts and sciences are guided by similar aesthetic-solving sensibilities, mandates, and preoccupations (Galison 1997; see also Jones and Galison 1998). Engineers and other craftspeople, such as repairpersons, also deploy similar problem-solving skills rooted in tinkering: they must engage with the limits, possibilities, and constraints of various material objects, and fiddle around to find a nonobvious solution (Orr 1996; Sennett 2008).

Hacker aesthetics share these above-mentioned dispositions, but differ in that hackers see ingenuity and cleverness, often expressed though humor, as far more than a means to regiment and guide technological innovation.[5] Among hackers, humor has a substantial life of its own. Hackers value craftiness and cleverness for their own sake. Whereas academic scientists tend to value referential cleverness as it concerns their work, hackers value cleverness as self-productive, and thus make it appropriate to nearly any context (mathematicians, though, are well known for their prolific humor that exceeds their discipline). Hackers idealize cleverness as a characteristic par excellence that transforms what they spend all of their time doing—creating technology and fixing problems in a great maelstrom of complexity and confusion—into an activity of shared and especially sensual pleasure.

Before extending my theoretical discussion on cleverness and humor, permit me to provide a few examples that are embedded in technical artifacts and one that arose during social interaction. Since much of hacker wit is so technically coded, it is difficult to translate it in any meaningful manner to a lay audience, and I am afraid it might not strike nongeek readers as all that humorous. Analyzing humor, after the fact, is also nearly never humorous, but hopefully it can still be analytically illuminating. I have chosen four examples that are more accessible to a nontechnical audience and supply at least a taste of the types of jokes common among hackers.

Peppering technical artifacts with clever quips occurs quite commonly in hacker technical naming conventions or documentation. For instance, most software applications also come with some sort of description of their purpose and functionality. Jaime Zawinski, the author of a software application called BBDB, portrays his creation via a smattering of jokes (most software applications include a description of their functionality):

> **BBDB** is a rolodex-like database program for GNU Emacs. **BBDB** stands for **Insidious Big Brother Database**, and is not, repeat, *not* an obscure reference to the Buck Rogers TV series.
> It provides the following features:
> Integration with mail and news readers, with little or no interaction by the user:
> easy (or automatic) display of the record corresponding to the sender of the current message; automatic creation of records based on the contents of the current message; [. . .]

While the "Insidious Big Brother Database" is an obvious and playful recognition of the common hacker mistrust of governmental authority, the Roger's reference is more esoteric and thus only a small fraction of hackers will be able to decipher it: those hackers who have watched the television series. With the cue offered in the documentation, those hackers will immediately catch the author's irony (that *this is* a reference to the show) and recognize that BBDB refers to the series' pint-size robot Twiki, whose preferred mode of communicating is a noise that sounds remarkably like "B-D-BBBB-D."

I am particularly fond of the next example contained in the manual (usually shortened to "man page") for Mutt, a popular email client among geeks. Man pages provide documentation and are included with almost all Unix systems. They typically follow a strict standard for conveying information about the program by designating a set of common categories under which programmers provide detailed information about the software, such as the name, synopsis, description, options, files, examples, and authors. One important category is bugs, where authors list the problems and glitches with the software. (Software can have a number of bugs and glitches yet still work. The bug category gives you a sense of what these glitches are and when they will emerge.) The Mutt man page exploits the fact that the word mutt can mean a mongrel dog. Notice the category of bugs:

NAME
      mutt—The Mutt Mail User Agent

SYNOPSIS
      mutt [-nRyzZ] [-e cmd] [-F file] [-m type] [-f file] [. . .]

DESCRIPTION
      Mutt is a small but very powerful text based program for reading electronic mail under Unix operating systems, including support color terminals, MIME, and a threaded sorting mode.

OPTIONS
      —A alias
         An expanded version of the given alias is passed to stdout.
      —a file
         Attach a file to your message using MIME. [. . .]

BUGS
      None. Mutts have fleas, not bugs.

FLEAS
      Suspend/resume while editing a file with an external editor does not work under SunOS 4.x if you use the curses lib in /usr/5lib. It does work with the S-Lang library, however. Resizing the screen while using an external pager causes Mutt to go haywire on some systems. [. . .]

My last example of this subtle integration of wit in a technological arti-fact comes in the form of a warning message. Many software programs and related artifacts are accompanied by dramatic warnings that appear during configuration. These are intended to alert the user that its integration into some software systems may produce unanticipated, drastic, and completely undesirable results (like breaking multiple parts of your software system that took five weeks to get "just right"). Often this happens because a piece of software is still experimental and riddled with bugs. The following help message is available in the 2.6 branch of Linux kernel configuration and refers to the RAID-6 device driver, which at the time was still under develop-ment and hence buggy:

> WARNING: RAID-6 is currently highly experimental. If you use it, there is no guarantee whatsoever that it won't destroy your data, eat your disk drives, insult your mother, or re-appoint George W. Bush

These three examples demonstrate that hackers value subtlety and irony of presentation. Hackers discretely embed nuanced, clever and frequently nonfunctional jokes within what are otherwise completely rational, con-ventional statements of function. Yet hackers never use jokes to undermine the functionality or trustworthiness of the code or documentation. These technical artifacts are judged seriously by geeks. The presence of wit only works to add to the value of the rational content by reminding the user that behind these highly systematized genres, there is a discriminating and creative individual.

Other instances of hacker wit occur in person and are less subtle. For ex-ample, at a security conference in 2001, Peiter Zatko, aka "Mudge," a com-puter security researcher, professional, and hacker (once part of the famous hacker association L0pht Heavy Industries), arrived in a terrycloth bathrobe to present on a panel on PDAs. This bold sartorial statement distinguished him from his nonhacker colleagues, also security researchers, but scientists. It prioritized hacker over scientific identity. Mudge's attire, however, per-formed a problematic public-private breach in the context of his talk, which focused on the changing use patterns of PDAs. "PDAs were designed for per-sonal use, but are now being used more for business," Zatko said. "There's a security boundary that's being crossed."[6] Zatko's robe embodied his argu-ment that the shift amounted to a breached security boundary: PDAs should not be used for sensitive, private data.

Though humor is found worldwide, instances like the ones just described are fruitful to the anthropologist because of their cultural particularity. As this playful practice usually induces laughter—a state of bodily affect that enraptures an audience—humor can potentially produce forms of collective awareness and shared sociality. Given these two properties, we can define humor, in the most general terms, as a play with form whose social force lies in its ability to accentuate the performer, and which at times can work to delineate in-group membership.

Apart from this, the meaning of humor is otherwise quite culturally specific. The power to enrapture and entangle people can lead to entirely contrary social effects. In certain cases and types of groups, joking can establish and maintain hierarchies as well as social boundaries by, say, delineating social roles (Gusterson 1998; Mulkay 1988; Radcliffe-Brown 1952). In other cultural and historical contexts, humor pushes the envelope of conceptual boundaries in ways that may be fleeting and frivolous (Douglas 1975), or politically subversive (Bakhtin 1984; Critchley 2002). In other words, because the effect, purpose, and even form of humor are deeply context dependent, culturally inflected, and historically moored, it is a useful tool for analyzing broader forms of cultural meaning.

Among hackers, humor is a distilled and parsimonious instantiation of the adoration of cleverness. It is an especially effective way of enacting hackers' commitment to wittiness precisely because, unlike the objects of hacker technical production, joking has no strict functional utility, and speaks to the inherent appeal of creativity and cleverness for their own sake. Joking is a self-referential exercise that designates the joker as an intelligent person and cleverness as autonomously valuable.

It bears repetition that hackers draw on their pragmatic ability to manipulate form to engage in this type of joking. These two elements—being good at hacking and valuing cleverness for its own sake—exist in a tight and productive symbiosis, a mutually reinforcing relation that produces an abundance of humor among hackers. There is a close kinship between hacking and humor.

Insofar as humor is tethered to the moment of its utterance, it exudes an auric quality of spontaneous originality (Benjamin [1936] 2005), which among hackers authenticates the self as a distinctive and autonomous individual. Humor is one of the starkest expressions of the hacker "ideal self." By telling jokes, hackers externalize what they see as their intelligence and gain recognition from technically talented peers.

Like hacker technological production, humor also works to implicitly confirm the relational self who is joined to others by a shared domain of practice, and a common stock of implicit cultural and explicit technical knowledge. Recall that many jokes, such as technical Easter eggs, are received as pleasurable gifts. They not only break the monotony and grind of sitting at the computer, usually for hours a day as one churns out code or resolves problems, but also remind hackers of their shared experiences. "One might say that the simple telling of a joke," writes philosopher Simon Critchley (2002, 18), "recalls us to what is shared in our everyday practices. [. . .] So, humor reveals the depth of what we share." If humor creates fine distinctions, it also levels the ground, because in the very moments of laughter, hackers implicitly recognize and celebrate the shared world of meaning in which they work. After all, like many instances of joking, much of hacker humor is so culturally coded (which here means technically inflected) that the only people who can routinely receive, and as such appreciate, their wit are other hackers. One must rely on the acknowledgment and judgment of those who can appreciate the performance of wit, because they share at least some of one's implicit values, explicit technical knowledge, and standards of creative evaluation.

To the extent that everyone enjoys laughter, humor functions much as a communal gift—the performance of which beckons others to follow suit. Indeed, once one hacker starts joking, many others will dive in. It also breaks the monotony and eases the strains of hacking, and so can also be seen as a mechanism to preserve hackers' humanity (and sanity) in the face of the merciless rationale of the machine they engage with everyday. When humor is woven into the actual code or technical artifacts animating the machine, it brings otherwise-mechanic language directly and unmistakably into the realm of human communication.[7] Once part of the apparatus of human communication, humor powerfully confirms a shared mode of being in the world; in other words, it affirms a lifeworld. The very expression of humor is seen as proof that despite their physical dispersion and sense of independence, hackers nonetheless cohabit a shared social terrain built around a lifelong intimacy with technology and technical thinking—one they have come to celebrate.

Among hackers, humor functions in multiple capacities and undoubtedly reflects the value they place on productive autonomy as well as the drive to perform cleverness. Much of their humor is ironic—a play with form. Its purpose is to arrive on the scene of the joke (often a technical object) unexpectedly. This is also the ideal nature of a great hack, insofar as it should surprise other hackers into a stance of awe. Humor, as Douglas (1975, 96) reminds us, is "a play upon form that affords an opportunity for realizing that an accepted pattern has no necessity." This definition bears a striking resemblance to the pragmatics of hacking; hackers are constantly playing on form, revealing that there is no single solution to a technical problem. And although hackers claim it is abominable to reinvent the wheel, in practice, they are constantly doing so as they follow their own creative instincts and visions.

In its ability to concurrently accentuate inclusiveness and exclusiveness, and make and level hierarchies, humor shapes conventions of sociality, ideals of creativity, and hackers' attitudes toward one another and outsiders. Now let's take a closer look at the tension between individuality and collectivism to which humor so delectably points us.

COMMUNAL POPULISM AND INDIVIDUAL ELITISM

If hacker pragmatics oscillate between a respect and disrespect for form, hacker sociality alternates between communal populism and individual elitism. Largely by way of F/OSS philosophy, hackers laud mutual aid and

cooperative reciprocity as vital features of technical collaboration. They
spend an inordinate number of hours helping each other. But there is also
an elitist stance that places an extremely high premium on self-reliance, individual achievement, and meritocracy.[8] While the populist stance affirms
the equal worth of everyone who contributes to an endeavor, the elitist one
distributes credit, rewarding on the basis of superior accomplishment, technical prowess, and individual talent—all judged meticulously by other hackers. Hackers will spend hours helping each other, working closely together
through some problem. Yet they also engage in agonistic practices of technical jousting and boasting with peers, and in turn, this works to create hierarchies of difference among this fraternal order of "elite wizards." Ullman
(1997, 101) condenses this tension into few words: "Humility is as mandatory as arrogance." The line between elitism and populism is not simply an
intellectual afterthought posed by me, the anthropologist, but also a living,
relevant, affective reality discussed and dissected by hackers.

This duality arises during the course of their work, and is openly discussed in ethical and pragmatic terms. On the one hand, hackers speak of
the importance of learning from others and construe knowledge production
as a collective enterprise—and this rhetoric is frequently matched in practice
by truly generous and copious acts of sharing. In any given minute of the
day, I can log into one of the developers' IRC channels, and there will be
some developers asking a question, getting an answer, and giving thanks, as
this example illustrates:

> \<zugschlus\> does anybody know how to configure sound in KDE4? [KDE
> is a desktop environment.]
> \<pusling\> Zugschlus: in systemsettings
> \<zugschlus\> pusling: applications =\> settings?
> \<kibi\> but AFAICT ["as far as I can tell"], what you have in svn helped me
> build various thingies against libqt4-dev and friends.
> \<pusling\> Zugschlus: computer \> s-ystemsettingns
> \<pusling\> KiBi: I think qt4 is now waiting in new.
> \<zugschlus\> pusling: that part only has home, network, root and trash.
> \<kibi\> pusling: oh, ok :(
> \<pusling\> Zugschlus: do you have the package systemsettings installed?
> \<pusling\> KiBi: so if you have special contacts to ftp team, feel free to use
> them.
> \<kibi\> pusling: yep, seen it.
> * kibi can try
> \<kibi\> Ganneff: mhy: ^^^ if you want to help kfreebsd-* folks get more
> packages built, fast-tracking qt4-x11 would really be great. Thanks for
> considering. :)
> \<zugschlus\> pusling: no, that was missing. thanks.
> \<pusling\> Zugschlus: you then probably want to make sure you have
> kde-minimal installed.

Guiding this practice is the idea that the free software project represents an endeavor that far exceeds any single person's efforts, and thus everyone's contribution is highly regarded, whether it involves filing a bug report or offering a significant, large-scale innovation.

On the other hand, hackers often express a commitment to self-reliance, which can be at times displayed in a quite abrasive and elitist tone. The most famous token of this stance is the short quip "Read the Fucking Manual" (RTFM). It is worth noting that accusations or RTFM replies are rarer than instances of copious sharing. Let me provide two examples of RTFM in action. In the first, "Error" drops into a new channel after asking a question in the #perl channel, where he got a prompt RTFM, after which everyone else went back to discussing the band Metallica. In this channel, they did not offer an RTFM but instead suggested going to the #metallica channel, which in this case, is a joke [IRC channels are designated by #name-of-channel].

> <813-error> i ask a question in #perl and get RTFM and they go back to
>   talking about metallica [. . .]
> <813-error> d Match digit character <that would be numbers right?
> * C4 knows nothing of perl
> <modem> same here :/
> <modem> ask in #metallica

The second example does not contain a joke but rather only a rebuke in the form of RTFM:

> <karsten> Ace2016: alsamixer / aumix are interactive ncurses programs
> <ace2016> so?
> <karsten> Ace2016: You may be able to steer 'em w/ stdin as well.
> <ace2016> can't they accept a command like aumix—volume decrease
>   10% or something like that?
> <karsten> Ace2016: RTFM
> <karsten> Ace2016: Which is to say, I don't know. Go look yourself.

These two poles of value reflect pervasive features of hacker social and technical production as it unfolds in everyday life. It only takes a few days of following hacker technical discussion to realize that many of their conversations, whether virtual or in person, are astonishingly long question-and-answer sessions. To manage the complexity of the technological landscape, hackers turn to fellow hackers (along with manuals, books, mailing lists, documentation, and search engines) for constant information, guidance, and help. Unlike academics—who at times religiously guard their data or findings until published, or only circulate them among a small group of trusted peers—hackers freely share their findings, insights, and solutions. More than ever, and especially in the context of free software projects, hackers see their productive mutual aid as the underlying living credo driving free software philosophy, and the methodology of collaboration and openness. Hackers maintain that this mode of production is responsible for better hackers and better technology.

Alongside technical question-and-answer sessions, developers dissect the ethics of their labor. For example, on a Debian mentors' mailing list discussion, one aspiring hacker asked, "How did you get from the middle ground to guru-dom?? Or is the answer that if I need to ask, I will never be a hacker!!??" A developer known for his humility and prolific contributions to the Debian project offered a lengthy response—a small section of which I quote below. In highlighting the importance of sharing, learning for others, and even coding for others, he affirms a populist stance, commonly expressed by many Debian developers:

> One other inspiration for me has been helping people. Though this has been spottier than I could hope, I do from time to time end up doing some program entirely because I can see other people need it. This tends to broaden experience a lot. Things like writing programs for an unfamiliar platform (microsoft), in a unfamiliar language (spanish), and needing to work closely with the people who would use it, cannot help but change how you look at things. My most valuable experiences in this area have been when I had direct contact with the people who would be using the program, rather than just noticing a hole and deciding I would try to go fill it like you did.[9]

Here he accords weight to pedagogy and collective interdependence in which learning from and even coding for others is a crucial component of technical progress as well as self-development.

During this discussion, though, other developers stressed the importance of independence by urging the questioner to follow his own particular interests necessary to cultivate technical independence. For example, one developer offered the following advice:

> I think you made two mistakes. [. . .] The first is looking to other people for problems to be solved. You'll never find the inspiration in solving problems that don't affect you. Since you don't feel the itch, you don't get much satisfaction from the scratch. Speaking for myself, I picked up a programming manual for my first computer and started reading; well before I was finished, I had two dozen ideas for programs to write. Those programs and their spinoffs kept me busy for a couple of years, and I loved it. Second, when an itch hits you, don't research to see if someone has already solved the problem. Solve it yourself. Mathematical texts aren't filled with answers right beside the problems; they teach you by making you work out the answers yourself.[10]

Simply in marking the question as misguided (because he looks to other people for problems to be solved), this developer asserts the value of self-determination. The original question violated what is the predominant (though not unquestioned) norm of self-sufficiency among developers—a norm that captures the isolated and individualistic phenomenology of much of their labor, which for many hackers commenced in childhood.

One developer, in answering a question I had about the significance of free software, expressed this stance of technical self-determination and independence in the following terms: "If I am cut off from the world, then in theory then I can maintain my own domain over software. I don't have to depend on anyone else; I can do it all myself. If my computing environment diverges from everyone else's in the world, I can still keep on going." This commitment to a fully autonomous, sovereign self who shuns any obvious signs of dependence on others is a common trait among developers. Given this mode of laboring, it is not surprising that hackers place so much emphasis on autonomy and self-sufficiency—qualities that are congenial to many hackers as they resonate so strongly with the very experience of intense periods of isolated labor.

Yet this statement of independence is based on a hypothetical scenario of being "cut off from the world"—something even this developer qualifies as unlikely.[11] In most practical instances, hackers are constantly plugged in, connected through various technical structures of communication. They work together as well as in complete isolation, for personal and joint public projects. Software theorist Matthew Fuller (2008, 5) describes how the freedom of coding gets subsumed by a host of conditions that always lay outside code proper: "Computation establishes a toy world in conformity with its axioms, but at the same time, when it becomes software, it must, by and large [. . .] come into combination with what lies outside of code."

Generally, the need to both work alone and with others is experienced free of contradiction, because the two needs are complementary and readily recognized as such by most hackers. To take another example from the mailing list discussion on what transforms a mediocre hacker into a great one, a developer captured this duality by describing how hacking tacks between two productive extremes—the collaborative and individual—that are not mutually exclusive:

> Creating a linux distribution is a group activity, but creating art is fundamentally a solitary, private experience. Turn off your internet connection; sit in a dark room, with nothing but the glow of a monitor, the warmth and hum of your computer, and the ideas will flow: Sometimes a trickle, sometimes a torrent.[12]

These two modes can clash, however. This is powerfully signaled through a form of stylized boasting that contrasts one's intelligence with the idiocy of "mere users" of software. While users of free software are often lauded as essential participants in the broader project of technical development because they provide insightful queries and bug reports (and also are seen as possible future hackers), at other times they are deemed second-class technical citizens.[13] This designation is frequently accomplished through the only way in which socially uncomfortable topics can be routinely discussed: by joking. On developer IRC channels, hackers playfully mock users. By complaining about stupid questions and queries, hackers depict users as less worthy contributors for lack of technical proficiency, or may display their complaints elsewhere, such as including humorous email signatures that taunt the wider universe of (l)users.[14] This condescending attitude is aptly and humorously conveyed in the following quote from a developers' email signature, originally formulated by Richard Cook: "Programming today is a race between software engineers striving to build bigger and better idiot-proof programs, and the Universe trying to produce bigger and better idiots. So far, the Universe is winning."

Users, though, are by no means the only type of persons subject to the humorous or more vitriolic accusation of technical incompetence. If a question is posed in the wrong register, is seen as uninteresting, or the answer can easily be found elsewhere, nearly anyone from a mere user to a "skilled" developer can receive the stylized and semihumorous RTFM rebuff. Stated on a hacker site with vivacious bite:

> [RTFM] is a big chromatic dragon with bloodshot beady eyes and fangs the size of oars. RTFM is me screaming at you as fireballs come out of my mouth to get off your precious no-good tush, march down to the local bookstore or MAN page repository, and get the eff off my back because I'm trying very hard to get some freakin' work done. Jeez.[15]

If you are better informed with the knowledge that there is "NO MAN-UAL," you can quickly defend your honor (i.e., intelligence) by pointing this out and gain substantial respect if you take it on yourself to write documentation. Otherwise, you will have to swallow the rebuke, google for the information, and hope for a better response next time (or simply find another IRC channel and ask elsewhere).

A complicated set of norms and conventions surround asking for help. They depend on the social context of the query and who is asking the question. For example, once someone has garnered a certain amount of trust and respect, they can usually get away with asking what is seen as a nonchallenging, uninteresting question. Developers who have not yet established trust will frequently get immediate help if the question is seen to be a challenge, but a basic questions will raise immediate eyebrows, especially among strangers or members who are technically unvetted, and therefore must maneuver with more caution and tact.

RTFM is a comedic, though stern, form of social discipline. It pushes other hackers to learn and code for themselves as well as affirms that effort has been put into documentation—an accessible form of information that benefits the group—but in a way that still requires independent learning. Many users and developers complain of the lack of adequate documentation for free software, faulting the tendency of some developers to exist in technical silos, "selfishly" coding only for themselves, and not attending to the needs of other users and developers by writing technically boring but necessary documentation. Many developers also note how the lack of extensive documentation can hinder collaborative technical work. Thus, when someone asks for information that in fact does exist in documentation, they often receive the RTFM rebuke, whose subtext says, "go learn for yourself, especially since others have already put in the work (i.e., documentation) to make this happen." To give too much aid is to deny the conditions necessary for self-cultivation.

The use of RTFM is disputed as well. During the 2005 Debian project leader election, the issue of documentation erupted during a mailing list debate. The subject of RTFM rebukes was broached directly. One developer argued that RTFM is an inflammatory, unproductive response to newcomers who may find themselves confused and overwhelmed with Debian's technical and procedural complexity. To make new users feel welcome, he believed that developers should refrain from replying with RTFM, and instead focus their efforts on achieving greater transparency and accessibility. While debating a Debian project leader candidate who had been with the project for years, he conveyed this commitment to corporate populism when he stated:

> You know a lot about the project [and its project internals], so it's all obvious to you. There are people among us who have not been part of Debian since 1.1, but who would like to know more about what's happening behind the curtains. However, those people are often told to RTFM or go spend time in the code, or just not taken seriously.[16]

In response, the Debian project leader candidate defended the general use of RTFM, concisely enunciating the value of self-determination:

> When the code is public, rtfm is the proper answer. One might add "document it properly afterwards" as well, though. When the data is available as well, that's best. Some data cannot be made available for legal or other binding obligations (new queue, security archive). If you feel that some bits are missing and need to be documented better, point them out and get them documented better, maybe by doing it on your own. I know a lot about the project because I've been involved in many parts. Other developers are involved in many parts as well. Some other developers mostly whine about not being involved without trying to understand. *sigh*[17]

In other words, if the requested information is public, it is incumbent on the developer to seek it out, and if unsatisfied with the current state of accessibility, then the next logical step is to make it happen—by yourself. If one does, one can display self-determination and self-development, the vehicles by which to gain the respect of accomplished peers on a similarly paved technical path.

If the subject of elitism erupts on mailing list discussions over project organization, a form of stylized boasting, taunting, cajoling, and elitist disdain is also frequently performed through code. Here I provide two examples. And again note how humor is used in both, to some degree working to soften the abrasive tone of these messages.

The first one is written in the style of an "I-can't-believe-how-idiotic-this-problem-I-have-to-solve-is rant" that disparages a bug in the Emacs email reader. Before addressing the significance of his code, permit me defer to the coder, Karl Fogel, to explain the context of the problem and the technical nature of his solution:

> Basically, the mailreader insisted on colorizing my mail composition window, even though I tried every documented method available to ask it not to do that. In desperation, I finally wrote code to go "behind the back" of the mailreader, and fool it into thinking that it had already done the colorization when it actually hadn't.[18]

The comments open with a statement of disbelief; take note of the naming of the variable, which I highlight in bold and italics:

```
;; I cannot believe what I have to do to turn off font locking in mail
   ;; and message buffers. Running "(font-lock-mode -1)" from every
   ;; possibly relevant gnus-*, mail-*, and message-* hook still left
   my
   ;; reply buffers font-locked. Arrrgh.
   ;;
   ;; So the code below fools font-lock-mode into thinking the buffer
   is
   ;; already fontified (so it will do nothing—see
   ;; font-lock.el:font-lock-mode for details), and then makes sure
   that
   ;; the very last thing run when I hit reply to a message is to turn
   ;; off font-lock-mode in that buffer, from post-command-hook.
   Then
   ;; that function removes itself from post-command-hook so it's
   not run
   ;; with every command.
   (defun kf-compensate-for-fucking-unbelievable-
   emacs-lossage ()
   (font-lock-mode -1)
   (remove-hook
   'post-command-hook
   'kf-compensate-for-fucking-unbelievable-emacs-lossage))

   (add-hook 'font-lock-mode-hook 'kf-font-lock-mode-hook)
   (defun kf-font-lock-mode-hook ()
```

```
(if (or (eq major-mode 'message-mode)
    (eq major-mode 'mail-mode))
(progn
(make-local-variable 'font-lock-fontified)
(setq font-lock-fontified t)
(add-hook 'post-command-hook
'kf-compensate-for-fucking-unbelievable-emacs-
lossage)
)))
```

By opening the comments with "I cannot believe what I have to do" and
ending with "Arrrgh," he signals the fact that this sort of trite problem is so
idiotically banal, it should have never appeared in the *first place*. Fixing it
is a waste of his superior mental resources. Lest there be any ambiguity as
to what the author really thought about the code, he continues to drive the
point home in his rant by naming the variable with an unmistakably deliberate insult: "compensate-for-fucking-unbelievable-emacs-lossage."

During the course of my early research, I was shocked at the disjoint
between the in-person real-world "codes of conduct" and the "codes of software conduct." Nothing about this coder's personality, who I got to know
very well over the course of five years, would indicate such haughty declarations. There is no need for such an indication because these enunciations
are rarely a matter of innate psychology. Instead, these are conventionalized
statements by which hackers declare and demarcate their unique contribution to a collective endeavor. They also represent culturally sanctioned
mechanisms for judgment.

Fogel's code is an apt example of "face work" (Goffman 1967, 5)—
when a hacker is sanctioned to perform a "line," which is the "pattern
of verbal and nonverbal acts by which he expresses his view of the situation and through this his evaluation of the participants, especially himself." Within such a presentation, hackers can declare and demarcate their
unique contribution to a piece of software while at the same time prof-
fering technical judgment. One may even say that this taunting is their
informal version of the academic peer-review process. In this particular
case, Fogel is declaring the code he patched as an utter failure of the
imagination.

Because these insults are critical evaluations of work, if hackers dare
to make such pronouncements, they also have to make them technically
clever enough to be accepted as accurate critiques. After a declaration is
made, a hacker should be ready to enter the arena of competitive jousting. If
one hacker judges some piece of code, it is almost guaranteed that another
hacker may reply with chutzpah of their own, often in humorous guise.

The second example demonstrates this type of competitive play of technical volleyball, a form of "antiphony" of "call and response" common to
jazz poetics (Gilroy 1993, 78). While jazz poetics may seem strange to apply

to hacking, I will expand on this connection later when addressing hacker notions of creativity. First, let's take a closer look at this portion of the code that shows the use of boasting to induce a response (I have highlighted the relevant section in italics):

```
/* Prime number generation
   Copyright (C) 1994 Free Software Foundation

This program is free software; you can redistribute it and/or
   modify it under the terms of the GNU General Public License as
   published by the Free Software Foundation; either version 2, or
   (at your option) any later version.

This program is distributed in the hope that it will be useful, but
   WITHOUT ANY WARRANTY; without even the implied warranty of
   MERCHANTABILITY or FITNESS FOR A PARTICULAR PUR-
   POSE. See the GNU General Public License for more details.

You should have received a copy of the GNU General Public License
   along with this program; if not, write to the Free Software
   Foundation, Inc., 675 Mass Ave, Cambridge, MA 02139, USA. */

#include <stdlib.h>
   #include <string.h>

/* Return the next prime greater than or equal to N. */
   int
   nextprime (int n)
   {
       static int *q;
       static int k = 2;
       static int l = 2;
       int p;
       int *m;
       int i, j;

       /* You are not expected to understand this. */

       if (!q)
          {
          /* Init */
          q = malloc (sizeof (int) * 2);
          q[0] = 2;
          q[1] = 3;
          }
```

Derived from the FSF's Hurd development project, which is its kernel project, the code is a prime number generator. Programmers have told me that the technical details are fairly intricate, so I refrain here from providing an explanation of the actual mechanics of the code, and for the sake of analysis it is not necessary. The important element is the author's comment: "/* You are not expected to understand this. */." It reveals how boasting is an open invitation to engage in technical jousting—a playful taunt that explicitly encourages the technical comeback that proves the expectation wrong.

The author's intentions are pretty clear in the code, but here is his retroactive explanation: "At this point I offered the function as a challenge to Jim Blandy. [. . .] That the function was intended to produce prime numbers was never hidden; the challenge was to explain its technique." Blandy took the call to technical arms and responded with his own exegesis of the algorithm. When the original author of the prime number function updated the code, he changed the taunt to "/* See the comment at the end for an explanation of the algorithm used. */," and at the end of the code, stated, "Jim produced the following brilliant explanation" and included it within the code (and again, I have indicated the relevant section in italics).

```
/* Prime number generation
   C [ . . . ]
   #include <stdlib.h>
   #include <string.h>
   /* Return the next prime greater than or equal to N. */ [ . . . ]
   /* See the comment at the end for an explanation of the algo-
   rithm
   used. */
   if (!q)
      {
      /* Init */ [ . . . ]
```
* *[This code originally contained the comment "You are not expected to understand this" (on the theory that every Unix-like system should have such a comment somewhere, and now I have to find somewhere else to put it). I then offered this function as a challenge to Jim Blandy. At that time only the six comments in the function and the description at the top were present.*
Jim produced the following brilliant explanation.]

The static variable q points to a sorted array of the first l natural prime numbers. k is the number of elements which have been allocated to q, l <= k; we occasionally double k and realloc q accordingly to maintain this invariant.

The table is initialized to contain a few primes (lines 26, 27, 34-40). Subsequent code assumes the table isn't empty.

> When passed a number n, we grow q until it contains a prime
> >= n
> (lines 45-70), do a binary search in q to find the least prime >=n
> (lines 72-84), and return that. [. . .]

If some hackers are ready to pounce on what they deem as the idiocy of others, they are also as likely to dole out recognition where they see fit. Hence, even while hackers are on a path toward *self-development*, this self-fashioning is intimately bound to others, not simply because of a love of tinkering or the dependence derived from collaboration, but because any meritocratic order based on expertise fundamentally requires others for constant evaluation as well. Hackers use the path of humor, taunt, jousting, boasting, and argument for such expressions of technical taste and worthiness, and in the process, cultivate themselves as expert hackers.

JUST FREEDOM

Given hackers' proclivity for expressing cleverness, acknowledgment that they build on the shoulders of giants, need to garner recognition from others, and dual penchant for lauding populist collectivism and individual self-determination, what might these attributes reveal about hacker notions of personhood, creativity, and authorship?

It is not surprising that in so much of the literature, hackers are treated as quintessentially individualistic (Levy 1984; Turkle 1984). "The hacker," Turkle (1984, 229) writes, "is the defender of idiosyncrasy, individuality, genius and the cult of individual." Some authors argue that this individualism is a close variant of a politically suspicious libertarianism (Borsook 2000). Hackers are perpetually keen on asserting their individuality through acts of ingenuity, and thus these statements are unmistakably correct. In most accounts on hackers, however, the meaning of this individualism is treated as an ideological, unsavory cloak or is left underspecified. Why the pronounced performance of individualism? What does it say about how hackers conceptualize authorship? What tensions does it raise?

Because hackers do not automatically treat software as solely derivative of one laboring mind but instead see it as derivate of a collective effort, the constant drive to perform ingenuity reflects the formidable difficulty of claiming discrete inventiveness. After all, much of hacker production is based on a constant reworking of different technical assemblages directed toward new purposes and uses—a form of authorial recombination rarely acknowledged in traditional intellectual property law discourse.

Because of the tendency, especially now more than ever, for hackers to recognize the reality of collaboration, it may seem that they are moving toward the type of politics and ethics of authorship that flatly reject the ideal of individualism altogether—a rejection famously explored in the works of Roland Barthes, Michel Foucault, and Dick Hebdige. In the F/OSS domain, hackers have not moved, even an inch, to decenter the persona of the author in the manner, say, most famously exemplified by Barthes, who in 1967 sought to dethrone the authority of an author: "To give a text an Author is to impose a limit on that text, to furnish it with a final signified, to close the writing."[19]

Instead, among hackers the authorial figure seems to speak slightly louder, clamoring for and demanding credit and recognition, established through oral histories of software or etched into the infrastructure of production. Hackers record contributions and attributions in common files included with source code, such as the Authors and Contributors files (Yuill 2008). This archival drive helps partially explain why certain hackers can also receive the legendary status they do. This everyday discourse and inscription develops a shared historical awareness about who contributed what—one that brings attention to the conditions of production or the nature of the contribution. Furthermore, accountability and credit are built into many of the technical tools that facilitate collaboration, such as CVS and Subversion—software systems used to manage shared source code. These systems give developers the ability to track (and potentially revert to) incremental changes to files and report the changes to a mailing list as they are made, and are often used concurrently by many developers. Since developers all have accounts, these technologies not only *enable collaboration* but also provide *precise details of attribution*. Over time, this record accumulates into a richly documented palimpsest. Though individual attribution is certainly accorded, these technological palimpsests reflect unmistakably that complicated pieces of software are held in place by a grand collaborative effort that far exceeds any one person's contribution.[20]

In contrast to many accounts on authorship, I find that a short description about the aesthetics of jazz and its "cruel contradiction" is eerily evocative of the hacker creative predicament:

> There is a cruel contradiction implicit in the art form itself. For true jazz is an art of individual assertion within and against the group. Each true jazz moment (as distinct from the uninspired commercial performance) springs from a context in which each artist challenges all the rest, each solo flight, or improvisation, represents (like the successive canvases of a painter) a definition of his identity: as individual, as member of the collectivity, and as link in the chain of tradition. Thus, because jazz finds its very life in an endless improvisation upon traditional materials, the jazzman must lose his identity even as he finds it. (Ellison 1964, 234; quoted in Gilroy 1993, 79)

Among hackers this cruelty, this difficulty in establishing discrete originality, is in reality not so cruel. It is treated like any interesting problem: an enticing hurdle that invites rigorous intellectual intervention and a well-crafted so-lution within given constraints. Hackers clearly define the meaning of the free individual through this very persistent inclination to find solutions; they revel in directing their faculty for critical thought toward creating bet-ter technology or more sublime, beautiful code. The logic among hackers goes that if one can create beauty, originality, or solve a problem within the shackles of constraints, this must prove a *superior* form of creativity, intel-ligence, and individuality than the mere expression of some wholly original work.

Not every piece of technology made by hackers qualifies as a hack. The hack is particularly the "individual assertion within and against the group" (Ellison 1964, 234), which may be easily attached to an individual even though it is still indebted to a wider tradition and conversation. Hackers certainly engage in a creative, complex process partially separated from hi-erarchy, enfolding a mechanics of dissection, manipulation, and reassembly, in which various forms of collaboration are held in high esteem. Much of their labor is oriented toward finding a good enough solution so they can carry forth with their work. But their form of production is one that also generates a practice of cordial (and sometimes not-so-cordial) one-upping, which simultaneously acknowledges the hacker's technical roots and yet at times strives to go beyond inherited forms in order to implement a better so-lution. If this solution is achieved, it will favorably reveal one's capacity for original, critical thought—the core meaning of individuality among hackers.

Hackers recognize production as the extension or rearrangement of in-herited formal traditions, which above all requires access to other people's work. This precondition allows one to engage in constant acts of re-creation, expression, and circulation. Such an imperative goes against the grain of current intellectual property law rationalizations, which assume that the nature of selfhood and creativity is always a matter of novel creation or individualized inventive discovery.

Among F/OSS hackers, the moral economy of selfhood is not easily re-ducible to modern "possessive individualism" (Graeber 1997; Macpher-son 1962). Nor does it entirely follow the craftsperson or the stand-alone romantic author figured by intellectual property jurisprudence but rather evinces other sensibilities that point to competing liberal concepts of in-dividualism and freedom. While hackers envisage themselves as free and rational agents, in the context of free and open-source hacking, most hack-ers place less emphasis on the freedom to establish relations of property ownership and exchange. Instead, they formulate liberty as the condition necessary for individuals to develop the capacity for critical thought and self-development.[21]

While the hacker interpretation of labor, creativity, and individuality strays from influential liberal understandings of personhood—possessive individualism—it does not represent a wholly novel take on these themes.

It aligns with the type of person presupposed in free speech theory, perhaps most lucidly in Mill's writings, which influenced the shape, content, and philosophy of free speech jurisprudence as it now exists in the United States (Bollinger and Stone 2002; Passavant 2002). Mill, influenced by the Romantic tradition (Halliday 1976), defines a free individual as one who develops, determines, and changes their own desires, capacities, and interests autonomously through self-expression, debate, and reasoned deliberation (Donner 1991). It is a vision that fuses utilitarian and romantic commitments, and is built on the idea of human plasticity and development—the ability of the self to grow and develop through creative expression, mental activity, and deliberative discussion, usually by following one's own personally defined path. As Wendy Donner argues, this form of liberal self-cultivation also requires the establishment of standards by which to judge the development of the human faculties. Mill's "transformed conception of utility necessitates a new method of value measurement which relies heavily on the judgment of competent agents," writes Donner (1991, 142), "and thus essentially rests on a doctrine of human development and self-development." What is notable is how Mill ([1857] 1991, 93) contends in his famous *On Liberty* that an individual must follow their own path of development, because "persons [. . .] require different conditions for their spiritual development." Even if this Romantic inclination prioritizes the individual, one can only develop the critical faculties along with moral and aesthetic standards via a process of training and open-ended argumentation in debate with other similarly engaged individuals.

Much of free software legal philosophy and moral sensibilities bear remarkable similarities to this Millian (and thus also Romantically informed) vision of personhood, self-development, and liberty, although there are differences and specifications tied to hacking's unique relations between persons, labor, and technology. Hackers place tremendous faith in the necessity and power of expressive activity that springs from deep within the individual self—an expression that acts as the motor for positive technical change. Progress depends on the constant expression and reworking of already-existing technology. Thought, expression, and innovation should never be stifled, so long as, many developers told me during interviews, "no one else is hurt"—a sentiment that is part and parcel of Millian free speech theories.

Free software developers have come to treat the pursuit of knowledge and learning with inestimable high regard—as an almost sacred activity, vital for technical progress and essential for improving individual talents. As one software developer observed, "I can use the code for my own projects and I can improve the code of others. I can learn from the code so that I can become a better programmer myself, and then there is all my code out there so that you can use it. It is just freedom." The spirit of this statement is ubiquitous among F/OSS developers. A utilitarian ethic of freedom and openness is increasingly seen as not only obvious but also indispensable in order to develop the "state of the art."

For developers, technical expression should always be useful. If it isn't, it denies the nature of software, which is to solve problems. Yet hackers also place tremendous value on the aesthetic pleasures of hacking, producing technology and software that may not have any immediate value but can be admired simply on its own elegant terms—as a conduit for personal self-expression.

Over years of coding software with other developers in free software projects where discourses about liberty run rampant, many developers come to view F/OSS as the apex of writing software, as we will see in the next chapter. It has, they say, the necessary legal and material features that can induce as well as fertilize creative production. In contrast to the corporate sphere, the F/OSS domain is seen as establishing the freedom necessary to pursue *personally* defined technical interests in a way that draws on the resources and skills of other individuals who are chasing down their own interests. In other words, the arena of F/OSS establishes all the necessary conditions (code, legal protection, technical tools, and peers) to cultivate the technical self and direct one's abilities toward the utilitarian improvement of technology. While many developers enjoy working on their corporate projects, there is always a potential problem over the question of sovereignty. One developer told me during an interview that "managers [. . .] decide the shape of the project," while the F/OSS arena allows either the individual or collective of hackers to make this decision instead. F/OSS allows for technical sovereignty.

The hacker formulation of individuality, as the pursuit of one's interest for the mutual benefit of each other and society, is an apt example of the general characterization of modern individualism as defined, according to Taylor (2004, 20), by "relations of mutual service between equal individuals." While much of liberal thought understands mutual service in terms of economic exchange, hackers relate to it through the very act of individual expression and technical creation—the only sound ways to truly animate the uniqueness of one's being.

CONCLUSION

As noted in the previous section, even though hackers tend to approach other hackers as equals, they also construct themselves as high-tech cognoscenti creating the bleeding edge of technology. This elitism follows from their commitment to the organizational ideal of meritocracy, a performance-based system that applauds individual skill, encourages respectful competition between peers, and sanctions hierarchies between developers, especially in the F/OSS project to be discussed at length in the subsequent chapter.

The meritocratic ideal, ubiquitous in liberal thought, has particular resonance in the US popular imaginary. The United States is often thought of
as a living embodiment of meritocracy: a nation where people are judged
on their individual abilities alone. The system supposedly works so well
because, as the media myth goes, the United States provides everyone with
equal opportunity, usually through public education, to achieve their goals.
As such, the hierarchies of difference that arise from one's ability (usually to
achieve wealth) are sanctioned by this moral order as legitimate.

In many senses, hackers have drawn from what is still a prevalent trope of
meritocracy to conceptualize how they treat one another and self-organize.
In his classic account of hackers, Levy (1984, 43) includes this principle as
one of the six elements that define the hacker ethic, noting that "hackers
should be judged by their hacking, not bogus criteria such as degrees, age,
race, or position," in which "people who trotted in with seemingly impres-
sive credentials were not taken seriously until they proved themselves at the
console of the computer."

Though written twenty years ago, this commitment to meritocracy still
holds undeniable sway in the way F/OSS hackers construct norms of sociality and envision selfhood, not because it exists in the same exact way,
but rather because hackers have given it new meaning by organizationally
building the institution of the free software project guided by a dedication
to meritocracies. Hackers who participate in free software projects routinely
asserted that F/OSS projects are run as meritocracies. The doors are open
to anyone, they insist; respect and authority are accorded along the lines of
superior and frequently individual technological contribution. As we will
see in the next chapters, F/OSS hackers may not build perfect meritocracies
and yet they are certainly motivated to implement them.

For F/OSS hackers, it is imperative to constantly and recursively equalize the conditions by which other hackers can develop their skills and prove
their worth to peers. As part of this equalization process, one must endow
the community of hackers with resources like documentation and the fruits
of one's labor: source code. The free software hacker does not privatize the
source of value created, even those exceptional pieces of code that are undeniably one's own and seen to emerge from sheer technical ability. Within
F/OSS, this value is fed back and circulated among peers, thereby contributing to an endowed and growing pool of resources through which other
hackers can constantly engage in their asymptotic process of self-cultivation.

This constant recirculation of value is one way in which hackers can
explicitly downplay their elitism and display their sound technical intentions to their peers. Their implementation of meritocracy contrasts markedly with the ideal of it in capitalist societies, where the privatization of
value is legitimate as long as one generates wealth (or gains other forms of
status) through one's personal ability. In fact, numerous issues over who
and what are responsible for equalizing the terrain of competition plague

liberal democracies marked by a meritocratic ideal. This leveling is often seen as secured through such avenues as public education. That, in turn, raises questions like, Should capitalist philanthropists (such as John Rockefeller in the past and Gates in the present), individuals, governments, or property tax fund public education? With hackers, these sets of thorny issues are minimized, partially resolved by their constant recirculation of value, notably software and documentation, as well as debates and conflicts over mentorship and helping.

Still, the predominant sentiment is that once knowledge has been released to the collective of hackers, individuals must, on their own two feet, prove their worth by creating new forms of value that can be fed back recursively to the community. If one seeks too much help, this violates the hacker implementation of the proper meritocratic order, and one might be subjected to a stylized rebuff such as the common RTFM.

Among hackers, the commitment to elitism and meritocracy historically has run fairly strong. There is still an ambivalent relationship to elitism and this meritocratic ideal, however, as I will explore in more detail in the next chapter. I will show how those vested with authority on software projects, because of their success, are usually met with some degree of suspicion, and thus jokes and sometimes accusations of cabals run rampant among hackers. This requires them to constantly perform their trustworthiness and demonstrate their good technical intentions to the community at large. I now turn to the institution, the free software project, where technological production unfolds, and where commitments to free speech and meritocracy are further specified under the aegis of a tremendously varied set of ethical practices.

CHAPTER 4

Two Ethical Moments in Debian

ಌಔ

F/OSS projects largely take place on the Internet. Varying in size from a couple of developers to a network of over one thousand, they are sites where programmers coordinate and produce high-quality software. A growing body of literature has addressed questions of developer motivation (Raymond 1999), project structures, and changing implications for software development along with factors that lead to success and failures in projects (Crowston and Howison 2005; O'Mahony and Ferraro 2007; Schweik and English 2012), open-source legality (McGowan 2001; Vetter 2004, 2007), utilitarian and rational choice incentive structures (Gallaway and Kinnear 2004; Lancashire 2001; von Hippel and von Krogh 2003), the economics of open-source software (Lerner and Tirole 2001; Lerner and Schankerman 2010; von Hippel 2005), and the noneconomic incentive mechanisms, cultural norms, and broader sociopolitical implications of F/OSS production (Benkler 2006; Berry 2008; Chopra and Dexter 2007; Ghosh 1998; Himanen 2001; Kelty 2008; Kollock 1999; Lessig 1999; Weber 2004).

Although a number of these studies tangentially discuss ethical questions (e.g., conflict resolution within F/OSS projects), they rarely address how developers commit themselves to an ethical vision through, rather than prior to, their participation in a F/OSS project. Much of the F/OSS literature, in other words, is heavily focused on the question of motivation or incentive mechanisms, and often fails to account for the plasticity of human motivations and ethical perceptions.

Many of these authors acknowledge the importance of shared norms, and usually address this by referring to or quoting the famous passage in Levy's *Hackers* where he defines the tenets of the hacker ethic. In a general sense, these principles still powerfully capture the spirit of ethical commitments. Nevertheless, by leaning so heavily on Levy, what we miss is how these precepts take actual form and how they change over time. The literature, crucially, has tended to ignore how hacker commitments are transformed by the lived experiences that unfold within F/OSS projects.[1]

This chapter uses the Debian project to demonstrate how free software development is not simply a technical endeavor but also a moral one. The analysis is informed by the work of the legal theorist Robert Cover, who examines the ways that "jurisgenesis," the production and stabilization of inhabited normative meanings, requires an ongoing and sometimes conflict- ing interpretation of codified textual norms. "Some small and private, others immense and public," these continual acts of reinterpretation and commit- ment establish what Cover (1993, 95) calls a nomos:

> We inhabit a *nomos*—a normative universe. We constantly create and maintain a world of right and wrong, of lawful and unlawful. [. . .] No set of legal institutions or prescriptions exists apart from the nar- ratives that locate it and give it meaning. For every constitution there is an epic, for each decalogue a scripture. Once understood in the con- text of the narratives that give it meaning, law becomes not merely a system of rules to be observed, but a world in which we live.

As Debian has organizationally matured, it has also concurrently devel- oped along legal and ethical lines, codifying key principles in two related documents: the Social Contract and DFSG. Developers continually draw on these texts to craft a dense ethical practice that sustains itself primarily via ongoing acts of narrative interpretation.

While the idea of nomos provides a useful general framework for under- standing how ethical stances are codified and internalized, for my purposes here, I specify its meaning by distinguishing among a repertoire of every- day micropractices that I group under two distinct (and contrasting) ethical moments: enculturation and punctuated crisis. While in practice these two moments exist in a far more complicated mixture and copresence, here they are separated for the sake of clarity and analytic value. Each one tells us a slightly different story about how people use narrative to adopt values, and then animate and transform them over time.

By ethical enculturation, I refer to a process of relatively conflict-free socialization. Among developers, this includes learning the tacit and explicit knowledge (including technical, moral, or procedural knowledge) needed to effectively interact with other project members as well as acquiring trust, learning appropriate social behavior, and establishing best practices. Al- though ethical enculturation is ongoing and distributed, the most pertinent instance of it in the Debian project is the New Maintainer Process (NMP)— the procedure of mentorship and testing through which prospective devel- opers apply for and gain membership in Debian. Fulfilling the mandates of the NMP is not a matter of a few days of filling out forms. It can take months of hard work. A prospective developer has to find a sponsor and advocate, learn the complicated workings of Debian policy and its techni- cal infrastructure, successfully package a piece of software that satisfies a set of technical standards, and meet at least one other Debian developer in person for identity verification. This period of mentorship, pedagogy, and testing ensures that developers enter with a common denominator of technical, legal, and philosophical knowledge, and hence become trusted collective members.

The other moment I investigate is crisis. As the number of developers in the Debian project has grown from one dozen to over one thousand, punctuated crises routinely emerge around particularly contested issues: matters of project transparency, internal and external communication, membership size, the nature of authority within the project, and the scope and limits of software licenses. Many of these crises have an acute phase (usually spurred by a provocative action or statement) in which debate erupts on several media all at once: mailing lists, IRCs, and blog entries. While the debate during these periods can be congenial, measured, rational, and sometimes even peppered liberally with jokes, its tone can also be passionate, uncharitable, and sometimes downright vicious.

During these times, we find that while developers may share a common ethical ground, they often disagree about the implementation of its principles. Though the content of these debates certainly matters (and will be discussed to some extent), my primary focus is on the productive affective stance induced by these crises. I argue that these are instances of assessment, in which people turn their attentive, ethical beings toward an unfolding situation and engage in difficult questions. In this mode, passions are animated while values are challenged and sometimes reformulated. Although these debates sometimes result in project stasis, demoralization, or exodus, they can produce a heightened and productive ethical orientation among developers. Crises can be evaluated as moments of ethical production in terms of not only their functional outcomes but also their ability to move people to reflexively articulate their ideals. Such dialogic, conflicted debate reflects the active engagement of participants who renew and occasionally alter their ethical commitments. As such, crises can be vital to establishing and reestablishing the importance of normative precepts.

The main purpose of this chapter is to explicate how different instances of ethical labor define the cohesive yet nonunitary moral commitments that developers hold toward Debian and its philosophy of freedom. It is necessary to first briefly introduce Debian's history and structure.

Thus, much of what is described in this part of the chapter is Debian's historical transition from an informal group (organized largely around charismatic leadership, personal relationships, and ad hoc decision making) to a stable institution. Most F/OSS projects in their infancy, including Debian, operate without formal procedures of governance and instead are guided by the technical judgments of a small group of participants. This informal technocracy is captured in a famous pronouncement by a hacker pioneer, David Clark, who helped develop the early protocols of the Internet: "We reject: kings, presidents and voting. We believe in: rough consensus and running code" (quoted in Hoffman 2011).[2] Even though an ideal of rough consensus still exists in Debian today, Debian developers have had to demarcate membership criteria, explicitly define roles, and implement a complicated voting protocol in order to successfully grow.

Although charismatic leadership, improvised actions, and informal relationships still exist in the project today, these have been supplemented by other modes of formal governance. Through Debian's tremendous growth, developers have cobbled together a hybrid organizational structure that integrates three different modes of governance—democratic majoritarian rule, a guildlike meritocracy, and an ad hoc process of rough consensus. It is unsurprising, then, that many of Debian's crises result from conflicts arising from differences in these three models. What I want to emphasize is how responses to these crises often clarify the purposes and limits of each mode of interaction.

Democratic voting reveals Debian's populist face; it is an acknowledgment that each developer is a valuable contributor to the project and deserves an equal say in its future. Yet democracy and especially majoritarian voting is frequently viewed as an ineffective, improper method for resolving technical matters, because the mediocrity of the majority can overrule the "right" technical decisions. For this reason, developers are notably committed to an open-ended process of argumentation, where vigorous debate, conducted over mailing lists, bug reports, and IRC channels, ideally clarifies the right solution and leads to enough rough consensus to proceed. In this mode, everyone is treated as an equal subject with the potential to convince others of the merit or demerit of a given technical solution, regardless of their status in the project.

This approach affirms two long-standing liberal dispositions. First, it displays the value placed on speech and debate in determining a nonpartisan resolution to collective problems, theorized, say, in the work of Jürgen Habermas (1981). This commitment also exhibits the preference that Debian developers hold for individually generated decision making in lieu of top-down regulation or management. These tendencies are not unique to Debian developers, though. For instance, Thomas Malaby (2009, 60) describes the mistrust of the hierarchical management that he routinely witnessed among the programmer employees of Linden Lab, makers of Second Life, which he portrays as a "politically charged disposition, one that tended to treat top-down or vertical decision making as the antithesis of empowered and creative action."[3]

However skeptical Debian hackers are of rigid, top-down authority, their system of equal opportunity nonetheless leads to some established modes and nodes of authority, and thus is also the basis for the hierarchies that inhere in meritocracies. Individual developers who over time come to demonstrate their technical worth through a combination of ability and dedication eventually obtain the status of a trusted technical guardian. As such, a meritocratic system arises that vests power in roles, such as delegates and various technical "masters" who hold power for unspecified periods of time.

As the very names of their roles suggest, guardians are not unlike the guild masters of times past who held the trust and respect of other guild members because of their wisdom, experience, and mastery of the craft.

If democratic rule is sometimes treated with overt suspicion and dislike, there is a far more subtle fear concerning the importance of meritocracy and the meritocrats it produces—namely, the fear of corruption. Specifically, there is discomfort with the idea that the technical guardians could (as they are vested to do) exercise their authority without consulting the project as a whole, thereby foreclosing precisely the neutral, technical debate that allowed them to gain their authority in the first place. Debian developers at times express their unease about the fact that delegates have the legitimate power to make decisions without consulting other developers. This anxiety is voiced indirectly through the humorous phrase "There is no cabal." It is manifested more critically when developers in positions of authority are seen to violate what I call "meritocratic trust"—the expectation that entrusted guardians act in good technical faith and not for personal interest.

The building of trust and novel organizational procedures has been central to the organizational growth of Debian as well as balancing its governance modes. These themes are recurrent in science and technology studies. Whether expressed through the trustworthiness of a noble character, as was the case in seventeenth-century British scientific enterprise (Shapin 1994), or the transformation of books into transparent and vetted objects of truthful knowledge (Johns 1998), trust has been essential to bringing coherence, order, and stability to emergent social institutions, objects, and technical practices. Within F/OSS projects, issues of trust are no less pressing (Kelty 2005). Questions of who and what to trust—whether delegates, voting procedures, a piece of code, a license, or a guideline—are central to the repertoire of ethical practices that are the primary focus of this chapter.[4]

DEBIAN AND ITS SOCIAL ORGANIZATION

Debian is a project, made up of just over a thousand volunteers at the time of this writing, that creates and distributes a Linux-based OS composed of thousands of individual software applications. As is the case with most mid- to large-size projects (i.e., those with over a couple of hundred developers), Debian is extraordinarily complex and has undergone considerable changes over the course of its history. In its nascency, Debian was run on an informal basis; it had fewer than two-dozen developers, who communicated primarily through a single email list. Excitement, passion, and experimentation drove the project's early development. In order to accommodate technical and human growth, however, significant changes in its policy, procedures, and structure occurred between 1997 and 1999. Now Debian boasts an intricate hybrid political system, a developer IRC, a formalized membership entry procedure (the NMP), and a set of charters that includes the Constitution, Social Contract, and Debian Free Software Guidelines (DFSG). Debian has produced detailed policy and technical manuals; controls development, testing, and mirroring machines located around the world; and manages bug-tracking and collaborative software. The project also publishes a newsletter, hosts a group blog, and organizes an annual conference.

The bulk of the volunteer work for Debian has always consisted of software packaging—the systematic compartmentalization, customization, and standardization of existing software into one system. (In local lingo, Debian is referred to as a distribution, the unit of software is called a package, and developers are often referred to as package maintainers.) Taken together, these packages constitute the Debian Linux distribution. Along with the package maintainers, teams of Debian developers support infrastructure and develop Debian-specific software, while others write documentation or translate documentation into various languages. Each Debian developer has at least one piece of software (and usually several) packages that they maintain.

Much of the work on Debian happens in an independent, parallel, distributed fashion through informal collaboration on IRC channels or mailing lists, where developers ask for and receive help.[5] Some collaboration is mediated by bug reports. Written by Debian developers or users, bug reports are filed on a publicly viewable bug-tracking system. Incoming reports can identify a technical problem with a piece of software and provide crucial details; they sometimes even supply the solution in the form of code to be incorporated as a patch.

While a maintainer holds no legal ownership of the software they package, Debian's norms of civility dictate that within the boundaries of the Debian project, it is their responsibility alone. The assumption that maintainers enjoy near-absolute control over their software package means that alterations should not take place without their explicit permission. If modifications are needed to eliminate a release-critical bug or fix a security problem, though, there is a socially accepted protocol for doing so: the Non-Maintainer Upload (NMU). This mechanism is designed to allow a nonmaintainer to upload a package in order to fix critical bugs, or compensate for a busy or missing maintainer. While many developers appreciate contributions provided by an NMU, seeing it as a handy mechanism to encourage coparticipation, others find the protocol annoying or even downright obnoxious insofar as it allows inexperienced developers to insert shoddy solutions into their software. Other developers view it in a slightly different light: as a means of exposing poor work. As one developer on IRC told me half jokingly, an NMU reveals "our laundry for public inspection."

If much of the project's work occurs through individualized but parallel efforts, work assumes a more collaborative and populist tone during the period before the release of a new Debian version: bug-squashing parties are held more regularly, and developers work round-the-clock on an IRC channel to resolve what have been identified as "release critical bugs" in the bug-tracking software. During this period, which can last anywhere from a few months to over a year, Debian's release managers sanction NMUs with much less stringent criteria, and they are correspondingly more frequent.[6]

Among the hacker and F/OSS publics, Debian's fame rests on four developments—two technical and two social. Technically, Debian is one of the best-equipped distributions, offering more than twenty-five thousand individual pieces of software, all with DFSG-approved licenses. Debian, relatedly, can currently run on eleven hardware architectures—more than any other Linux distribution. This is one of the reasons it has earned the title of the "Universal OS." On the social side, Debian holds the distinction of having more individual members than any F/OSS project. It is also known for its strong commitment to the ethical principles of free software, as elaborated in two key documents— the Social Contract and DFSG. These documents figure prominently in the NMP I discuss below. They are also the foundational texts that orient the project's sense of identity. Now let's take a closer look at the Debian charters and governing structures that have emerged in the last decade.

Social Charters and Governance

Dissatisfied with the then-existing distribution and inspired by the Linux kernel project, Murdock founded the Debian project in August 1993. He attracted a group of volunteers, who began to design a package management system that could integrate the contributions of *every single developer* who chose to maintain the package. I emphasize this point because it marked an important shift in the history of the Unix collaborative ethical temperament—one that explicitly honored transparency, accessibility, and openness for the purpose of facilitating as well as encouraging participation. It represented a new historical chapter in how hackers conceived of and implemented meritocracy.

One longtime Debian developer, who came of age as a hacker well before the Linux era, powerfully captured the spirit of this change in a short comment he made during a Debian history roundtable at the Debian annual conference. He described how collaboration on Unix proceeded before the Linux era, at the University of California at Berkeley (and other locations) where the Berkeley Unix distribution was partially developed:

> There was a process by which you wrote some code and submitted in the "I-am-not-worthy but I-hope-that-this-will-be-of-use-to-you supplication mode" to Berkeley, and if they kinda looked at it and thought, "Oh, this is cool," then it would make it in, and if they said, "Interesting idea, but there is a better way to do that," they might write a different implementation of it.

While the Berkeley Unix gurus accepted contributions from those who were not already participating on the project, it was difficult to pierce the inner circle of authority and become an actual team member. This, from the point of view of the developers participating in the roundtable, produced an unacceptable form of project participation, characterized by a degraded elitism that failed to equalize the terrain on which developers could prove their worth. As I argued earlier, the F/OSS hacker system of meritocracy compels individuals to release the fruits of their labor in order to constantly equalize the conditions for production, so that others can also engage in the lifelong project of technical self-cultivation within a community of peers. When Torvalds and Murdock developed their own projects (the Linux kernel and Debian, respectively), they did things differently than the earlier cadre of Unix hackers by fostering a more egalitarian environment of openness and transparency. Participation was encouraged, and recognition was given where it was due. Accepting more contributions was also, of course, seen as a way to improve and encourage technical efficiency.

Murdock, who took on a great deal of the early work on Debian, acted as the project's leader. Debian in this sense was not unusual. Many of the early free software projects worked and still work along this logic of informal leadership by extension of a work ethic charisma (O'Neil 2009). Authority and respect is established through the sheer amount of work one puts into the project; participants in return offer their loyalty to it. But what crucially distinguished Debian from earlier collaborative efforts was that everyone who technically contributed to the project could potentially become a member. By 1995, there was a software package system in place that harnessed the power of individuality to produce a distribution that far exceeded the contributions of any single person.

In 1996, Debian grew in size to 120 developers and released a version of the OS that contained about 800 packages. Around this time, Murdock passed on the reins of leadership to Perens, who along with a handful of other developers, became responsible for the bulk of the project's technical work. Perens, already famous in the geek public sphere for both his passionate commitment to the principles of free software and desire to make free software more visible in the business sector, had a marked impact on the organization of Debian, in ways recalled as both positive and negative.[7] Perhaps most significant for my purposes here, Perens helped coordinate the drafting of the Social Contract and DFSG, which were first suggested by Schuessler.

The genesis of the Social Contract is worth briefly recounting, for it reveals the explicit sense of responsibility and accountability to a larger commonwealth of users and developers that has characterized the project since its inception (when Murdock first articulated these values in "The Debian Manifesto"). Schuessler proposed the idea for the Social Contract after a conversation at a conference with Bob Young, the cofounder of a then-emergent commercial Linux distribution, Red Hat. When Schuessler suggested that Red Hat might want to guarantee in writing that as it grew larger, it would always provide GPL software, Young replied, "that would be the kiss of death," implying that such an assurance made to the users of free software could prove disastrous to his business, given that at the time, the commercial future of free software was entirely uncertain. Schuessler (himself a business owner) was both amused and disturbed by Young's answer, and with other developers at the conference, he decided that it would behoove Debian to offer such a written guarantee.

If immediate inspiration for the Social Contract was a conversation that brought to light two divergent interpretations of accountability to a wider community of technical users, the time was quite ripe in Debian for users to accept such a contract. As the project grew larger, many felt that the group had outgrown "The Debian Manifesto." Many developers felt it was especially important to clarify their position on free software, for there was a small group clamoring to distribute nonfree software or risk losing users to the other distributions that did so. Thus when the Social Contract was proposed, it seemed like an ideal opportunity to clarify the project's goals to both outsiders and newcomers joining in large numbers.

Led by Perens, who wrote large chunks of the document, developers produced a statement of intent that helped define Debian's unique role within a larger field of production. A crisp and short document, the Social Contract makes four promises and gives one qualification:

"Social Contract" with the Free Software Community

Debian Will Remain 100% Free Software

We promise to keep the Debian GNU/Linux Distribution entirely free software. As there are many definitions of free software, we include the guidelines we use to determine if software is "*free*" below. We will support our users who develop and run non-free software on Debian, but we will never make the system depend on an item of non-free software.

We Will Give Back to the Free Software Community

When we write new components of the Debian system, we will license them as free software. We will make the best system we can, so that free software will be widely distributed and used. We will feed back bug-fixes, improvements, user requests, etc. to the "*upstream*" authors of software included in our system.

We Won't Hide Problems

We will keep our entire bug-report database open for public view at all times. Reports that users file on-line will immediately become visible to others.

Our Priorities Are Our Users and Free Software

We will be guided by the needs of our users and the free-software community.

We will place their interests first in our priorities. We will support the needs of our users for operation in many different kinds of computing environment. We won't object to commercial software that is intended to run on Debian systems, and we'll allow others to create value-added distributions containing both Debian and commercial software, without any fee from us. To support these goals, we will provide an integrated system of high-quality, 100% free software, with no legal restrictions that would prevent these kinds of use.

Programs That Don't Meet Our Free-Software Standards

We acknowledge that some of our users require the use of programs that don't conform to the *Debian Free Software Guidelines*. We have created "contrib." and "non-free" areas in our FTP archive for this software. The software in these directories is not part of the Debian system, although it has been configured for use with Debian. We encourage CD manufacturers to read the licenses of software packages in these directories and determine if they can distribute that software on their CDs. Thus, although non-free software isn't a part of Debian, we support its use, and we provide infrastructure (such as our bug-tracking system and mailing lists) for non-free software packages.

This charter is a strong statement of intent concerning Debian's role, commitments, and goals, declared notably beyond the Debian project to the users of this distribution. It elevates the virtues of transparency and accountability, and seeks to foster a commonwealth that upholds the production of free software and the pragmatic needs of users. Although the charter affirms a well-defined moral commitment to free software and a community of users, it also formulates, in its last provision, the pragmatic limits to such "ideological" adherence, sanctioning to a limited degree the use of nonfree software by providing a place for it. In part, this decision reflected the state of free software during the period when the Social Contract was composed as well as an existing desire to ground Debian's shared moral commitments within technical pragmatism. At the time the charter was drafted, there were a number of important software applications like browsers and word processors that simply had no robust free software equivalent. For example, while Netscape existed and was free as in beer, it was not free as in speech; the source was unavailable for use, modification, and circulation.

Following the creation of free software equivalents to these programs over the years, Debian has routinely debated dropping its support of non-free programs; this has even led to a "General Resolution" (resolutions are voted on by the entire project) to eliminate such programs. A resolution in March 2004 reaffirmed Debian's commitment to this provision, though given the voluminous debate it generated, it is an issue that I imagine will be revisited again in the near future. Drawing the line between pragmatism and utility, on the one hand, and ideological purity, on the other, is a task that Debian developers are constantly struggling with, as we will see later in this chapter.

The DFSG is the legal corollary to the Social Contract. For a license to meet the standard of free, it must meet the following criteria:

1. Free Redistribution
The license of a Debian component may not restrict any party from selling or giving away the software as a component of an aggregate software distribution containing programs from several different sources. The license may not require a royalty or other fee for such sale.

2. Source Code
The program must include source code and also allow distribution in source code as well as compiled form.

3. Derived Works
The license must allow modifications and derived works, and must allow them to be distributed under the same terms as the original software's license.

4. Integrity of the Author's Source Code
The license may restrict source code from being distributed in modified form *only* if the license allows the distribution of patch files with the source code for the purpose of modifying the program at build time. The license must explicitly permit the distribution of software built from modified source code. The license may require derived works to carry a different name or version number from the original software.

5. No Discrimination against Persons or Groups
The license must not discriminate against any person or group of persons.

6. No Discrimination against Fields of Endeavor
The license must not restrict anyone from making use of the program in a specific field of endeavor. For example, it may not restrict the program from being used in a business or for genetic research.

7. Distribution of License
The rights attached to the program must apply to everyone to whom the program is redistributed without the need for execution of an additional license by those parties.

8. License Must Not Be Specific to Debian
The rights attached to the program must not depend on the program's being part of a Debian system. If the program is extracted from Debian, and used or distributed without Debian but otherwise

within the terms of the program's license, all parties to whom the program is redistributed should have the same rights as those that are granted in conjunction with the Debian system.

9. License Must Not Contaminate Other Software
The license must not place restrictions on other software that is distributed along with the licensed software. For example, the license must not insist that all other programs distributed on the same medium must be free software.

The DFSG both generalizes and specifies the GPL's four freedoms (access, use, modification, and distribution). It generalizes them so that the DFSG can act as a pragmatic standard to determine the relative "freeness of a license" or as the baseline to create a new license. At the same time, it specifies the meanings of freedom, largely by including an explicit language of nondiscrimination—one of the document's most salient themes. The DFSG has been assiduously excavated for discussion and debate on Debian legal and other mailing lists to help developers decide whether a piece of software they want to package and maintain has a DFSG license, or what changes to an existing license need to be made to make it DFSG free (to be explored in the next chapter).

Along with these two seminal documents, Debian also has an explicit Constitution, which was drafted after a failed first election and in an effort to prevent the type of authoritarian leadership that some developers identified with Perens.[8] The Debian Constitution outlines in great detail the group's organizational structure, which includes nonelected and elected roles and responsibilities. Contained within this document is a representation of Debian's overall system of governance—its combination of majoritarian democracy, meritocracy, and ad hoc consensus.

Debian's democratic commitments are apparent in its voting protocols. Using a version of the Condorcet method (which guards against simple majority rule by means of a complicated ranking system), the project now votes every year for the Debian project leader, and any developer can propose a General Resolution relating to technical, policy, or procedural matters for a projectwide vote. These two provisions demonstrate the populist commitment to give all developers a voice, and acknowledge that regardless of their level or quality of contribution, all developers, once accepted into the project, deserve some decision-making influence. That said, the Debian project leader has assumed a decidedly nontechnical role, not vested with power to make technical decisions for the project at large, and proposing General Resolutions to resolve technical disputes is fastidiously discouraged. Strictly technical problems are not seen as appropriate objects for democratic voting.

For instance, in 2004 when one developer proposed a technically based General Resolution (calling for the support of a new architecture), this suggestion was ripped to shreds on the mailing lists and effectively halted by many contributors, including some of the most respected and visible Debian developers. One response conveyed the distrust of political inclusion within the technical arena that many developers hold and will consistently give voice to: "I won't even consider this proposal until you or someone else explains to me why we should use the voting system to decide an issue like this. [. . .] If recent experience has shown us anything, it's that votes HURT Debian. Please don't take us further down this path." Voting, in other words, blocks open and ongoing debate, the proper and most popular means by which technology should be revisioned and improved.

If the Debian project leader is not a technical position, then what is that person empowered to do? Most developers agree that the project leader acts as a public spokesperson at conferences and other events. Within the Debian community, the project leader acts to coordinate and facilitate discussion, perhaps most vitally opening blocked pathways of communication and aiding in conflict resolution. Their most significant power lies in the ability to assign or legitimate nonelected official roles in the form of delegates and teams—typically technical guardians, who garner respect because of their superior talents and dedication to the project. These teams and delegates perform much of the Debian-wide work, such as administering mailing lists, accepting new members, running votes, and maintaining and integrating new software into the master archive. There is general faith that the Debian project leader either legitimates teams already in existence because of the work they do or assigns roles to people already doing the work.

If it is incumbent on developers to make decisions, there are nonetheless types of developers empowered with special authority to make certain kinds of decisions, usually by virtue of holding nonelected posts as individual delegates, or within teams or committees.[9] While the Debian project leader can assign a Debian developer as a delegate, and in theory is empowered to revoke any existing position, this action has never been taken within the last five years and possibly ever. This is significant. While in theory the project leader or a General Resolution can revoke the position of a technical guardian, in practice this would never happen. Guardianships are vetted positions, and there is strong pressure to let these people remain in their positions so long as they are doing work and desire to remain there.[10]

These positions are largely technical in nature. Current teams include the release manager and team, listmasters, Webmasters, Debian admin team, NMP team, security team, and policy team. These teams coordinate in order to work on larger-scale infrastructural or organizational structures as well as procedures. Important among these individuals are the FTP masters, who existed before there were Debian project leaders assigning teams; they review by hand all new submitted pieces of software packages for technical and licensing glitches, and integrate them into the "master archive."[11]

I was repeatedly told that those who hold these nonelected positions do so because they initially undertook the work necessary to accomplish the tasks of the position. For example, some FTP masters hold their position because they coded the software used to handle package uploads and verification, or the package repository software. Power, in other words, is said to closely follow on the heels of personal initiative and its close cousins: quality technical production and personal dedication to the project.

Even if most developers prefer meritocracy to democracy—in fact, nearly every developer interviewed stated with pride that Debian is meritocratic—this form of power is nonetheless shrouded in some level of distrust. Positions of authority, like the FTP masters, undeniably represent a form of centralized and potentially lifelong authority, potentially subject to corruption or—just as dangerous—knowledge specialization and hoarding. Hackers generally tend to honor decentralization and the distinct power of the individual to trump authority, so *any* centralized authority is bound to act as a lightning rod for reflection and debate.

There is a more specific reason for distrust, though. To fully appreciate the texture of controversies that emerge over authority, we must revisit the argument laid out earlier. Debian developers operate within a social imaginary rooted in a Millian conception of liberal individualism that requires them to cultivate their skills, improve technology, and prove their worth to other hackers within their elite fraternity. Figures of central authority, such as team members and delegates, represent a potential threat to the conditions for this perpetual process of technical self-fashioning. As Donner (1991, 152) maintains in her discussion of Mill's model of self-development, those who gain authority because of merit nonetheless "can only act as guides to others," never as "authorities"; if they attempt to impose "judgments of value on others," this "paradoxically undermines that claim to development." Everyone, not a select order of people, must be able to exercise their capacity for thought, discrimination, and critical intervention, and at all times.

The anxiety that power could potentially corrupt those who enjoy privileges and block conditions for public self-development (by making choices) as well as institute a rigid form of vertical authority emerges from time to time, although in a less coherent and sustained fashion than the critiques of Debian's democratic elements. It is far more common to joke about the existence of what is called the cabal, usually stated as a denial: "There is no cabal." Long before Debian existed, this was a running joke on Usenet, where a similar discomfort over the potential for corruption by meritocratic leaders played out (Pfaffenberger 1996).[12]

In Debian joking enjoys a wide purview, and playful joking about the cabal is littered everywhere. For example, the evening before the 2005 Debian project leader winner was to be announced, a group of developers, including a project leader candidate and the release manager, casually slipped jokes about the cabal into the discussion, unprompted by anything except the announcement by the project secretary that there were twenty-four hours to go until the voting period was over:

<markel> less than 24 hours to go
<crawlspace> cue sinister music
<mickmac> I expect it all to be a conspiracy
<mickmac> The cabal will already have chosen their candidate
<jabberwalkie> mickmac: Nah, there's still time; got your last-minute
    bribes ready? ;)
<mickmac> JabberWalkie: Well, uh, no.
<mickmac> Damnit.
<jabberwalkie> mickmac: Better luck next year. :)
<mickmac> I can offer you beer if you come to Debconf?

*vapor-b shakes his fist at the cabal

Developers use cabal humor to express chronic anxieties about the general corruptibility of meritocracy and their distrust of top-down authority. More specifically, it points to the way Debian "must reconcile the central notion of each developer's autonomy [. . .] with the constraints deriving from the complex system with quality standards of the highest order," as Mathieu O'Neil (2009, 134) has so aptly put it. Most of the time, these jokes are playful. They work like a safety valve to diffuse tension, and are used as a creative and oblique reminder to those in positions of authority that their intentions must be transparent for them to receive the continued trust of the developer population.

At other times, developers couch discussions of the cabal as accusations, seeking more trustworthy behavior from meritocrats, which is usually expressed in claims for greater transparency, accountability, and accessibility. In the recent Debian project leader debate, for example, one developer wrangled with an FTP master over what could be done to increase the project's transparency and equalize the access conditions. The developer invoked the specter of the cabal:

> I see Debian as a meritocracy, and the way to receive privileges is to contribute and be pro-active. However, it cannot be the goal to expect from willing users to figure out everything about a job all by themselves prior to being able to gain recognition for the contributions they make—if they are lucky enough to be considered useful by current holders of the position strived for. If this is actually intended, then it is highly inefficient. If it is not intended, then maybe Debian wants to do something about it, and if not only to stop cold those rumours about an alleged cabal.[13]

This developer felt that Debian developers could do more to increase transparency in order to facilitate and encourage participation from new members. Many of the developers he was arguing with (those in positions of power) disagreed, saying that there was enough transparency and that it was incumbent on interested members to take responsibility for their own self-education, independent of the help of others. This is conveyed in the email below, where one FTP master responded to the claim that Debian policy and organization is too obscure:

> > What you fail to see is that there is something daunting about
> > a project of this size and complexity to those who are trying to
> > understand it top-down, rather than having been part of building it
> > bottom-up.

> What you fail to see is that the bits are available and that you "only" have to build the large picture. If you're too lazy to do so, it's not the job of the people working on essential corners of the project to edu-cate every random Johnny Sixpack for the sake of it.[14]

Even when there is pressure to equalize the conditions for access, which is manifested in jokes about the cabal, equalization within a meritocracy, as I discussed in chapter 3, must proceed by specific methods. Many (though not all) developers feel that if too much help is given to newcomers, it will un-dercut their ability to prove their worth and intelligence within a group that values precisely this sort of performance of self-reliance. The line between the equalization of conditions and too much assistance is constantly being negotiated in Debian, and perhaps more so than in other projects because of its populist bent.

Debian's meritocratic guardians find themselves in a paradoxical position with respect to hackers who accord tremendous weight to liberal individual-ism, especially constant acts of technical self-fashioning and the open-ended process of nonpartisan technical debate. Granted the authority to act with-out the community's prior consent, the guardians rarely can do so without displaying good and pure intentions. In this way, these developers, much like the early natural philosophers of Britain's Royal Society studied by Steven Shapin (1994), must constantly garner the trust of peers through the perfor-mance of character virtues and other related acts.

If the natural philosophers of the Royal Society displayed good faith through a combination of humility, detachment, generosity, and civility, how do the meritocratic guardians of Debian perform their good intentions and navigate this dilemma? Delegates and teams manifest their pure technical intentions through a wide range of practices (and humility is not always one of those, although it certainly can be). Many can display their intentions simply through ongoing technical work—a form of labor that speaks to their unwavering commitment to the project. They are supposed to com-municate openly with developers, and in some periods, developers voiced their dissatisfaction by clamoring for more transparency and accountability from a few of the delegates. These arguments follow a predictable arc: some developers complain about a lack of transparency among the guardians; on the other hand, the guardians feel suffocated under the weight of their obligations, so that the work necessary to communicate and increase the transparency of the role becomes an impossible, unnecessary additional burden; then the developers will offer to help share the workload; and typically the guardians' exasperated response is that integrating and training new people would require more work than they can take on, or the developers need to take the initiative themselves.

Nonetheless, there are some established routines for increasing the visibility and transparency of different working groups, including emails sent out to all developers on the debian-devel-announce mailing list (a required subscription for developers) that summarize the most recent activities of the different technical teams. These informal updates are sent periodically to project members and forge a connection with the body politic of Debian. One former FTP master, James Troup, known more for his technical prowess and dedication than for his communicative access, once sent such a status report titled "Bits from the FTP Master Team" after there had been several months of debate on the mailing lists about the opacity of the FTP master's exact role and complaints that the FTP masters were becoming roadblocks to the project in failing to fulfill their duties. His email, drafted by a number of team members, announced the addition of new members to the team and provided some clarification over the exact responsibilities of each member. Following this information, Troup and the other FTP masters ended the email with a humorous, bitingly sarcastic remark that asserted their goodwill while discounting the complaints as overblown: "We hope this has made your day more pleasant, and your nights less filled with the keening wails of the soulless undead."[15] Its ironic and sardonic subtext is clear: Troup has heard and registered the complaints, is humored that people thought that the situation was so hellishly torturous, and is revealing that there is nothing to worry about, because he is acting in good faith and this unnecessary email serves as his merciful act of grace releasing souls from the unbearable suffering that they were experiencing.

Along with consistent communication, delegate technical proposals must be carefully framed to reflect project and not personal goals. In many instances, it is imperative to let certain decisions be made through an ad hoc, consensual process in which the merit of the outcome emerges via a processes of collective debate rather than as a mandate from those with vested authority (even if the outcome falls entirely within their purview).

An interesting site to examine is the committee invested with the greatest technical power: the Technical Committee. Its role is defined in the Constitution as "the body which makes the final decision on technical disputes in the Debian project," and its members perform their good intentions largely by way of inaction.[16] In the period during which I followed Debian (2000–2005), for instance, this committee rarely exercised its authority.

A hands-off approach is thus how committee members establish their good intentions toward the very process that afforded them the right to become part of the Technical Committee. It reflects the general ideal that those in authority should first defer to the developer community so that differences of opinions can be solved through debate and consensus. The Technical Committee Web site enunciates this notion clearly under the heading "Some Caveats about Contacting the Committee": "A sound and vigorous debate is important to ensure that all the aspects of an issue are fully explored. When discussing technical questions with other developers you should be ready to be challenged. You should also be prepared to be convinced! There is no shame in seeing the merit of good arguments."[17]

The argumentative consensus advocated by the Technical Committee is the third mode of governance in Debian—a mode that is understood as a form of self-governance because it stems from the debate, contributions, and actions of independent-minded, consenting individuals. A tremendous faith is placed in the power of what might be called "technical rhetoric" to convince others of the logic of decisions that have been made. Technical rhetoric is about technical work, and frequently includes a presentation of the code, a corollary written statement, or a justification as to why no change should be made.

These debates happen on IRC, bug-tracking software, and mailing lists; on IRC, the process of argumentation is informal. Developers usually seek the advice of others and move on to do the work. Many times such advice seeking produces robust debate, and when there are especially pronounced differences of opinion, this transforms civil heartiness into vibrant, sometimes-vicious flame wars—outbursts of dissent that are characterized by inflammatory language or direct accusations of incompetence. The Debian bug-tracking system is another site where technical jousting happens, and since there is a formal system that allows developers to rate bugs according to a spectrum of severity from a wish list to severe, these debates can be tracked more systematically. The attention a given bug received can be easily tracked by the length of debate contained therein along with the multiple reassignments of different levels of severity, closing, and reopening. Some bug debates have reached legendary status because of multiple reassignments of severity, their length, and their lack of closure. It is often during such contestations over technical questions that developers most explicitly raise issues of authority, and renegotiate the lines between democracy, consensus, and meritocracy that define their system of governance.[18]

Two Moments of Ethical Cultivation

In terms of governance alone, Debian exhibits an extraordinarily complex moral and technical environment. It should come as no surprise that the way new members integrate themselves within this community, and learn the proper codes of conduct and procedures by which to contribute effectively to the project as well as gain the trust of other developers, is not a simple one. Although many prefer coding over organizational building, Debian developers have nonetheless concocted an interesting social solution to this problem of integration and trust building—the NMP. This process addresses problems following from growth: how to build trust and encourage accountability in the space composed solely of bits and bytes along with a growing number of participants.

Building Trust through the NMP

Essentially a gateway for new members, the NMP defines what is morally and technically expected of them. As such, it works powerfully as a centripetal force of ethical enculturation. It is the framework within which new members first confront the sociopolitical and organizational milieu of Debian. This process represents the first time that some new members meet another Debian developer in person or "ethically voice" their commitment to free software through the prolific writing that is required of them.

Already explicitly committed to a vision of free software, Debian is to some degree a self-selecting organization, unlikely to attract programmers with a staunch commitment to upholding the current status of intellectual property law. But the NMP is unique insofar as it requires prospective Debian developers not only to study detailed texts on the ethics of free software (such as the GPL, Social Contract, and DFSG) but also to produce their own texts on the subject. Through the NMP, developers produce ethically relevant discourse. The extensive narrative work of the NMP makes Debian's codified values personally relevant, and this in turn breeds social commitment to the project.

As Debian grew quickly, the project found itself in the midst of a crisis that peaked between 1998 and 1999. New members were being admitted at rates faster than the project's ad hoc social systems could integrate them. Some longtime developers grew skeptical of the quality of incoming developers, complaining that they introduced more bugs into the system than helpful contributions. The populism of open membership began to come under attack. Some developers suggested that Debian had reached its saturation point.[19]

In response to these problems, the Debian account manager (who creates accounts for new members) waged a silent revolt by halting the processing of new maintainer accounts—essentially preventing any new members from being able to join the project. This move eventually led the account manager to officially stop accepting members under the informal procedures. Instead, the manager proposed formalized procedures that could systematically ensure the trustworthiness of new members as members of the community.

The procedure developed was Debian's NMP. First presented in October 17, 1999, as a proposal on a mailing list, its preamble (quoted below) indicates that the "growing pains" Debian had been experiencing were not merely technical but also ethical. A small group of developers had been clamoring to loosen the commitment to free software and integrate nonfree software in order to be competitive with commercial distributions whose ethical commitments were less stringent. Even though the constitutional charter was already established, the spirit of free software was seemingly losing its potency with the addition of each new wave of developers. The Debian project leader listed the following criteria by which to select new members, and note that the first line is intentionally repeated:

—needs to have a *strong* oppinion [sic] for free software
—needs to have a *strong* oppinion [sic] for free software
—he needs to be able+willing to make long distance phone calls [for an interview]
—He needs to know what he's doing, that new people need some guidance,
we have to prevent ourselves from trojans etc.
—we need to trust him—more than we trust *any* other active person
—He *has to* understand that new-maintainer is *more* than just creating dumb accounts on n [n being a numerical variable] machines

Out of this initial proposal and the establishment of an NMP team, the NMP created a standard that all developers must meet. The NMP is structured not only as a test but also as a process for learning, mentoring, and integrating prospective developers into the project by making them work on packaging a piece of software closely with at least one older, "trusted," project member.

Before prospective developers formally enter the NMP, they are first asked to identify the contributions they plan to make to Debian. They are encouraged to demonstrate their commitment to the project, express why they want to join, and display some level of technical proficiency. For most developers, this involves making a software package and—because only existing developers can integrate a piece of software into the larger GNU/Linux distribution—finding an existing developer to "sponsor" their work. New maintainers work closely with their sponsors, who check their work for common errors and take partial responsibility for the new maintainer. This supervision is important, because in addition to gaining technical skills, the new volunteer begins to participate in the project's social sphere. Prospective developers are encouraged to join mailing lists and IRC channels that provide the medium for technical as well as social communication.

A new maintainer's sponsor often acts as the new applicant's advocate when the maintainer applies for project membership. Advocates are existing developers who vouch for new developers along their history of and potential for contributions to the community. Early in the NMP, the issue of establishing trust is crucial. After the applicant's advocacy has been approved, that person officially becomes part of the NMP, and then an application manager is assigned to guide the new developer through the remainder of the process. It is this manager who handles the rest of the process by acting simultaneously as a mentor, examiner, and evaluator. While it is certainly the case, as phrased condescendingly by one Debian developer, that a "village idiot can't join Debian," this mentorship is the NMP's implicit concession to the limits of a meritocratic imperative that would otherwise require a person to prove their worth entirely on their own.

The NMP includes three steps and requires considerable work on the part of applicants. The process is used to confirm the new maintainers' identity, knowledge and position on free software philosophy, and proficiency with the established Debian policies and procedures as well as their overall technical expertise and knowledge.[20]

The identify verification is accomplished by obtaining *the cryptographic signature* of at least one existing Debian developer on their personal GNU privacy guard key. This key is encrypted with a pass phrase that is known only to the person holding that key. When properly unlocked with the pass phrase, a signature can be generated, and that signature can then in turn be attached to a particular email message, text, or piece of software. With an attached signature, it is proof that it originated from the person possessing the key. When key owners meet in person, they establish their identity to each other by exchanging pieces of government-issued picture identification and the key fingerprint, which uniquely identifies the key itself. Having traded and verified this information, developers later place their unique cryptographic signature on each other's keys to confirm to others that they have connected the key being signed with the individual in possession of those identity documents. This is a process of identity verification that can then be used over the Internet to confirm, with certainty, that an individual is who they say they are.

By requiring new developers to obtain the signature of an existing Debian developer, the NMP integrates them into what they call a cryptographic "web of trust." Because nearly every hacker within Debian has a key signed by at least one existing developer, and because many developers have keys signed by numerous others (the stronger the connected set of signatures is, the more trustworthy it is considered), nearly all maintainers are connected. Debian can use cryptographic algorithms to prove that most every developer met at least one other developer, who in turn met at least one other developer, and so forth, until every developer is linked. Debian's administrative software depends heavily on these keys to identify users for the purposes of integrating software into the distribution, for controlling access to machines, allowing access to a database with sensitive information on developers, and restricting publication to announce-only email lists.

The importance of meeting in person to sign the keys is illustrated in the following anecdote, which begins with the controversial claim of one Debian developer:

> I have a potentially controversial thesis. My thesis is that the "Raul Miller" who is a Debian Developer and sits on the Technical Committee (and was, for a time, its chairman) doesn't actually exist.
>
> You see, Mr. Miller joined the project before we had the current procedures for vetting developers' identities, and even before we had the semi-informal ones under which I myself was admitted to the project in 1998. Interestingly, there are no signatures on Mr. Miller's PGP key other than his own. A remarkable accomplishment for someone who's been with the project this long, but not so surprising for someone whom no other developer has, as far as I can tell, ever claimed to have met in person.[21]

When it became clear that Miller, who occupied a crucial technical position in the project at that time, was outside the web of trust, there was such alarm that within three days, two developers drove to meet the individual in question and succeeded in bringing him into the cryptographic network. The developers' strong reactions demonstrated the *essential nature* of these infrequent face-to-face interactions and significance of verifying the identity of one of their technical guardians.

Integration into Debian's web of trust is thus a vital first step in new maintainers' integration into the Debian project. This process connects and leads into the second and often most rigorous part of the NMP: philosophy and procedures. The first part of the application requires that new maintainers provide a declaration of intention, a proof of some contribution or skill they could bring to the project, and undergo the philosophy and procedure testing, which includes a biographical narrative of why and how they became involved in free software and Debian.

During this philosophy step in the NMP, application managers ask prospective developers a series of questions regarding free software and Debian philosophy. While general knowledge of the definition and philosophy related to F/OSS is essential, the questions revolve around Debian's Social Contract and DFSG. New maintainers are asked a series of questions—some culled from a standard template, and others created anew—to demonstrate their familiarity with these documents, ability to apply and synthesize the concepts encapsulated within them, and capacity to articulate their agreement with as well as commitment to the Debian ideals.

Although each new maintainer must agree to the Social Contract, the philosophy test does not require developers to hold a homogeneous view on free software. Rather, it seeks to ensure that all Debian developers are knowledgeable about, interested in, and dedicated to its basic principles. Open-ended questions frequently turn into longer email conversations between application managers and prospective developers in which the subtleties about licensing along with free software philosophy are dissected. While I have heard some developers complain of the "wait" and "bureaucracy" introduced by the NMP, or even the absurdity of some of the technical questions, I have never heard an objection levied against this part of the application. In fact, most developers recall the philosophy section as enjoyable and rewarding.

In particular, the initial biography allows developers to take an inventory of their technical past, in a way that starts to imbue it with a decidedly ethical dimension. It is worth quoting large blocks of an application here to offer a sense of the remarkable detail and nuance of these writings. Below I quote a short section from a developer answering the biographical question:

> This is my story about free software: In the first times I was excited by the idea of something to which everybody could contribute, just like that Internet that I was discovering at the same time. I could also see that it had a future, because of that part that said that all the contributions would remain free. Wow! At the same time, I was seeing many closed softwares rise and fall (DOS, Windows 3.x, OS/2, compiler environments, BBS software, Office suites, hardware drivers, proprietary format backup suites, whatever), and everytime they got superseded by some other thing, support fell, bugs remained unfixed, data became unreadable and nobody could do anything about it except spending lots of time and resources relearning everything and porting or even restarting their works from scratch. [. . .]
> I realized that Free Software was and is the only thing that potentially allows you to be free of the risks that (usually silly) external events pose on your know-how and on the software that you depend on. [. . .]
>
> This is about me and my time for Debian:
> Between five and six years have passed running Debian, and my experience with it has grown. I got used to the Debian phylosophy [sic], did some experience with the BTS [bug-tracking system], read some mailing lists, the DWN, got curious and somewhat knowledgeable on how Debian works, read pages, policies, discussions, I even went to the LSM and Debian One. [. . .]
> The packages that I used to create, however, were not perfect, and I would have needed to better study the various Debian policies and manuals to do some better job. Willing to do that, I thought it was silly not to become an official maintainer, and start contributing to the project myself, so that others could take advantage of that knowledge I was about to acquire.

The first section usually sticks to a standard technical life history, gesturing toward the ethical uniqueness of F/OSS, yet it is told in a mode hinged to practical life experiences with technology. Often told in a confessional tone, such essays are as much a biography about not only one's own discovery of this specific project but also how one arrived at the principles upheld in Debian itself.

The philosophy aspect of the philosophy and procedures section also covers the Social Contract and DFSG, and it is here where the ethical voicing becomes strikingly pronounced. In contrast to the descriptive register of the biographical section, here prospective developers are required to formulate their personal views on free software, moving from personal experiences toward reflective generalizations regarding the legal and ethical principles they are committing to in joining this project. Let me first share the text before commenting on its implications. Below is an excerpt from a different application than the one quoted above. This applicant, responding to the question "Please explain the key points of the Social Contract and the DFSG—in your own words," remarks:

> The Social Contract is the commitment the Debian project makes to its members and users. It is about fostering a community so committed to software freedom, so open, and so supportive that no one would have need to go elsewhere. Debian's members and users benefit from the fact that Debian is completely free software and that nothing in the Debian process is hidden from them.
>
> Debian also provides an outlet for new free software and a "channel" for contributing changes back to the original developers. It also takes the realistic view that some users may still be using non-free software and that providing this software actually helps Debian's users and indirectly the free software community.
>
> The Debian Free Software Guidelines is the set of concrete rules that help determine if a piece of software complies with the Social Contract and the Project's goals. The rules in the DFSG are chosen to make sure software accepted into Debian maintains the user's freedoms to use, distribute, and modify that software now and forever. This is not just for Debian's users but anyone who might take software in Debian and modify it, create CDROMs, or even create a derivative distribution. [. . .]
>
> \> Also, describe what you personally think about these documents.
>
> The Social Contract and the DFSG represent a very unique idea. In this day and age where society (at least in the US and some other first world countries) encourages individualism and tries to divide the people and control them it is very refreshing to read the Debian Social Contract. Proprietary software made by commercial software companies/developers is exactly that, commercial. Those companies/developers are only about profit or advancing their agenda and will do what they need to in order to maximize that. Often this conflicts with doing the right thing for the user and here are some examples,
>
> —If a company/developer sells a piece of proprietary software that, as all software does, has bugs and they also sell incident based support contracts then what incentive do they have for fixing bugs in the software?

—If a company/developer's revenue stream is based on selling new versions of their proprietary software, what incentive do they have for fixing bugs in the old one rather than forcing users to pay for a new upgrade they may not want. [. . .]

—Imagine a company/developer that develops a proprietary application that initially meets the users needs so well and is priced reasonably that they gain a monopoly on the market. With the competition gone they can raise their prices or bundle additional unwanted applications into their software, or do pretty much anything they want.

—Now imagine a company/developer that uses that monopoly in one market to gain entry and into other markets and attacking users' freedoms in those as well.

In all these examples the company/developer benefits at the expense of the users.

In order to prevent situations like this one of the things the Social Contract/ DFSG effectively says is this,

"Our users are so important to us that we are setting these ground rules to protect their freedoms. If you can develop software that meets these rules then not only do we invite you to include it in Debian, but we accept you into the our community and will expend our resources to distribute your software, help keep track of bugs it may have and features that could be added, and help you improve and support it."

In addition to that statement several of the DFSG's clauses have the effect of saying,

"We are so committed to doing the right thing and working together with anyone in an open manner to resolve differences and always do the right thing for the users that we're willing to let you have all the work that we've done. You can do whatever you wish with it as long as you obey the original author's license." [. . .]

These are very powerful ideas that can't be taken away or subverted by someone who wants to extort or control users. Personally, I think my interest in getting involved with Debian is an extension of my overall views and this is the only way that I want to use and develop software.

While the content of this narrative certainly matters, I want to stress the type of ethical labor being produced by this text. The developer takes the vision ensconced in the Debian charters and adds value to it in numerous personalized ways: he reformulates its key principles in his own words; to hone down his points, he makes a fairly sophisticated contrast between proprietary and free software development largely along the ethical lines that matter to him—transparency, openness, and accountability; and he poignantly concludes with a succinct commitment to this style of development.

What we see here with these applications is what Cover, in his discussion of a nomos, describes as a simultaneous process of subjective commitment to and objective projection of norms, or a bridging that emerges out of a narrative mode. "This objectification of the norms to which one is committed frequently," Cover (1993, 145; emphasis added) observes, "perhaps always entails a narrative—a story of how the law, now object, came to be, and more importantly, *how it came to be one's own*." This is precisely what occurs during the NMP. Developers affirm their commitment to the principles enshrined in their key charters largely by way of a specific gravitational pull: the force of their life experiences is brought to bear directly on these documents, thereby rendering them objectively real, but in a way that subjectively matters within one's personal orbit of life experiences. This is followed by a second move, which betrays subjective personalization. Developers voice the broader importance of these principles and clarify the social implications of their commitments. Neither purely subjective nor objective accounts, these narratives form a bridge between them.

Moreover, the narratives are at the basis of temporal movement and personal transformation. They take people to new locations, and past, present, and future come together in a moment of ethical assessment. The past is weaved into the present, and the voicing of commitment in the application becomes the path toward a future within the project. It is a step that brings a developer closer to a new social localization within a larger ethical and technical project of developers who have also undergone the same reflective exercise.

Through this reconfiguration of temporality, developers after the NMP can be said to share at least three connections: they are technologically linked through the web of trust that requires them to meet at least one other developer; they share the experience of a common ritual of entry; and finally, they have started to learn a Debian-specific vocabulary with which to situate themselves within this world, formulate the broader implications of freedom, and continue the conversation on freedom, licensing, and their craft, with a wider body of developers.

Although the philosophy aspect of the NMP often results in voluminous expository output, it is by no means the bulk of the process; in fact, it is only half of step three of a five-step process. The other half of the philosophy step is known as procedures, in which applicants must demonstrate what the general policies are as well as their ability to perform whatever individual responsibilities they wish to take on within the project itself. Once the philosophy and procedures step is deemed appropriately passed, the applicant moves on to the rigorous tasks and skills step. This step confirms that the applicant has the necessary skills to carry out the job that they will take on as a Debian developer. These tests vary depending on what the applicant will be doing, but typically involve many technical questions. The overall process generally results in several dozen pages of exhaustive responses along with many back-and-forth discussions and clarifications over months (and sometimes up to a year) with the assigned application manager.

If accepted into the project, some developers slip into relative obscurity. Some do not actively participate in Debian's dynamic culture of debate and dialogue. Some follow only as spectators, while others could care less about what are perceived as overly dramatic conversations and concentrate wholly on their technical contributions. But for most developers, in ethical terms, the NMP is a highly condensed version of what flows and follows in the social metabolism of the project, though in a slightly altered version. The narrative work that transforms codified norms into meaningful ones continues within the project itself, and the knowledge gained during the process is necessary for newcomers to integrate effectively into the project.

Interactions among developers in the ongoing debates tend to be less concerned with the nature of the principles they committed to in the NMP than with the *implications* of these principles. In other words, common principles start to diverge into a multiplicity of newly generated ethical meanings, some of which alter the basic procedures and structures of the project. Even if their interpretations of principles diverge, developers usually refer to the charters or shared precepts in arguments, and as such, these precepts are kept actively relevant. Divergence and disagreement is thus the basis for moral coexistence. I turn next to one such moment of group crisis.

CRISIS AND ETHICAL RENEWAL

Punctuated moments of distrust and despair are responsible for a great deal of the existing framework of Debian itself. Crises occur when there are fundamental disagreements over some issue. These can range from governance to legality, but many consistently revolve around a limited set of themes: project transparency, major technical decisions, the meaning and scope of freedom, and the relations between ordinary developers and those with vested power. These grievances are expressed on mailing lists, IRCs, and blogs; the writing that unfolds during moments of crisis is both voluminous and markedly passionate.

These punctuated moments are eminently precarious: the nomos is under threat, populated by all sorts of pitfalls and dangers. The drama of disease can spread uncontrollably like a virus, channeling the potent energy of dissatisfaction into a pit of destabilizing disgust or despair. Tempers flare, leading to inflammatory remarks that burn bridges, and people sometimes cling too literally to codified norms, blinding them to a unique situation that yearns for its own unique response. The crisis may be of such great magnitude that it overshadows the positive energy that moves the project toward a solution.

Despite their riskiness, however, periods of crisis are also among the most fertile instances of ethical production, articulation, and transformation; their mere expression is proof that people are ethically "on call." People would not be willing to take sides if they did not feel personally invested in changing what is collectively diagnosed as a problem. Crisis periods are incipient calls for movement and realignment, and hence reveal commitments that, if acted on, can lead to positive solutions and a profound renewal of the organization.

The formal attributes of crisis—its drama, high-pitched emotional nature, and kinetic energy—have an ethical subtext that speaks to the fact that an altered situation or unsatisfactory event has arisen that demands immediate, overt attention. A crisis demands a response —one that a charter or code cannot fully provide but rather must be sculpted through a fraught process of voicing, debate, and action.

Because the emotional tone of communication induced by a crisis can diverge significantly from the way many developers expect or desire communication to unfold, I run the risk of portraying crisis as a positive force that can contribute to moral cohesion. Many developers adhere to a Habermasian (and so quite liberal) ideal of communicative interaction that requires participants to shed personal interest and passion in favor of sober rational discussion, where clarity is achieved because "all participants stick to the same reference point" (Habermas 1987, 198). While communication can certainly happen along those lines and be ethically productive, it downplays the inherently risky nature of many communicative acts (Butler 1997; Gardiner 2004). Judith Butler (1997, 87–88) in *Excitable Speech* probably states this most poignantly when she argues that the Habermasian project is self-limiting, possibly undermining its democratic aspirations, because of its insistence on eliminating personal interest and the inherent risk in the act of communication:

> Risk and vulnerability are proper to the democratic process in the sense that one cannot know in advance the meaning that the other will assign to one's utterance, what conflicts of interpretation may well arise, and how best to adjudicate the difference. The effort to come to terms is not one that can be resolved in anticipation but only through a concrete struggle of translation, one whose success has no guarantees.

Now let us take a look at one legendary "concrete struggle of translation"— one whose resolution looked quite tenuous at the time of its unfolding.

Portrait of a Crisis

The first story of ethics in Debian that I presented began with an ending: the NMP was a solution to a crisis over the integration of new members. In fact, it created a social architecture that, while imperfect, continues to sustain a baseline level of trust and coherence, and helps to absorb and lessen the shocks of future crises. Yet punctuated periods of distrust or malaise invariably recur, and here I focus on one of the most memorable to have hit Debian in the last ten years. So as the opening of this section on ethical moments began with the story of an ending, the closing of this section will end with a beginning.

There are a number of events that I could have chosen to illustrate the social metabolism of a crisis in Debian. I have picked this one because of the rich multiplicity of issues it raises, and because I actually witnessed and closely followed its ebb and flow from the instant it began to its current recession.

Let me provide some background on the project's status at the time in March 2005. Debian was in the process of choosing a new leader. There were several candidates, and the ideas they brought to the table concerned fundamental questions of governance that could alter the nature of the Debian project leadership, communications issues, the role of women in the project, transparency, a perceived hostile working climate, growing pains, and the uncertain threat of a new Linux project based on Debian (Ubuntu). The project was gearing up to complete a new release, and given this, there was a heightened sense of pressure. It was in this frenetic climate that a single email began the crisis.

The Debian release manager sent this email to the developer list, announcing the final plans for releasing Debian's latest distribution. An in-person meeting in mid-March had convened in Vancouver, Canada, bringing together the FTP masters, the release team, and members of the security team to hammer out a plan that offered a concrete vision for Debian's technical future. In addition to information about the upcoming release, proposals were advanced detailing how to handle the release after that, called "etch." The participants in the Vancouver meeting had concluded that the era of universal architecture support was over. Debian did not have the technical or human resources to support as well as maintain so many different versions of Debian at the time. These "ports," as these different versions are called, run on different hardware architectures, ranging from i386 to AMD64:

> The much larger consequence of this meeting, however, has been the crafting of a prospective release plan for etch. The release team and the FTP masters are mutually agreed that it is not sustainable to continue making coordinated releases for as many architectures as Sarge currently contains, let alone for as many new proposed architectures as are waiting in the wings. The reality is that keeping eleven architectures in a releasable state has been a major source of work for the release team, the d-i team, and the kernel team over the past year; not to mention the time spent by the DSA/build admins and the security team. It's also not clear how much benefit there is from doing stable releases for all of these architectures, because they aren't necessarily useful to the communities surrounding those ports. Therefore, we're planning on not releasing most of the minor architectures starting with etch. They will be released with Sarge, with all that implies (including security support until Sarge is archived), but they would no longer be included in testing. This is a very large step, and while we've discussed it fairly thoroughly and think we've got most of the bugs worked out, we'd

appreciate hearing any comments you might have. [. . .]
Note that this plan makes no changes to the set of supported release architectures for Sarge, but will take effect for testing and unstable immediately after Sarge's release with the result that testing will contain a greatly reduced set of architectures, according to the following objective criteria:

—it must first be part of (or at the very least, meet the criteria for) scc. debian.org (see below)
—the release architecture must be publicly available to buy new
—the release architecture must have N+1 builds where N is the number required to keep up with the volume of uploaded packages
—the value of N above must not be $> 2^{22}$

At first glance it may be unclear what in this technical, matter-of-fact email would have led to a crisis. The meeting's participants included the technical guardians of Debian, and their advice is usually held with respect. But before I explain why such a seemingly benign proposal produced such an event, first let me describe the response, for it was nothing short of monumental—even by Debian standards of crisis. Within the first day there were over five hundred email messages in response, and within three days, there were over nine hundred emails. This text of mailing lists, if taken together, could probably fill one or possibly two multivolume dissertations. On IRCs, conversation was bubbling nonstop about this debacle. Posts analyzing the event and its significance appeared on Planet Debian, the group Debian blog that aggregates individual developer's blogs. I had to spend days reading this material.

The cascade of responses was astonishing. It is first worth portraying the atmosphere of utter paradox that arose, in which synchronicity sat alongside unsettling discordance. The project was in one of the most pronounced moments of unity that I had seen in a long time. Hundreds and hundreds of developers gave the problem their due attention in the form of numerous writings—on mailing lists, IRCs, and blogs. For days the project felt like it was riding the same but nevertheless dangerously large and unstable collective wave. This was also a moment of pronounced dis-ease and thus discordance, where differences of opinion rang loud and overblown accusations prevailed, as if a furious legion of frenzied and rabid hydra had suddenly appeared on the scene, with each individual head screeching, rearing, and rending in all directions.

It felt as if Debian was coming apart at its seams. But a duality of centrifugal discordance *and* centripetal synchronicity defines crisis. Crisis sits at a crossroads, a moment of betwixt and between when outcomes are decidedly uncertain. During this period, people were brought together to express their deep dissatisfaction, but pulled apart from one other by different sets of conflicting opinions—including over the very reaction—with unity under dire threat. There was a sense that this crisis was at once remarkably silly and overblown, a distraction from the work required by the immanent release, yet fully important and serious, as if some line had been crossed. Why? What was it about this particular email that caused such collective alarm?

The crisis rested on several factors. Notably, the developers were able to suture a wide range of concerns to this email, but one of the most significant complaints, stated over and again, was about *its tone*: its disharmonious resonance struck the wrong collective chord, working to resurrect the project's perennial discomfort over the corruptibility of meritocratic authority. Other precipitating factors included its timing and content. Last but not least was the email's content, which many developers found shocking. Over the course of many years, Debian had built an image of being a Universal OS, special among its class because it ran on more architectures than any other Linux distribution. Developers had informally animated the edifice of the DFSG's nondiscrimination clause to include architecture support. The announcement that the era of technical universality was perhaps soon to be part of its past was a huge blow to Debian's sense of collective pride.

Complaints about the email's tone centered on the following sentence: "The release team and the FTP masters are mutually agreed that it is not sustainable to continue making coordinated releases for as many architectures as Sarge currently contains, let alone for as many new proposed architectures as are waiting in the wings." Even though the email was stated as a proposal, below is a short excerpt from an IRC discussion that articulated the shock that the email produced:

> <kivet> mm, I certainly didn't expect the meeting to be quite so wide-ranging; in advance, I rather expected it to be mostly "ok, let's sort out Sarge; [. . .] oh, and in the five minutes we have left, how can we look to avoid this in the future?"
>
> <yaarr> vapor-b: if you wanted open discussion, you should have stopped in your tracks when it became apparent that other people might be interested in the subject. Don't do shadowy meetings on your part and request open discussion from us.
>
> <stig> Yaarr: but that is what happened: they put out a proposal and now it can be discussed.
>
> <yaarr> yeah, sure
>
> <markel> and the announcement, signed off by all the people who do the work, and most future dpl candidates, had an unfortunate ring of finality. If indeed this is a proposal, that is open to serious discussion (as opposed to "this is the way it is, unless you happen to convince all of us of something else, despite the hours of discussion where we hammered it all out"), than [sic] perhaps a follow-up is in order.
>
> <markel> stig: I don't know about you, but my comprehension of the English language has been often deemed adequate, and my take of the announcement was a fait accompli.

> <yaarr> stig: as I told you before, the idea is for our statement to be con-
> structive, in that it'll try to suggest some modifications that will make
> this mess a bit less of a problem to us.

What this discussion demonstrates is that by presenting a fairly significant technical change in a way that *seemed* like an established decision, the delegates violated the norms of acceptable and appropriate behavior. In this proposal, many developers found it difficult to believe in the "pure technical intentions" of entrusted members. What had failed here was a necessary performance of the goodwill that normally acts to limit anxieties about corruption in meritocracies, especially those with hierarchies like Debian.

What this event revealed is that Debian's implementation of meritocracy, like all meritocracies, is a fragile framework easily overtaken by the threat of corruptibility. In the case of Debian, this threat is particularly onerous, for it can potentially block the conditions for rough technical consensus; this event ostensibly edged too close to such corruption for the project's comfort zone.

Within Debian, the delegates and teams hold a similar form of authority as the mythical philosopher king and his guardians presented in one of the most favorable accounts of meritocratic rule, Plato's *Republic*. In this imagined world, rulers are granted authority for life by virtue of their talents, their passion for the inherent good of ruling, and a well-cultivated character that breeds the proper "intent" for rule. Leaders are those who are "full of zeal to do whatever they believe is for the good of the commonwealth and never willing to act against its interest. They must be capable of possessing this connection, never forgetting it or allowing themselves to be either forced or bewitched into throwing it over" (Plato n.d.). This sentiment is eerily descriptive of the ways in which Debian developers conceive of proper meritocratic rule. Team members and delegates are entrusted to hold technical authority for as long as they want to (insofar the Debian project leader has never removed someone from these positions), because they display their "zeal" to do good for the "technical commonwealth" of Debian through superior acts of technical production.

In Plato's imaginary republic, rulers were kept in check by being subject to a highly public presence and the demands of rigorous ascetic life—little property and no domestic relations. These components confirmed and sustained proper intent. But in Debian, there are few formal mechanisms to curb the excesses of power of those who have been granted positions of technical authority. Teams and delegates, in theory, are fully trusted members who no longer have to perform their intent in order to prove their worth and make decisions. The teams that convened in Vancouver were empowered to make the significant technical decisions that they proposed. Yet in practice (as this crisis made clear), such decisions would be difficult to pull off without first consulting and building technical consensus. The guardians are bound by the informal codes discussed earlier in this chapter by which they must be seen to act not out of a self-interest but instead always in the interest of the Debian project.

Given this, the overwhelming response to the Vancouver prospectus was a reaction to the perceived violation of meritocratic trust, and during this period, accusations of a cabal proliferated. It seemed to some as if the myth, the joke, of "smoky backrooms" in Debian was perhaps no joke at all. But if the crisis raised the specter of mistrust, it was also the very mechanism by which trust was rebuilt again. The overt public voicing and revoicing that the Vancouver meeting "smacks too much of deals in smoky backrooms, where a seat at the table is by explicit invitation," was a moment of collective clarification. The backlash and conversations that called Debian's philosopher kings to task served to call attention to what was seen as potentially inappropriate exercises of technical meritocratic authority as well as an opportunity for Debian guardians to assert that no such thing had ever happened.

Through an overwhelming tide of emails, many of these delegates were forced to explain the reasoning behind their recommendation that Debian limit architecture support. In turn, developers contributed their own views on what would have been the proper way to approach the problem, and others contributed discussions and proposals about how to technically proceed. The release manager and another member of the participating teams were remarkably attentive: they wrote emails and talked to developers on IRCs to appease fears, explained technical details, took into account the recommendations of others, revealed what happened at the meeting, and especially, reaffirmed that nothing was written in stone. In essence, they conformed to the stipulation by Plato (n.d.) that "[the guardians] must be capable of possessing this connection, never forgetting it or allowing themselves to be either forced or bewitched into throwing it over." In contrast with Plato's *Republic*, what this crisis shows is how in Debian, anyone can theoretically become a philosopher king so long as they posses the right intent and skill, and so long as the channels for dialogue are kept open. As a result of these often-passionate outpourings, the proposal was transformed into a proposition awaiting further discussion. In the end, although it took a blow, trust was reestablished.

One participant and member of the FTP team posted the following explanation, which provided a window into the meeting's organic development and affirmed the proposal's openness:

As it happened, James and I were staying at Ryan's, and after dinner on Friday night (before the meeting proper started, but after we'd met everyone), we chatted about the topic and came to the opinion that removing a bunch of architectures from being release candidates would be necessary—for reasons I hope are adequately explained in the announcement, or that will be on –devel as people ask. As it turned out, when we got to the actual meeting the next day, this was more or less exactly what Steve was wanting to propose, and he seemed to be expecting most of the objections to come from James, Ryan and/or me. So instead of that, we then spent a fair while discussing criteria for what support architectures would/should receive.

Hopefully the above provides some useful specifics for people to talk about.

>As a result, the rest of the project had little input into
>the decision-making process.

That's why it's posted on the lists now—it [is] never too late to get input into something in Debian; even after we've committed to something, *we can almost always change our minds* [emphasis added].

Due to these outpourings, many of which were wildly passionate, any ambiguity as to the proposal's status was dispelled, transforming it to an unambiguous proposition waiting to be further explored.

When the acute phase of the Vancouver crisis was over, energy was diverted back to releasing the subsequent version of Debian: Sarge. Certainly, there remains a tremendous amount of work to be done on the technical problem of architecture support in Debian, and there are many broader questions about governance that this crisis raised. Even if it was affirmed that entrusted members of Debian should consult the entire project before proposing radical changes, there seems to be a growing unease among many developers over the scalability of technical consensus. The rough consensus that so many developers are proud of seems to have gotten rougher with the addition of each new developer, and eventually Debian developers may have to start thinking about novel social solutions to accommodate these changes. For that period, however, the work laid out by the Vancouver prospectus was entrusted to anyone who has a stake in the process. The field had been momentarily leveled despite the hierarchies of power that emerge from a meritocratic system.

If much of the work performed during this crisis reopened the decision-making process to the whole project, it also allowed developers to collectively affirm that the values they tend to desire from technology (accountability, openness, and access) are those that they also expect from project governance and members of their project, especially those who hold vetted positions of power. Nonetheless, Debian is a dynamic organization. It changes. And through these types of unforeseen conflicts, the door to a reflective process of assessing is frequently opened, allowing developers to revoice their commitment to informal norms of governance and begin the design work to reach new solutions within these norms.

While the charters codify these values, the texts do not fully determine their significance within the everyday life of the project. The values must be enacted in various guises—one of which is a passionate outpouring of commitments during moments of dis-ease. Mikhail Bakhtin's discussion of ethical situationalism can help account for the necessity and importance of the crisis as a moment in which preexisting norms and codes break down, and then need to be rearticulated. In *Toward a Philosophy of the Act*, Bakhtin offers an ethical theory of action that repudiates the implications of formalistic theories of ethics, particularly Immanuel Kant's categorical imperative. Formalism requires what Bakhtin interprets as a suspect allegiance to universally conceived theoretical precepts standing above time and place.[23] Bakhtin argues that an overallegiance to theoretical precepts misdirects and thus disables responsibility instead of channeling it toward an active confrontation with the living moment in its full-blooded complexity. The effect of such "acts of abstraction," says Bakhtin (1993, 7; emphasis added), is to be "controlled by [. . .] autonomous laws" in which people are "*no longer present in it as individually and answerable active human beings.*"

Although Bakhtin's dismissal of codified norms is somewhat overstated—in fact as I have been contending here, norms are more practical then he suggests; they are necessary guiding abstractions that establish a common ground for action and social cohesion—his critique nonetheless clarifies a number of key points. For Bakhtin, the most problematic aspect of formal ethics is that they provide a false sense of security, "an alibi" for an actual ethical being that downplays the inherent risk and conflict of making decisions along with the necessity of working toward solutions. The hard labor of ethics, its demanding phenomenology, is an outgrowth of taking risks, putting in the effort to engage with others, and choosing to confront the situation at hand in its specificity.

Despite Bakhtin's repudiation of theoretical dogmatism, he is careful to steer away from advocating moral relativism. As Michael Gardiner (2004, 39) maintains, Bakhtin rejects relativism for its shaky theoretical presumption that "a priori the mutual incomprehension of view [. . .] renders authentic dialogue superfluous." Rather, Bakhtin asserts that individuals can potentially achieve some level of consensus because they are situated within a shared world of meaning. Despite clear differences in opinion that are unquestionably made evident during periods of crisis, people participating in a collective endeavor are nevertheless situated in a shared social space and committed to a baseline set of goals. As a result of Debian developers' common participation in the project and shared rituals of entry such as the NMP, common participation within the broader hacker public, and participation in public events like conferences, they can draw on a set of shared experiences to work toward resolving crisis. This is an important condition of possibility that speaks to a potential, though not a guarantee, for consensus. To reach agreement, ethical labor must still be performed.

CONCLUSION

Given what I have written in this chapter, I hope it is clear that the praxis of ethics among Debian developers is diverse and ongoing; the making of a nomos is a dynamic affair. At times, ethical work occurs as an implicit form of enculturation, and in other moments, it takes shape as a reflective voicing through which a series of temporally and personally significant transformations are declared as well as achieved. For example, the new maintainer narratives allow developers to reevaluate their lives, making them into life histories that publicly offer a current and future commitment to a commonwealth. Crises represent moments of limits; charters and even routine narrative discussion are never enough to confront the emergent realities of new situations. In the simplest terms possible, an ethical life demands constant attention, response, reevaluation, and renewal.

A critical question remains: Can we generalize Debian to illuminate the ethical processes of other virtual or F/OSS projects? With such a stark adherence to well-established ethical precepts, is Debian in fact just the radical black sheep of development projects? Or do other projects exhibit similar social, organizational, and ethical processes? It is worth noting that with over one thousand developers, Debian is the largest free software project and thus not simply sitting on the margins. Furthermore, each project has its own peculiar idiosyncrasies, so it is impossible to use any one project to generalize about all of them. If the processes I discussed here exist on a spectrum, Debian undoubtedly resides on one end by virtue of its articulation of strong moral commitments whereas others, such as the Linux kernel project, steer clear from explicit moral language.

But other endeavors evince many of the elements explored here. Every large project is dynamic, and has had to deal with the problems of trust and scalability. Most of the large ones have had to routinize, like Debian, by devising formal procedures for entry that require prospective members to undergo mentorship and training. Many medium- to large-size projects have drafted key documents that define their goals and vision. In the case of Debian, they have formalized this into the Social Contract. Similar to developers who labor in distinct places, in other free software projects to large technology firms, Debian developers also seek to strike a balance between individually initiated decision making and vertical authority, yielding to the latter to some qualified degree, even if clearly preferring the former. The ways in which this balance is reached—when and if it is—never follow a predictable, unitary path, although the general attempt is a crucial conduit for articulating and embodying this commitment.

PART III

THE POLITICS OF AVOWAL
AND DISAVOWAL

✦

We do not act because we know.
We know because we are called upon to act.
—Johann Gottlieb Fichte, *The Vocation of Man*

The final two chapters engage directly with the politics of free software. Chapter 5 examines the politics of avowal and popular protest, and the conclusion looks at the disavowal of broadly conceived politics among many free software hackers.

Chapter 5 explores two different conditions under which free software developers learn about the law. It contrasts everyday legal pedagogy as it unfolds in Debian with a lively series of political protests, which I describe as a moment of political avowal because of the way hackers and programmers took to the streets between 1999 and 2003 to insist on their free speech rights to create as well as circulate software unencumbered by current legal restrictions. During this period, F/OSS hackers enunciated more reflexively than ever before their free speech rights to produce and distribute software, thereby working to stabilize a relatively new cultural claim in which source code came to be imagined as a species of free speech.

In contrast to this period of lively political protest, the conclusion examines what I consistently witnessed during my fieldwork: a reluctance to signify free software beyond a narrow politics of software freedom. I start by discussing how and why this is articulated, but quickly move on to look at the consequence of this political disavowal. A central feature of F/OSS has been its political agnosticism, which has facilitated, I argue, its spread and adoption, allowing it to attain a position where it can circulate widely and perform a political message. Through its visibility and its use by multiple publics, F/OSS thus makes apparent the assumptions that dominate the moral landscape of intellectual property law and mainstream economic theory. An important element here is the transposability of F/OSS, or its power to enjoin others to become part of its performance in various ways—through the use of F/OSS artifacts and licenses, participation in projects, reflections on the larger meaning of collaboration, and the reconfigurations of licenses for other nontechnological objects. Its most profound political effect has been to devitalize the hegemonic status of intellectual property law and catalyze a series of transformations in the arena of intellectual property law.

CHAPTER 5

Code Is Speech

⋯◈⋯

Like many computer aficionados today, Seth Schoen writes all of his software as free software to ensure that the source code—the underlying directions of computer programs—will remain accessible for other developers to use, modify, and redistribute. In so doing, Schoen not only makes technology but also participates in an effort that redefines the meaning of liberal freedom, property, and software by asserting in new ways that code is speech. A tiny portion of a 456-stanza haiku written by Schoen (2001), for example, makes just this claim:

> Programmers' art as
> that of natural scientists
> is to be precise,
>
> complete in every
> detail of description, not
> leaving things to chance.
>
> Reader, see how yet
> technical communicants
> deserve free speech rights;
>
> see how numbers, rules,
> patterns, languages you don't
> yourself speak yet,
>
> still should in law be
> protected from suppression,
> called valuable speech![1]

Schoen's protest poem not only argued that source code is speech but also demonstrated it: the extensive haiku was in fact a transcoding of a short piece of free software called DeCSS, which could be used to decrypt access controls on DVDs in violation of current copyright laws. Schoen did not write this poem simply to be clever. His work was part of a worldwide wave of protests following the arrest of DeCSS' coauthor, Johansen, and the lawsuits launched against some of those who published the software.

In this chapter, I examine how F/OSS developers like Schoen are reconfiguring what source code and speech mean ethically, legally, and culturally, and the broader political consequences of these redefinitions. I demonstrate how developers refashion liberal precepts in two distinct cultural "locations" (Gupta and Ferguson 1997): the F/OSS project, already covered in detail in the last chapter, and the context of much broader legal battles.

First, I show how F/OSS developers explore, contest, and specify the meaning of liberal freedom—especially free speech—via the development of new legal tools and discourses within the context of the F/OSS project. I highlight how developers concurrently tinker with technology and the law using similar skills, which transform and consolidate ethical precepts among developers. Using Debian as my primary ethnographic example, I suggest that these F/OSS projects have served as an informal legal education, transforming technologists into astute legal thinkers who are experts in the legal technicalities of F/OSS as well as proficient in the current workings of intellectual property law.

Second, I look at how these developers marshal and bolster this legal expertise during broader legal battles to engage in what Charles Tilly and Sidney Tarrow (2006) describe as "contentious politics." I concentrate on a series of critical events (Sewell 2005): the separate arrests of two programmers, Johansen and Sklyarov, and the protests, unfolding between 1999 and 2003, that they provoked. These events led to an unprecedented proliferation of claims connecting source code to speech, with Schoen's 456-stanza poem providing one of many well-known instantiations. The events are historically notable because they dramatize what normally exists more tacitly and bring visibility to two important social processes. First, they publicize the direct challenge that F/OSS represents to the dominant regime of intellectual property (and thus clarify the democratic stakes involved), and second, they make more visible and hence stabilize a rival liberal legal regime intimately connecting source code to speech.

The Ethics of Legal Contrast

Debian developers, like other F/OSS developers, are constituted as legal subjects by virtue of being extremely active *producers* of legal knowledge. This is an outgrowth of three circumstances. For one, developers have to learn basic legal knowledge in order to participate effectively in technological production. They must ascertain, for instance, whether the software license on the software application they maintain is compliant with licensing standards, such as the DFSG. Second, developers tend to closely track broader legal developments, especially those seen as impinging on their practices. Is the Unix company SCO suing IBM over Linux? Has the patent directive passed in the EU Parliament? Information regarding these and other relevant developments is posted widely on IRC channels, mailing lists, and especially Web sites such as Slashdot, Boing Boing, and Reddit. These channels form a crucial part of the discourse of the hacker public. Third and most important, developers largely produce their own legal artifacts, and as a result, there is a tremendous body of legal exegesis (e.g., charters, licenses, and legal texts) in the everyday life of their F/OSS projects. Projects adopt the language of the law to organize their operations, adding a legal layer to the structural sovereignty of these projects.

To be sure, there are some developers who express an overt distaste for discussions of legal policy and actively distance themselves from this domain of polluting politics. But even though the superiority of technical over legal language, even technical over legal labor, is acknowledged among hackers—some hackers will even claim that it is a waste of time (or as stated a bit more cynically yet humorously by one developer: "Writing an algorithm in legalese should be punished with death [. . .] a horrible one, by preference")—it is critical to recognize that geeks are in fact nimble legal thinkers. One reason for this facility, I suggest, is that the skills, mental dispositions, and forms of reasoning necessary to read and analyze a formal, rule-based system like the law parallel the operations necessary to code software. Both, for example, are logic oriented, internally consistent textual practices that require great attention to detail. Small mistakes in both law and software—a missing comma in a contract or a missing semicolon in code—can jeopardize the system's integrity and compromise the author's intention. Both lawyers and programmers develop mental habits for making, reading, and parsing what are primarily utilitarian texts. As noted by two lawyers who work on software and law, "coders are people who write in subtle, rule-oriented, specialized, and remarkably complicated dialects"—something, they argue, that also pertains to how lawyers make and interpret the law (Cohn and Grimmelmann 2003).[2]

This helps us understand why it has been relatively easy for developers to integrate the law into everyday technical practice and advocacy work, and avoid some of the frustration that afflicts lay advocates trying to acquire legal fluency to make larger political claims. For example, in describing the activists who worked on behalf of the victims of the Bhopal disaster, Kim Fortun (2001, 25–54) perceptively shows how acquiring legal fluency (or failing to adequately do so) and developing the correct legal strategy is frustrating, and can lead to cynicism. Many hackers are similarly openly cynical about the law because it is seen as easily subject to political manipulation; others would prefer not to engage with the law as it takes time away from what they would rather be doing—hacking. Despite this cynicism, I never encountered any expression of frustration about the actual process of learning the law. A number of developers I worked with at the Electronic Frontier Foundation or those in the Debian project clearly enjoyed learning as well as arguing about a pragmatic subset of the law (such as a particular legal doctrinal framework), just as they did with respect to technology. Many developers apply the same skills required for hacking to the law, and as we will see, technology and the law at times seamlessly blend into each other.

To offer a taste of this informal legal scholarship—the relationship between technical expertise and legal understanding, and how legal questions are often tied to moral issues—in one free software project, I will describe some of Debian's legal micropractices: its routine legal training, advocacy, and exegesis. In order to deepen this picture of how developers live in and through the law, I proceed to a broader struggle—one where similar legal processes are under way, but also are more visible because of the way they have circulated beyond the boundaries of projects proper.

"Living Out Legal Meaning"

Just over a thousand volunteers are participating in the Debian project at this time, writing and distributing a Linux-based OS composed over twenty-five thousand individual software applications. In its nascency, Debian was run entirely informally; it had fewer than two dozen volunteers, who communicated primarily through a single email list. To accommodate growth, however, significant changes in policy, procedures, and structure took place between 1997 and 1999. The growth of Debian, as discussed in the last chapter, necessitated the creation of more formal institutional policies and procedures. Central to these procedures is the NMP, which not only screens candidates for technical skills but also serves as a form of legal education.

Several questions in the NMP application cover what is now one of the most famous philosophical and legal distinctions in the world of free software: free beer versus free speech. Common among developers today, this distinction arose only recently, during the early to mid-1990s. A prospective Debian developer comments on the difference in an NMP application: "Free speech is the possibility of saying whatever one wants to. Software [that is] free as in beer can be downloaded and used for free, but no more. Software [that is] free as in speech can be fixed, improved, changed, [or] be used as building block for another [sic] software."[3] Some developers also note that their understanding of free speech is nested within a broader liberal meaning codified in the constitutions of most liberal democracies: "Used in this context the difference is this: 'free speech' represents the freedom to use/modify/distribute the software as if the source code were actual speech which is protected by law in the US by the First Amendment. [. . .] '[F]ree beer' represents something that is without monetary cost."[4] This differentiation between free beer and free speech is the clearest enunciation of what, to these developers, are the core meanings of free—expression, learning, and modification. Freedom is understood foremost to be about personal control and autonomous production, and decidedly not about commodity consumption or "possessive individualism" (Macpherson 1962)—a message that is constantly restated by developers: free software is free as in speech, not in beer.

This distinction may seem simple, but the licensing implications of freedom and free speech are complicated enough that the NMP continues with a series of technically oriented questions whose answers start to enter the realm of legal interpretation. Many of these questions concern the DFSG, a set of ten provisions by which to measure whether a license can be considered free. Of these questions, one or two are fairly straightforward, such as:

"Do you know what's wrong with Pine's current license in regard to the DFSG?"

After looking at the license on the upstream site it is very clear why Pine is non-free. It violates the following clauses of the DFSG:

1. No Discrimination Against Fields of Endeavor—it has different requirements for non-profit vs. profit concerns.
2. License Must Not Contaminate Other Software—it insists that all other programs on a CD-ROM must be "free-of-charge, shareware, or non-proprietary."
3. Source Code—it potentially restricts binary distribution [binary refers to compiled source code].

The sample license for an e-mail program, Pine, violates a number of DFSG provisions. With different provisions for nonprofit and for-profit endeavors, as an example, it discriminates according to what the DFSG calls "fields of endeavor."

Developers are then asked a handful of far more technical licensing questions, among them: "At http://people.debian.org/~joerg/bad.licenses.tar.bz2 you can find a tarball of bad licenses. Please compare the graphviz and three other (your choice) licenses with the first nine points of the DFSG and show what changes would be needed to make them DFSG-free." The answer clearly demonstrates the depth of legal expertise required to address these questions: "Remove the discriminatory clauses [. . .] allow distribution of compiled versions of the original source code [. . .] replace [sections] 4.3 with 4.3.a and 4.3.b and the option to choose."[5]

After successfully finishing the NMP, some developers think only rarely about the law or the DFSG, perhaps only tracking legal developments of personal interest. Even if a developer is not actively learning the law, however, legal discourse is nearly unavoidable because of the frequency with which it appears on Debian mailing lists or chat channels. Informal legal pedagogy thus continues long after the completion of the NMP.

As an illustration, below I quote from an arcane discussion on IRC wherein a developer proposed a new Debian policy that would clarify how non-free-software packages (those noncompliant with their license guidelines) should be categorized so as to make it absolutely clear how and why they cannot be included in the main software repository, which can only have free software. I do not want to emphasize the exact legal or technical details but rather how, late on a Friday night (when the conversation happened), a developer made a policy recommendation, and his peers immediately offered advice on how to proceed, talking about the issue with such sophisticated legal vocabulary that to the uninitiated, it will likely appear as obscure, obtuse, and hard to follow. This is simply part of the "natural" social landscape of most free software projects.

> <dangmang> Markel: what is your opinion about making a recommenda-
> tion in policy that packages in non-free indicate why they're in non-
> free, and what general class of restrictions the license has?
> <markel> dangmang: well, I am not too keen on mandating people
> do more work for non-free packages. but it may be a good practice
> suggestion.
> <jabberwalkie> dangmang: Then I would suggest that the ideal approach
> would be to enumerate all the categories you want to handle first, giv-
> ing requirements to be in those categories.
> <dangmang> Markel: true. could the proposal be worded so that new
> uploads would have to have it? [. . .]
>
> <jabberwalkie> dangmang: You don't want to list what issues they fail;
> you want to list what criteria they meet. [. . .]
>
> <jabberwalkie> dangmang: X-Nonfree-Permits: autobuildable, modifiable,
> portable.
> <markel> the developers-reference should mention it, and policy can
> recommend it, for starters.
> <markel> dangmang: we need to have well defined tags.
> <jabberwalkie> mt3t: "gfdl," "firmware." [. . .]
>
> <jabberwalkie> mt3t: No "You may not port this to _____."
> <jabberwalkie> mt3t: You wouldn't believe what people put in their
> licenses. :)
> <dangmang> Markel: right. [. . .] I think I'll start on the general outline of
> the proposal, and flesh things out, and hopefully people will have com-
> ments to make in policy too when I start the procedure.

More formal legal avenues are also employed. Debian developers may contact the original author (called the upstream maintainer) of a piece of software that they are considering including and maintaining in Debian. Many of these exchanges concern licensing problems that would keep the software out of Debian. In this way, non-Debian developers also un-dergo informal legal training. Sometimes developers act in the capacity of legal advocates, convincing these upstream maintainers to switch to a

DFSG-compliant license, which is necessary if the software is to be included in Debian.

The developers who hold Debian-wide responsibilities must in general be well versed in the subtleties of F/OSS licensing. The FTP masters, who integrate new software packages into the main repository, must check every single package license for DFSG compatibility. Distributing a package illegally could leave Debian open to lawsuits.

One class of Debian developers has made legal matters their obsession. These aficionados contribute prolifically to the legal pulse of Debian in debian-legal—a mailing list that because of its legal esoterica and large number of posts, is not for the faint of heart. For those who are interested in keeping abreast but do not have time to read every message posted on debian-legal, summaries link to it in a weekly newsletter, *Debian Weekly News*. Below, I quote a fraction (about one-fifth) of the legal news items that were reported in *Debian Weekly News* during the course of 2002 (the numbers are references linking to mailing list threads or news stories):

> **GNU FDL a non-free License?** Several [22] people are [23] discussing whether the [24] GNU Free Documentation License (GFDL) is a free license or not. If the GFDL is indeed considered a non-free license, this would [25] render almost all KDE·and many other well known packages non-free since they use the GNU FDL for the documentation. Additionally, here's an old [26] thread from debian-legal, which may shed some light on the issue.[6]

> **RFC: LaTeX Public Project License.** Claire Connelly [4] reported that the LaTeX Project is in the process of considering changes to the LaTeX Project Public License. She tried to summarize some of the concerns that Debian people have expressed regarding the changes. Hence, Frank Mittelbach asked for reviews of the draft of version 1.3 of the [5] LaTeX Public Project License rather than of the current version (1.2).[7]

> **Enforcing Software Licenses.** Lawrence Rosen, general counsel for the [20] Open Source Initiative, wrote an [21] article about the enforceability of software licenses. In particular, he discusses the issue of proving that somebody assented to be bound by the terms of a contract so that those terms will be enforced by a court. Authors who wish to be able to enforce license terms against users of their source code or compiled programs may find this interesting.[8]

> **Problematic BitKeeper License.** Branden Robinson [3] pointed out that some of us may be exposed to tort claims from BitMover, Inc., the company that produces BitKeeper, the software that is the primary source management tool for the Linux kernel. Your license to use BitKeeper free of charge is revoked if you or your employer develop,

produce, sell, or resell a source management tool. Debian distributes rcs, cvs, subversion and arch at least and this seems to be a [4] different case. Ben Collins, however, who works on both the Linux kernel and the subversion project, got his license to use BitKeeper free of charge [5] revoked.[9]

These are newsletter summaries, which are read by thousands of developers outside the Debian community proper as well as by Debian developers. Practical and immediate concerns are layered on global currents along with more philosophical musings. Some discussions can be short, breeding less than a dozen posts; other topics are multiyear, multilist, and may involve other organizations, such as the FSF. These conversations may eventually expand and reformulate licensing applications.

It is also worth noting how outsiders turn to Debian developers for legal advice. One routine task undertaken in debian-legal is to help developers and users choose appropriate licensing, by providing in-depth summaries of alternative licenses compliant with the DFSG. One such endeavor I witnessed was to determine whether a class of Creative Commons licenses (developed to provide creative producers, such as musicians and writers, with alternatives to copyright) was appropriate for software documentation. Debian developers assessed that the Creative Commons licenses under consideration failed to meet the DFSG's standards, and suggested that Debian developers not look to them as licensing models. The most remarkable aspect of their analysis is that it concluded with a detailed set of recommendations for alterations to make the Creative Commons licenses more free according to the Debian licensing guidelines. In response to these recommendations, Lessig of Creative Commons contacted Evan Prodromou, one of the authors of this analysis, to try to find solutions to the incompatibilities between the DFSG and some of the Creative Commons licenses.

There is something ironic, on the one hand, about a world-renowned lawyer contacting a bunch of geeks with no formal legal training to discuss changes to the licenses that he created. On the other hand, who else would Lessig contact? These developers are precisely the ones making and therefore inhabiting this legal world. These geeks are training themselves to become legal experts, and much of this training occurs in the institution of the free software project.

Debian's legal affairs not only produce what a group of legal theorists have identified as everyday legal awareness (Ewick and Silbey 1998; Mezey 2001; Yngvesson 1989). The F/OSS arena probably represents the largest single association of amateur intellectual property and free speech legal scholars ever to have existed. Given the right circumstances, many developers will marshal this expertise as part of broader, contentious battles over intellectual property law and the legality of software—the topic of the next section.

CONTENTIOUS POLITICS

If hackers acquire legal expertise by participating in F/OSS projects, they also use and fortify their expertise during broader legal battles. Here I examine one of the most heated of the recent controversies over intellectual property, software, and access: the arrests of Johansen and Sklyarov. These arrests provoked a series of protests and produced a durable articulation of a free speech ethic that under the umbrella of F/OSS development, had been experiencing quiet cultivation in the previous decade. Intellectual property has been debated since its inception (Hesse 2002; Johns 2006; McGill 2002), but as media scholar Siva Vaidhyanathan (2004, 298) notes, in recent times intellectual property debates have "rarely punctured the membrane of public concern." It was precisely during this period (1999 to 2003), and in part because of these events, that a more visible, notable, and "contentious politics" (Tilly and Tarrow 2006) over intellectual property emerged, especially in North America and Europe.

Before discussing how the emergence of this contentious politics worked to stabilize the connection between speech and code, some historical context is necessary. At the most general level, we can say a free speech idiom formed as a response to the excessive copyrighting and patenting of computer software. Prior to 1976, such an idiom had been rare. The first widely circulated paper associating free speech and source code was "Freedom of Speech in Software," written by programmer Peter Salin (1991). He characterized computer programs as "writings" to argue that software was unfit for patents, although appropriate for copyrights and thus free speech protections (patents being for invention, and copyright being for expressive content). The idea that coding was a variant of writing was also gaining traction, in part because of the popular publications of Stanford Computer Science professor Donald Knuth (1998; see also Black 2002) on the art of programming. During the early 1990s, a new ethical sentiment emerged among Usenet enthusiasts (many of them hackers and developers) that the Internet should be a place for unencumbered free speech (Pfaffenberger 1996). This sensibility in later years would become specified and attached to technical artifacts such as source code.

Perhaps most significantly, what have come to be known as the "encryption wars" in the mid-1990s were waged over the right to freely publish and use software cryptography in the face of governmental restrictions that classified strong forms of encryption as munitions. The most notable juridical case in these struggles was *Bernstein v. U.S. Department of Justice*. The battles started in 1995 after a computer science student, Daniel J. Bernstein, sued the government to challenge international traffic in arms regulations, which classified certain types of strong encryption as munitions and hence subjected them to export controls. Bernstein could not legally publish or export the source code of his encryption system, Snuffle, without registering as an arms dealer. After years in court, in 1999 the judge presiding over the case concluded that government regulations of cryptographic "software and related devices and technology are in violation of the First Amendment on the grounds of prior restraint."[10]

What is key to highlight is how neither Salin's article nor the Bernstein case questioned copyright as a barrier to speech. With the rise of free software, developers began to launch a direct critique of copyright. The technical production of free software had trained developers to become legal thinkers and tinkerers well acquainted with the intricacies of intellectual property law as they became committed to an alternative liberal legal system steeped in discourses of freedom and, increasingly, free speech. If the first free speech claims among programmers were proposed by a handful of developers and deliberated in a few court cases in the early to mid-1990s, in the subsequent decade they grew social roots in the institution of the F/OSS project. Individual commitments and intellectual arguments developed into a full-fledged collective social practice anchored firmly in F/OSS technical production.

Unanticipated state and corporate interventions, though, raised the stakes and gave this rival legal morality a new public face. Indeed, it was only because of a series of protracted legal battles that the significance of hacker legal expertise and free speech claims became apparent to me. I had, like so many developers, not only taken their free speech arguments about code as self-evident but also taken for granted their legal skills in the making of these claims. Witnessing and participating in the marches, candlelight vigils, street demonstrations, and artistic protests (many of them articulated in legal terms), among a group of people who otherwise tend to shy away from such overt forms of traditional political action (Coleman 2004; Galloway 2004; Riemens 2003), led me to seriously reevaluate the deceptively simple claim: that code is speech. In other words, what existed tacitly became explicit after a set of exceptional arrests and lawsuits.

POETIC PROTEST

On October 6, 1999, a sixteen-year-old Johansen used a mailing list to release a short, simple software program called DeCSS. Written by Johansen and two anonymous developers, DeCSS unlocks a piece of encryption by the name of CSS (short for content scramble system), a form of Digital Rights Management (DRM) used to regulate DVDs. CSS "is a lock rather than block" (Gillespie 2007, 170) preventing a DVD with CSS from being played on a device that has not been approved by the DVD Copy Control Association (DVD CCA), the organization that licenses CSS to hardware manufactures. Before DeCSS, only computers using either Microsoft's Windows or Apple's OS could play DVDs; Johansen's program allowed Linux users to unlock a DVD's DRM to play movies on their computers. Released under a 'free software license, DeCSS soon was being downloaded from hundreds or possibly thousands of Web sites. In the hacker public, the circulation of DeCSS would transform Johansen from an unknown geek into a famous "freedom fighter"; elsewhere, entertainment industry executives saw his program as criminal and sought Johansen's arrest.

Although many geeks were gleefully using this technology to bypass a form of DRM so they could watch DVDs on their Linux machines, various trade associations sought to ban the software because it made it easier to copy and potentially pirate DVDs (Gillespie 2007). In November 1999, soon after its initial spread, the DVD CCA and the MPAA sent cease-and-desist letters to more than fifty Web site owners and Internet service providers, requiring them to remove links to the DeCSS code for its alleged violation of trade secret and copyright laws, and in the United States, the DMCA. Passed in 1998 to "modernize" copyright for digital content, the DMCA's most controversial provision outlaws the manufacture and trafficking of technology (which can mean something immaterial, such as a six-line piece of source code, or something physical) capable of circumventing copy or access protection in copyrighted works that are in a digital format. The DMCA outlaws the trafficking and circulation of such a tool, even if it can be used for lawful purposes (such as fair use copying) or is never used. "Now with the DMCA," media scholar Tartelton Gillespie (2007, 184) perceptively notes, "circumvention is prohibited, meaning that the technologies that automatically enforce these licenses are further assured by the force of the law."

In December 1999, alleging trade secret misappropriation, the DVD CCA filed a lawsuit against hundreds of individuals, and eventually two cases from this batch moved forward.[11] In 2000, the MPAA (along with other trade associations) sued the well-known hacker organization and publication *2600* along with its founder, Eric Corley (more commonly known by his hacker handle, Emmanuel Goldstein), claiming violation of the DMCA.[12] Corley would fight the lawsuits, appealing to *2600*'s journalistic free speech right to publish DeCSS. As frequently happens with censored material, the DeCSS code at this time was unstoppable; it spread like wildfire.

Simultaneously, the international arm of the MPAA urged prosecution of Johansen under Norwegian law (the DMCA, a US law, had no jurisdiction there). The Norwegian Economic and Environmental Crime Unit took the MPAA's informal legal advice and indicted Johansen on January 24, 2000, for violating an obscure Norwegian criminal code. Johansen (and since he was underage, his father) was arrested and released on the same day, and law enforcement confiscated his computers. He was scheduled to face trial three years later.

Hackers and other geek enthusiasts discussed, debated, and decried these events, and a few consistent topics emerged. The influence of the court case discussed above, *Bernstein v. U.S. Department of Justice*, was one such theme. This case established that software could be protected under the First Amendment, and in 1999, caused the overturning of the ban on the exportation of strong cryptography. Programmers could write and publish strong encryption on the grounds that software was speech.

F/OSS advocates, seeing the DeCSS case as a similar situation, hoped that the courts just might declare DeCSS worthy of First Amendment protection. Consider the first message posted on dvd-discuss—a mailing list that would soon attract a multitude of programmers, F/OSS developers, and activist lawyers to discuss every imaginable detail concerning the DeCSS cases:

> I see the DVD cases as the natural complement to Bernstein's case. Just as free speech protects the right to communicate results about encryption, so it protects the right to discuss the technicalities of decryption. In this case as well as Bernstein's, the government's policy is to promote insecurity to achieve security. This oxymoronic belief is deeply troubling, and worse endangers the very interests it seeks to protect.[13]

There were, it turned out, significant differences between Bernstein and DeCSS. In the Bernstein case, hackers were primarily engaged spectators. Furthermore, many free software advocates were critical of Bernstein's decision to copyright, and so tightly control, all of his software. In the DeCSS and DVD cases, by contrast, many F/OSS hackers became participants by injecting into the controversy notions of free software, free speech, and source code (a language they were already fluent in from F/OSS technical development). Hackers saw Johansen's indictment and the lawsuits as a violation of not simply their right to software but also their more basic right to produce F/OSS. As the following call to arms reveals, many hackers understood the attempt to restrict DeCSS as an all-out assault:

> Here's why they're doing it: **Scare tactic.** [. . .] I know a lot of us aren't political enough—but consider donating a few bucks and also mirroring the source. [. . .] This is a full-fledged war now against the Open Source movement: they're trying to stop [. . .] everything. They can justify and rationalize all they want—but it's really about them trying to gain/maintain their monopoly on distribution.[14]

Johansen was, for hackers, the target of a law that fundamentally challenged their freedom to tinker and write code—values that acquired coherence and had been articulated in the world of F/OSS production only in the last decade.

Hackers moved to organize politically. Many Web sites providing highly detailed information about the DMCA, DeCSS, and copyright history went live, and the Electronic Frontier Foundation launched a formal "Free Jon Johansen" campaign. All this was helping to stabilize the growing links between source code and software, largely because of the forceful arguments that computer code constitutes expressive speech. Especially prominent was an amicus curiae brief on the expressive nature of source code written by a group of computer scientists and hackers (including Stallman) as well as the testimony of one of its authors, Carnegie Mellon computer science professor David Touretzky, a fierce and well-known free speech loyalist. Just as they dissected free software licensing, F/OSS programmers quickly learned and scrutinized these court cases, behaving in ways that democratic theorists would no doubt consider exemplary. *Linux Weekly News*, for example, published the following overview and analysis of Touretzky's testimony:

> His point was that the restriction of source is equivalent to a restriction on speech, and would make it very hard for everybody who works with computers. The judge responded very well to Mr. Touretzky's testimony, saying things like [. . .] *"I think one thing probably has changed with respect to the constitutional analysis, and that is that subject to thinking about it some more, I really find what Professor Touretzky had to say today extremely persuasive and educational about computer code."* [. . .]
> Thus, there are two rights being argued here. One is that [. . .] we have the right to look at things we own and figure out how they work. We even have the right to make other things that work in the same way. The other is that code is speech, that there is no way to distinguish between the two. In the U.S., of course, equating code and speech is important, because protections on speech are (still, so far) relatively strong. If code is speech, then we are in our rights to post it. If these rights are lost, Free Software is in deep trouble.[15]

In this exegesis, we see again how free software developers wove together free software, source code, and free speech. These connections had recently been absent in hacker public discourse. Although Stallman certainly grounded the politics of software in a vocabulary of freedom, and Bernstein's fight introduced a far more legally sophisticated idea of the First Amendment for software, it was only with the DeCSS case that a more prolific and specific language of free speech would come to dominate among F/OSS developers, and circulate beyond F/OSS proper. In the context of F/OSS development in conjunction with the DeCSS case, the conception of software as speech became a cultural reality.

Much of the coherence emerged through reasoned political debate. Cleverness—or prankstership—played a pivotal role as well. Prodromou, a Debian developer and editor of one of the first Internet zines, *Pigdog*, circulated a decoy program that hijacked the name DeCSS, even though it performed an entirely different operation from Johansen's DeCSS. Prodromou's DeCSS stripped cascading style sheets data (i.e., formatting information) from HTML pages:

Hey, so, I've been really mad about the recent spate of horrible witch hunts by the MPAA against people who use, distribute, or even LINK TO sites that distribute DeCSS, a piece of software used for playing DVDs on Linux. The MPAA has got a bee in their bonnet about this DeCSS. They think it's good for COPYING DVDs, which, in fact, it's totally useless for. But they're suing everybody ANYWAYS, the bastardos!

Anyways, I feel like I need to do something. I've been talking about the whole travesty here on Pigdog Journal and helped with the big flier campaign here in SF [. . .] , but I feel like I should do something more, like help redistribute the DeCSS software.

There are a lot of problems with this, obviously. First and foremost, Pigdog Journal is a collaborative effort, and I don't want to bring down the legal shit-storm on the rest of the Pigdoggers just because I'm a Free Software fanatic.

DeCSS is Born

So, I decided that if I couldn't distribute DeCSS, I would distribute DeCSS. Like, I could distribute another piece of software called DeCSS, that is per-fectly legal in every way, and would be difficult for even the DVD-CCA's lawyers to find fault with. [. . .]

Distribute DeCSS!

I encourage you to distribute DeCSS on your Web site, if you have one. [. . .] I think of this as kind of an "I am Spartacus" type thing. If lots of people dis-tribute DeCSS on their Web sites, on Usenet newsgroups, by email, or what-ever, it'll provide a convenient layer of fog over the OTHER DeCSS. I figure if we waste just FIVE MINUTES of some DVD-CCA Web flunkey's time looking for DeCSS, we've done some small service for The Cause.[16]

Thousands of developers posted *Pigdog*'s DeCSS on their Web sites as flak to further confuse law enforcement officials and entertainment industry ex-ecutives, since they felt these people were clueless about the nature of soft-ware technology. Dozens of these developers (including Johansen) received cease-and-desist letters demanding they take down a version of DeCSS that was completely unrelated to the decryption DeCSS.

Clever re-creations of the original DeCSS source code (originally written in the C programming language) using other languages (such as Perl) also began to proliferate, as did translations into poetry, music, and film. A Web site hosted by Touretzky, called the Gallery of CSS DeScramblers, show-cased a set of twenty-four of these artifacts—the point being to demonstrate the difficulty of drawing a sharp line between functionality and expression in software.[17] Touretzky, an expert witness in the DeCSS case, said as much in the introductory statement to his gallery:

If code that can be directly compiled and executed may be suppressed under the DMCA, as Judge Kaplan asserts in his preliminary ruling, but a textual description of the same algorithm may not be suppressed, then where exactly should the line be drawn? This web site was created to explore this issue.[18]

Here is a short snippet (about one-fifth) of the original DeCSS source code written in the C programming language:

```
void CSSdescramble(unsigned char *sec,unsigned char *key)
{
unsigned int t1,t2,t3,t4,t5,t6;
unsigned char *end=sec+0x800;
t1=key[0]^sec[0x54]|0x100;
t2=key[1]^sec[0x55];
t3=(*((unsigned int *)(key+2)))^(*((unsignedint *)(sec+0x56)));
t4=t3&7;
t3=t3*2+8-t4;
sec+=0x80;
t5=0;
while(sec!=end)
{
t4=CSStab2[t2]^CSStab3[t1];
t2=t1>>1;
t1=((t1&1)<<8)^t4;
t4=CSStab5[t4];
t6=(((((((t3>>3)^t3)>>1)^t3)>>8)^t3)>>5)&0xff;
t3=(t3<<8)|t6;
t6=CSStab4[t6];
t5+=t6+t4;
*sec++=CSStab1[*sec]^(t5&0xff);
t5>>=8;
}
```

Compare this fragment to another one written in Perl, a computer language that hackers regard as particularly well suited for crafting poetic code because longer expressions can be condensed into much terser, sometimes quite elegant (although sometimes quite obfuscated) statements. And indeed the original DeCSS program, composed of 9,830 characters, required only 530 characters in Perl:

```
#!/usr/bin/perl -w
# 531-byte qrpff-fast, Keith Winstein and Marc Horowitz
# <sipb-iap-dvd@mit.edu>
# MPEG 2 PS VOB file on stdin -> descrambled output on stdout
# arguments: title key bytes in least to most-significant order
$_='while(read+STDIN,$_,2048){$a=29;$b=73;$c=142;$t=255;@
t=map{$_%16or$t^=$c^=($m=(11,10,116,100,11,122,20,100)
[$_/16%8])&110;$t^=(72,@z=(64,72,$a^=12*($_%162?
0:$m&17)),$b^=$_%64?12:0,@z)[$_%8]}(16..271);if((@
```

```
a=unx"C*",$_)[20]&48){$h=5;$_=unxb24,join"",@
b=map{xB8,unxb8,chr($_^$a[—$h+84])}@ARGV;s/ [ . . . ]
$/1$&/;$d=unxV,xb25,$_;$e=256|(ord$b[4])<<9|ord$b[3];$d=$d>
>8^($f=$t&($d>>12^$d>>4^$d^$d/8))<<17,$e=$e>>8^($t&($g
=($q=$e>>14&7^$e)^$q*8^$q<<6))<<9,$_=$t[$_]^(($h>>=8)+=
$f+(~$g&$t))for@a[128..$#a]}print+x"C*",@a}';s/x/pack+/g;eval
```

If Perl allows programmers to write code more poetically (in this case, being terse) than other computer languages, Schoen took up the challenge of publishing a bona fide poem in the form of an epic haiku—456 individual stanzas written over the course of just a few days. Schoen, who was inspired by the clever re-creations of DeCSS compiled in the gallery, wrote the poem to deliver a stark and clear political message. The author asserts that source code is not a metaphor or similar to expression but rather *is* expression, and he makes this point by re-creating the original DeCSS program as a poem. This bit of poetry is now well known among hackers as an exemplary hack for displaying the cleverness that hackers collectively value. Schoen opens his poem by thanking Touretzky and then moves immediately to abandon his "exclusive rights" clause of the copyright statute, indexing the direct influence of F/OSS licensing.

How to Decrypt a DVD: In Haiku Form
(Thanks, Prof. D. S. T.)

(I abandon my
exclusive rights to make or
perform copies of

this work, U. S. Code
Title Seventeen, section
One Hundred and Six.)

Muse! When we learned to
count, little did we know all
the things we could do

some day by shuffling
those numbers: Pythagoras
said "All is number"

long before he saw
computers and their effects,
or what they could do

by computation,
naive and mechanical
fast arithmetic.

It changed the world, it
changed our consciousness and lives
to have such fast math

available to
us and anyone who cared
to learn programming.

Now help me, Muse, for
I wish to tell a piece of
controversial math,

for which the lawyers
of DVD CCA
don't forbear to sue:

that they alone should
know or have the right to teach
these skills and these rules.

(Do they understand
the content, or is it just
the effects they see?)

And all mathematics
is full of stories (just read
Eric Temple Bell);

and CSS is
no exception to this rule.
Sing, Muse, decryption

once secret, as all
knowledge, once unknown: how to
decrypt DVDs.

Here, the author first frames the value of programming in terms of mathematics along with its antagonists in the entertainment industry, intellectual property statutes, lawyers, and judges—all of which use software without recognizing, much less truly understanding, the embedded creative labor and expressive value. This critique is made explicit through a question: "Do they understand the content, or is it just the effects they see?" The author then launches into a long mathematical description of the forbidden CSS code represented in DeCSS. The expert explains the "player key" of CSS, which is the proprietary piece that enacts the access control measures:

So this number is
once again, the player key:
(trade secret haiku?)

Eighty-one; and then
one hundred three—two times; then
two hundred (less three)

> Two hundred and twenty
> four; and last (of course not least)
> the humble zero

The writer states the access control mathematically, but using words. From these lines alone a proficient enough programmer can deduce the encryption key. Thus the poem makes a similar point to the one made in the amicus brief—namely, that "at root, computer code is nothing more than text, which, like any other text, is a form of speech. The Court may not know the meaning of the Visual BASIC or Perl texts [. . .] but the Court can recognize that the code is text."[19]

The author then conveys that many F/OSS programmers conceive of their craft as technically precise (and so functional) yet fundamentally expressive, and as a result, worthy of free speech protection. In formally comparing code to poetry in the medium of a poem, Schoen displays a playful form of clever and recursive rhetoric valued among hackers; he also articulates both the meaning of the First Amendment and software to a general public:

> We write precisely
> since such is our habit in
> talking to machines;
>
> we say exactly
> how to do a thing or how
> every detail works.
>
> The poet has choice
> of words and order, symbols,
> imagery, and use
>
> of metaphor. She
> can allude, suggest, permit
> ambiguities.
>
> She need not say just
> what she means, for readers can
> always interpret.
>
> Poets too, despite
> their famous "license" sometimes
> are constrained by rules:
>
> How often have we
> heard that some strange twist of plot
> or phrase was simply
>
> "Metri causa," for
> the meter's sake, solely done
> "to fit the meter"?

Although this haiku contains novel assertions (the tight coupling between source code and speech), it is also through its inscription into a tangible and especially culturally captivating medium (a hack with playful, recursive qualities) that the assertion is transformed into a firm social fact. Or to put it another way, here a recondite legal argument makes its way into wide and public circulation as well as consumption. This is how discourse meant for public circulation, as Warner (2002, 91) has noted, "helps to make a world insofar as the object of address is brought into being partly by postulating and characterizing it."

FREE DMITRY!

The protests, poetry, and debate demonstrate how programmers and hackers quickly became active participants in the drama of law and free software in the digital age. This narrative process by which the law takes on a meaning to individuals through a period of contentious politics would accelerate thanks to the simultaneous (although completely unrelated) DMCA infraction and arrest of another programmer, Sklyarov. Because Sklyarov faced up to twenty-five years in jail, programmers in fact only grew more infuriated with the state's willingness to police technological innovation and software distribution through the DMCA. After Sklyarov's arrest, protest against the DMCA and the hacker commitment to a discourse of free speech only increased in emotional intensity, and worked to extend and fortify the narrative process already under way.

This case would also prove far more dramatic than Johansen's because of the timing and place of the arrest. As mentioned earlier, Sklyarov was arrested while leaving Defcon, one of the largest hacker conferences in the world. During the conference, he had presented a paper on security breaches and weaknesses within the Adobe e-book format. He purportedly violated the DMCA by writing a piece of software for his Russian employer, Elcomsoft, that unlocks Adobe's e-book access controls and subsequently converts the files into PDF format. For the FBI to arrest a programmer at the end of this conference was a potent statement. It showed that federal authorities would act on corporate demands to prosecute hackers under the DMCA.

FBI agents attend Defcon, but there is a well-known, although tacit, agreement that these agents, immediately identifiable by their L. L. Bean khaki attire (normal Defcon regalia leans toward black clothing, T-shirts, and body piercings), not interfere with the hackers. Despite their presence since the con began in 1993, FBI agents had never arrested a hacker at Defcon. (Typically, any arrests were local, and due to excessively rowdy and drunken behavior.) The first-ever FBI arrest of a hacker signaled a one-sided renegotiation of the relationship between legal authority and the hacker world.

On July 17, 2001, as Sklyarov was leaving the conference, federal agents whisked him away to an undisclosed jail in Nevada. Weeks later, he was released in the middle of a fervent Free Dmitry campaign. Sklyarov's arrest and related court hearings also prompted conversations built on those

So he's a "hacker", right?

At no time in the U.S. (or as far as we know anywhere else) did he illegally steal information, break into a computer system, or do anything destructive as one might expect from a "hacker". He was conducting himself in what he believed was a legal and respectable manner for a visitor to the U.S. to behave. He was personally targeted for arrest by the FBI, rather than, as one might reasonably expect, a U.S. distributor of the software might have been. This arrest pushes the interpretation of the law into very controversial and threatening grounds, and is widely considered a travesty of justice by both experts and lay-people.

FIGURE 5.1. So he's a "hacker," right?
Original pamphlet produced by Barrington King, http://www.
wyrdwright.com/sklyarov/ (accessed on September 10, 2010). Excerpt and photo taken from *Free Version A*, produced with ps2pdf
(pdf v 1.3 compatible) by Mike Castleman.

initiated by Johansen's arrest and the resultant DeCSS lawsuits. But the Free Dmitry campaign was organized more swiftly, was more visible, and directly attacked Adobe, the company that had urged the US Department of Justice to make the arrest. Its success, argues media scholar Hector Postigo (2010), followed in part from how quickly activists organized the campaign, which framed the issues in strong but accessible language, and actively sought to distance the association between Dmitry and "hacker," as an excerpt from one of the organizing pamphlets makes clear, reinforced by the featured family photo included in the flyer (see figure 5.1).

Developers organized protests across US cities (such as Boston, New York, Chicago, and San Francisco) and in Europe as well as Russia. San Francisco, where I was doing my fieldwork at the time, was a hub of politi-cal mobilization. Even though Sklyarov was in no fashion part of or identi-fied with the world of F/OSS development, local F/OSS developers were behind a slew of protest activities, including a protest at Adobe's San Jose headquarters, a candlelight vigil at the San Jose public library, and a march held after Linux World on August 29, 2001, that ended up at the federal prosecutor's office.

At a fund-raiser that followed the march to the prosecutor's office, Stall-man, the founder of the FSF, and Lessig, the superstar activist-lawyer, gave impassioned speeches. Sklyarov, in a brief appearance, thanked the audience for their support. The mood was electric in an otherwise-cool San Francisco warehouse loft. Lessig, who had recently published his *Code and Other Laws of Cyberspace*, a book that was changing the way F/OSS developers understood the politics of technology, fired up the already-animated crowd with charged declarations during his speech:

Now this is America, right? It makes me sick to think this is where
we are. It makes me sick. Let them fight their battles in Congress.
These million-dollar lobbyists, let them persuade Congressmen about
the sanctity of intellectual property and all that bullshit. Let them have
their battles, but why lock this guy up for twenty-five years?[20]

Most programmers agreed with Lessig's assessment: the state had gone too
far in its uncritical support of the copyright industries. The protests had an
immediate effect. Adobe withdrew its support of the case, and eventually,
the court dropped all charges against Sklyarov on the condition that he
testify in the subsequent case against his employers, which he did. In December 2002, the jury in that case acquitted Elcomsoft, Sklyarov's employer.
Johansen was acquitted just over a year later because the charges against
him were seen as too shaky for prosecution (the law he was arrested under
had nothing to do with DRM). Johansen still writes free software (including
programs that subvert DRM technologies) as well as a blog, So Sue Me, and
is admired among F/OSS hackers.

The DeCSS lawsuits were decided between 2001 and 2004, and even
though the courts were persuaded that the DeCSS was a form of speech,
they continued to uphold copyright law and deemed DeCSS unfit for First
Amendment protection. In one of the 2600 cases, *Universal City Studios
Inc. v. Reimerdes*, Judge Lewis A. Kaplan went so far as to declare that the
court's decision meant to "contribute to a climate of appropriate respect for
intellectual property rights in an age in which the excitement of ready access
to untold quantities of information has blurred in some minds the fact that
taking what is not yours and not freely offered to you is stealing."[21]

Many developers and hackers were deeply disappointed with these decisions, which equated DeCSS with theft, and were shocked about how
narrow the consequences of Bernstein turned out to be. Many developers,
however, emboldened and galvanized by the collective outpouring they organized or witnessed, continued to assert, in passionate and often considerable legal detail, a different narrative to that of piracy and stealing. Schoen,
the DeCSS haiku author who questioned the cultural assumptions and stereotypes at play with Judge Kaplan's doctrinal reasoning, published one of
the most incisive accounts:

It's hard to avoid the inherent *sympathy* Judge [Marilyn Hall] Patel bears toward Professor Bernstein (a speaker whose expression is
crushed by the awesome might of government bureaucracy) or the
equally apparent suspicion with which Judge Kaplan regards Emmanuel Goldstein (a self-avowed hacker seemingly hell-bent on trouble).
These attitudes seem to me to be visible behind all the doctrinal questions; without committing myself for all time to a position in a contentious area of legal theory, I would say that Judge Patel fought to show
why her case was a free speech case and that Judge Kaplan fought to

show why his was not. The question of which approach seems natural would then be not primarily a question of legal doctrines, standards, or precedents. It would instead be a conceptual, cultural battle: shall programs be compared to epidemics of disease (evil, menacing, worthy only of quarantine) or to books in libraries (the cornerstones of our culture and our civilization)?[22]

Even if the court cases never declared source code as First Amendment speech, the arrests, lawsuits, and protests cemented this connection. Hackers, programmers, and computer scientists would continue to be motivated to transform what is now their cultural reality—a rival liberal morality—into a broader legal one by arguing that source code should be protectable speech under the US Constitution and the constitutions of other nations.

Conclusion

The law, in its formal and informal dimensions, clearly saturated this story, acting as a double-edged sword that constrains and enables (and produces) new possibilities. In an article on liberal law, Jane Collier, Bill Maurer, and Liliana Suarez-Navaz note how liberal law, riddled with productive contradictions, works to sanction an individuated identity. If "bourgeois law is constructed as a system of rules that people are required to obey, whatever their personal desires," at the same time it also encourages "expressions of individual contention or will, particularly in private contract that legal agencies enforce" (Collier, Maurer, and Suarez-Navaz 1997, 4). While liberal law certainly individuates its citizens (and private contract has been one privileged route by which this is accomplished), free software is just one example of what we might think of as a type of legal populism, especially prevalent in the United States since the civil rights era, under which collectives take the law into their own hands, and whereby the content of the law matters as much as its formal attributes to recharge and change cultural meaning. If the law, to use the formulation offered by Geertz (1983, 184), is "part of a distinctive manner of imagining the real," what I have shown in this chapter is how the law *becomes* social reality, and in effect, constitutes particular cultural meanings related to personhood, expression, creativity, and thought.

This period of political protest and avowal, like much of hacker activity, is rooted initially in a defense of the existing hacker lifeworld, insofar as intellectual property law in basic ways challenges the capacity of hackers to do their work. Yet this defense does not merely leave the hacker lifeworld untouched; it in fact transforms it in significant ways, most especially by bringing hackers into more quotidian, though quite persistent, contact with the language of law. Software developers have now deployed and also contested the law to reconfigure central tenets of the liberal tradition—and specifically the meaning of free speech—to defend their productive autonomy.

Many hackers, understood to be technologists, became legal thinkers and tinkerers, undergoing legal training in the context of the F/OSS project while building a corpus of liberal legal theory that links software to speech and freedom. By means of lively protests and prolific discussions, almost continuously between 1999 and 2003, hackers as well as new publics debated the connection between source code and speech. This link became a staple of free software moral philosophy, and has helped add clarity in the competition between two different legal regimes (speech versus intellectual property) for the protection of knowledge and digital artifacts. Now other actors, such as activist lawyers, are consolidating new projects and bodies of legal work that challenge the shape along with the direction of intellectual property law.

To be sure, the idea of free speech has never held a single meaning across the societies that have valued, instantiated, or debated it. Yet it has come to be seen as indispensable for a healthy democracy, a free press, individual self-development, and academic integrity. It is, as one media theorist aptly puts it, "as much cultural commonplace as an explicit doctrine" (Peters 2005, 18). F/OSS is an ideal vehicle for examining how and when technological objects, such as source code, are invested with new liberal meanings, and with what consequences. By showing how developers incorporate legal ideals like free speech into the practices of everyday technical production, I trace the path by which older liberal ideals persist, albeit transformed, into the present.

This is key to emphasize, for even if we can postulate a relation between a product of creative work—source code—and a democratic ideal—free speech, there is no necessary or fundamental connection between them (Ratto 2005). Many academics and programmers have argued convincingly that the act of programming should be thought of as literary—"a culture of innovative and revisionary close reading" (Black 2002, 23; see also Chopra and Dexter 2007). As with print culture of the last two hundred years (Johns 1998), this literary culture of programming has often been dictated and delineated by a copyright regime whose logic is one of restriction. New free speech sensibilities, which fundamentally challenge the coupling between copyright and literary creation, must therefore be seen as a political act and choice, requiring sustained labor and creativity to stabilize these connections.

Hackers have been in part successful in this political fight because of their facility with the law; because of years of intensive technical training, they have not only easily adopted the law but also tinkered with it to suit their needs. This active and transformative engagement with the law raises a set of pressing questions about the current state of global politics and legal advocacy. As Jean Comaroff and John Comaroff (2003, 457) note, the modern nation-state is one "rooted in a culture of legality"—a culture that in recent years has become ever more pervasive, especially in the transnational arena. Whether it is the constitutional recognition of multiculturalism across Latin America and parts of Africa, or new avenues of commoditization like the patenting of seeds, these new political and economic relationships are "heavily inscribed in the language of the law" (ibid.). Given the extent to which esoteric legal codes dominate so many fields of endeavor, from pharmaceutical production to financial regulation to environmental advocacy, we must ask to what extent informal legal expertise, of the sort exhibited by F/OSS developers, is a necessary or useful skill for social actors seeking to contest such regimes, and where and how advocates acquire legal literacy. Legal pedagogy keeps the issues of freedom present, sometimes through the minuscule redefinitions that occur through discussion, legal exegesis, and the production of legal artifacts such as legal tests and guidelines. We must remain alert to these amateur forms of legalism and the alternative social forms that they imply.

The Cultural Critique of
Intellectual Property Law

ೲ☉ഌ

> The door that is at least half-open, when it appears
> to open onto pleasant objects, is marked hope.
> —Ernst Bloch, *The Principle of Hope*

This book concludes by examining one of the most significant, although unintended, political consequences of F/OSS technical production: the way it worked to fundamentally refigure the politics of intellectual property law. Using this material, I will revisit various themes raised throughout previous chapters and draw some preliminary conclusions about the importance of what I designate here as a material politics of cultural action.

A paradox is at work here: How can a movement narrowly configured around a technical craft to ensure software freedom help catalyze broader political and economic transformations? Although F/OSS is foremost a technical movement based on the principles of free speech, its historical role in transforming other arenas of life is not primarily rooted in the power of language or the discursive articulation of a broad political vision. Instead, it effectively works as a politics of critique by providing a living counterexample, or in the words of free software's most famous legal counsel, Eben Moglen: "Practical revolution is based upon two things: proof of concept and running code."[1] Returning to the terminology offered by Bruno Latour (1993, 87), F/OSS production acts as a "theater of proof" that economic incentives are unnecessary to secure creative output—a message that attained visibility as various groups were inspired to follow in the footsteps of free software, and extend the legal logic of free software into other domains of artistic, academic, journalistic, and economic production. Equally crucial was that free software production was never easily shackled to a Right versus Left political divide, despite numerous attempts early in its history by its critics to portray it as communist. In an era when identification with Right or Left, conservative or liberal, often functions as a politically paralyzing form of ideological imprisonment, F/OSS has been able to successfully avoid such polarization and thus ghettoization.

Even if some hackers write and release free software for political reasons, many developers tend to divorce an official, broadly conceived political stance outside software freedom from their *collective* laboring (with the exception of free software projects defined primarily by political aspirations). This tight coupling between a particular version of freedom and its instantiation in technology—mediated by licensing within F/OSS—paves the way for certain sociopolitical travels. We might say that F/OSS has attained such legibility not so much because of the material nature of source code but rather because of licensing arrangements socially enveloping the source code: F/OSS technology is free (as in beer as well as in speech) for people to use, learn from, and modify.[2] Further, because these technical and legal artifacts are hinged on a politics of free software—and not traditional Right-Left political divides—others have taken hold of free software artifacts and recoded the meaning of freedom, access, and collaboration in new ways.

As the idea of free software spread into other domains of social life, it gained significant social visibility and notoriety. Through the legibility and use of free software by multiple publics, its status has shifted dramatically. What was once an odd, exceptional, and subcultural practice has acquired a more authoritative position. Through its translations into different terms, the very practice of free software, both as a mode of production and a set of licenses, has been legitimated and brought from the subcultural background into the political foreground (largely between 2000 and 2005). In this new state of near ubiquity, free software has been well positioned to perform an embedded critique of the assumptions that dominate the moral geography of intellectual property law. If court case after court case, economist after economist, and all sorts of trade associations stipulate that economic incentives are absolutely (or self-evidently) necessary to induce labor and secure creativity, hackers counterstipulate such views, not simply through the power of rhetoric, but also through a form of collective labor that yields high-quality software (software that happens to power much of the Internet). Thousands and thousands of individual developers' laboring to make software *libre* constitutes a social performance of collective work that contrasts with as well as effectively chips away at some of the foundational assumptions driving the continual expansion of intellectual property law.

In the rest of this chapter I describe how and why developers of the Debian project insist on a narrow politics of software freedom, and then compare F/OSS's translation into three different spheres. Specifically, I examine how F/OSS has become the corporate poster child for capitalist technology giants like IBM, how it has served as a technological and philosophical weapon of anticorporate activists in the Indymedia counterglobalization movement, and finally, how it has provided a pragmatic template for a nascent movement to create an intellectual commons as part of a larger liberal critique of neoliberal capitalism. I conclude by exploring in more detail how F/OSS has worked to defamiliarize a set of assumptions concerning intellectual property law.

THE POLITICAL AGNOSTICISM OF F/OSS

During a discussion about the most common free software license, the GPL, the following F/OSS developer described free software as an economy working in absence of copyrights: "Free software should create a sort of economy in which things are the way they would be if there were no copyrights at all." He subsequently fleshes out how F/OSS developers conceive of software freedom as a condition that also demands a form of restraint, neutrality, and political disavowal:

> In other words, when I write free software, I renounce the ability to control the behavior of the recipient as a condition of their making copies or modifying the software. The most obvious renunciation is that I don't get to demand money for copies. But I also don't get to demand that the person not be a racist; I don't get to demand that the person contribute to the Red Cross. I don't get to demand that the recipient contribute to free software. I renounce the little bit of control over the other person which copyright law gives me and in that way, I enhance their freedom. I enhance it to what it would be without copyright law.[3]

To secure the practice of free software, in other words, this developer claims that one must disassociate licensing along with its requirements from other ideologies, demands, and affiliations, whether they are economic, religious or political.

This sort of political denial came as a great surprise at first. When I started my fieldwork in 2001, the bifurcation of free software and open source was already firmly in place. Because open source represents an *explicit* and firm denial of not only politics but also even the ethics of software freedom, it led me to believe that among Debian developers, I would encounter a political sensibility exceeding software freedom. Because of their dense ethical commitment to software freedom, which I covered in chapter 4, I was startled to instead encounter a form of political disavowal whereby Debian developers routinely police collective claims so as to prevent certain forms of political associations from entering *official* project policy and even at times informal discourse. To put it another way, rather than an absolute distinction between politically engaged hackers and neutral corporate promoters of the world of open source, I had encountered something more complicated that blurred the well-known distinction between these two positions.

The strongest evidence of this disavowal emerges from what is rarely talked about. Despite the prolific discussions on project mailing lists covering an endless stream of topics—technical problems, project politics, licensing issues, mentoring, and project policy—conversations about the role of Debian in supporting widespread political change or social justice are nearly nonexistent—except, of course, on the rare occasions when someone suggests otherwise.

For example, in the segment here, a developer is vehemently disagreeing with another developer, who in 2003, suggested that Debian should officially participate in a World Social Forum event:

> Look, when I signed up for this project and agreed to adhere to the Social Contract, it didn't say anything about Christianity, genetically modified beef, Microsoft, war in Iraq, or anything else like that. It said we agree to work on Free Software. That's the *only* common belief you're guaranteed to find among Debian developers.[4]

Most other developers participating in this heated, contentious conversation over the project's political scope agreed with this assessment and pounced on the developer who had dared suggest the existence of a politics beyond software freedom itself. Certainly some hackers write free software to fulfill political agendas, and more than ever, they simply cannot deny the vibrant political life that they themselves have engendered. There is a small crop of Debian developers who are also technology activists, channeling their energies primarily toward social justice causes by running technology collectives bearing unmistakably leftist names like, as mentioned earlier, Riseup and Mayfirst (and using 100 percent free software to do so). But as part of their commitments to freedom of expression and nondiscrimination, many developers, especially in the context of large projects, divorce a traditional and overt political stance outside software freedom from official project discourse. Since each developer has their own personal opinion about politics as well as personal reasons for writing free software, hackers believe those sentiments should remain personal, and it behooves them not to attribute a universal political message to their collective work. This message was voiced by many in the email discussion on the World Social Forum, but was captured particularly well in the following statement:

> You must realize that your personal views on other issues are political, and therefore inherently controversial, and are almost certainly not agreed to by every other developer in this project. So let's leave the other politics to the other organizations devoted to them, and keep Debian focused on what it does best.[5]

Here we see how politics are deemed problematic because they are personal and "inherently controversial," and as such, should be left in the private, not public realm. Pragmatically, the inclusion of politics writ large may generate unnecessary project strife and interfere with the real task at hand: the production of superior, free software, articulated as what Debian "does best."

While Debian provides one of the most crystalline instances of how political disavowal emerges during the course of everyday social interaction, it is by no means unique. Debian only stands out and serves as such a useful ethnographic example because it is regarded as the project with the starkest ethical standards. Many other software developers, especially those who identify with the utilitarian principles of open-source software, are reluctant to conceptualize their collective labor in ethical terms, much less expansive political vocabularies (Ross 2006).

Avowed neutrality is of course a central feature of how segments of liberalism function as a moral philosophy for it enshrines certain fundamental principles—notably tolerance and free speech—as residing outside the sphere of the proper domain of politics (Brown 2006; Marcuse 1965). These precepts are seen as apolitical vehicles of sorts, necessary for a healthy democracy and the marketplace of ideas. As Stanley Fish (2002, 219–20) argues, one important idea animating free speech theory is that a "reward" will follow free expression, which "will be the emergence of general and self-evident truths."[6] By supporting free expression, hackers also seek to secure a marketplace of ideas that will help establish self-evident truths. Yet as the work of Kelty (2005, 2008) keenly demonstrates, these truths are generally limited to what hackers love to obsess over: the functionality, elegance, and worth of technology, and increasingly, the technical means of connection—the Internet—that allows them to collectively associate.

As should be clear by now, I do not seek to reveal the fallacy of liberal neutrality; the critical literature on liberalism has convincingly shown the construction and consequences of such an ordering (Brown 2006; Fish 1994; Marcuse 1965). Nor am I assuming the perspective of normative liberal theory that posits a clear connection between the marketplace of ideas and democracy writ large. What I am more interested in is demonstrating how these eclipses acquire meaning within technological social contexts (as opposed to more formal jurisprudence or abstract liberal theory), and what sorts of unexpected consequences they may have in transforming other domains of social, political, and legal life.

Although this disavowal is intriguing in its own regard and could be discussed at further length, I have described it to get at one of the most crucial results of the disavowal itself. Although some free software hackers disavow politics among themselves, the effects of doing so have spilled far beyond this realm of technoscience to transform the politics of intellectual property law more generally. Take, for one, Microsoft's repeated attempts in the early 2000 to tag free software and open source as a cancerous force of communism.[7] Despite the fact that some Microsoft employees tried to portray F/OSS as fundamentally about polluting politics—usually some variant of socialism or communism—ultimately and surprisingly, their red baiting failed (surprisingly, as it is a remarkably effective political tactic in the United States). What happened instead is that F/OSS became a beacon, and inspired a range of groups and actors to embrace some facet of free software, allowing the idea and practices associated with free software to travel far beyond the technological field. And when free software traveled, it also garnered new and distinct types of associations.

THREE MOMENTS OF TRANSLATION

In using the term translation, I invoke the work of Latour, who has extensively theorized the microprocesses of social translation as part and parcel of the extension of technoscientific networks. Latour's model reveals how, through a process of gradual enrollment, social actors recruit various allies to extend a network of meanings, objects, and institutions. Though his model pays attention to nonhuman actors (like artifacts or techniques), a number of critics have argued that he puts too much weight on the capacity of individuals to extend networks, thus overlooking how semiotic processes may shape the conditions for translatability (Downey 1998; Haraway 1997). Donna Haraway (1997, 33), for instance, characterizes Latour's account as a perverse elevation of "heroic action." My discussion below makes it clear there are examples of human-initiated translation, notably the lawyer-advocate Lessig; but there are other mechanisms at work, such as the semiotics of translation.

To understand why and how the semiotics of translation matters in the case of free software, Gyan Prakash's study of science in the Indian colonial era is instructive. While colonial rulers heralded science as a sign of Western reason, ideologically used to justify their presence and undemocratic rule, Prakash shows how this association between despotic rule and technoscientific projects did not determine how others grasped as well as represented the politics of science. Because the sign of science is able to "spill beyond its definition as a body of methods, practices, and experimental knowledge" (Prakash 1999, 7), a cadre of Indian nationalists reenvisioned the meaning of technoscience instead to justify and direct an anticolonial national liberation movement. In other words, the flexibility of the sign of science was an important precondition for the radical redirection of its meaning and the ability of Indian nationalists to take science down a new political path.

The sign of science is not unique in having such semiotic flexibility; the term freedom is loaded with a similar elasticity. Of course, as a number of theorists insist, all language, words, and especially dialogue tend toward a type of indefiniteness, openness, and multiplicity (Bakhtin 1981; Butler 1997; Silverstein 2004; Wittgenstein 1953). But since the sign of freedom (as well as related ideals of liberal enlightenment, such as the public or science) rests atop a trope of universalism, its ambiguity is accentuated, and so is its ability to take on various configurations of meaning (Joyce 2003; Warner

2002). Furthermore, since the time of the Enlightenment, freedom has acted as a master trope by which to prop up a vast array of political theories and imaginaries, ranging from anarchism to socialism as well as liberalism (Lakoff 2006; Hardt and Negri 2000), and also underwrites contemporary notions of personhood (Rose 1999).

Drawing on these various insights, we might say that the ideas of free software and freedom are similarly endowed with semiotic surplus and elasticity. The meaning of free software is further specified, although also transformed, as different types of actors—journalists, educators, scientists, artists, lawyers, and businesspeople—have taken the idea or objects of free software to justify new practices. To put it in slightly different terms, F/OSS acts as an icon as well as a transposable set of practices for openness, collaboration, and alternative licensing schemes that are tactically adopted by others to justify divergent political and economic practices and imaginaries. I now present three examples of F/OSS's wider adoption, each of which has also shifted the ways that many F/OSS developers conceptualize and engage in F/OSS production.

OPEN-SOURCE CIRCULATION WITHIN CAPITAL: IBM

Now a massive multinational corporation, IBM has dominated a wide array of technology-based markets for more than a century. Deriving much of its revenue through the tight control of its vast intellectual property holdings, the company has boasted that it files thousands of patents each year, or up to 75 percent more than the next most active filer.[8] In 2000, IBM started to sell the freely available OS GNU/Linux on its enterprise servers in place of its internally developed proprietary operating system, AIX; this change made big waves in the news.

In 2001, attempting to link its name with the growing surge of popularity for Linux, IBM ran a multimillion-dollar advertising campaign featuring three recognizable icons, the peace symbol, a heart, and Tux the GNU/Linux penguin, that together conveyed the message of "Peace, Love, and Linux."

Big Blue, as IBM is sometimes called, hired marketing firms to perform guerrilla marketing tactics as part of this ad campaign, such as chalking and spray painting these icons on the sidewalks of several major cities (Kenigsberg 2001).

In this advertising campaign, IBM connected using and buying F/OSS-based enterprise solutions with countercultural ideals of sharing, empowerment, and openness, on the one hand, and market agility and dominance, on the other hand. This campaign drew from an already-established advertising tradition, introduced and perfected by the Apple Computer television commercials of the 1980s that equated computing with personal empowerment and even social revolution.

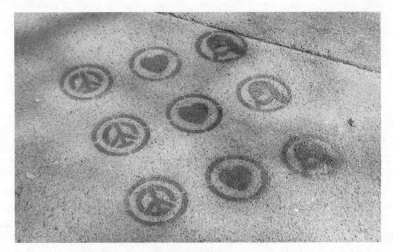

FIGURE 6.1. Peace, Love, and Linux
https://secure.flickr.com/photos/kino-eye/39036635/in/photostream
(accessed October, 23, 2011). Photo: David Tames.

IBM's adoption of F/OSS, while uniquely visible, represents a much larger corporate espousal that translates F/OSS principles into a neoliberal language of market agility, consumer choice, and an improved bottom line. While F/OSS is not universally embraced in the corporate world, IBM's integration of F/OSS is part of a much larger corporate push toward open-source software as the basis of a service-based business model characteristic of post-Fordist capitalism.

By leveraging volunteer work, IBM uses F/OSS as a labor- and resource-saving measure. Yet they also hire a cadre of F/OSS developers to work in-house on F/OSS software. In this respect, they are not unique: Red Hat employs a number of the top Linux kernel developers, Hewlett-Packard employs a small number of Debian developers, and other companies have similar practices.[9] Being neither totally independent nor completely directed, F/OSS development in corporations represents a hybrid between volunteer self-directed labor and paid, directed forms of labor that significantly speed the pace of development for some F/OSS projects (Lerner and Schankerman 2010).

As I have argued, while F/OSS developers are critical of a range of particular corporate practices (a lack of transparency, abuse of intellectual property law, the tendency to obscure bugs, and onerous nondisclosure agreements), many see the corporate adoption of F/OSS as proof that their software is technically sound and superior. Many developers also personally value salaried work developing F/OSS as it affords them the luxury of hacking full-time on what was once only a hobbyist pursuit.

It is clear that the licensing terms for F/OSS technologies allow IBM to adopt, repackage, modify, and sell F/OSS (such as make peace with, make love to, and sell Linux). The politically neutral form of freedom associated with F/OSS facilitates the reenvisioning of what F/OSS means. In the process of such adoptions and translation, new meanings are born, and the F/OSS network is extended and made more visible. In particular, many of the IBM Linux ads, like the one featuring Muhammad Ali that aired during the Super Bowl of 2004, made Linux an unforgettable household name. In the ad, a young blond boy (presumably Torvalds) is sitting in a sterile white room watching a white computer featuring black-and-white footage of a young but feisty Ali, who after a winning fight, proclaims, "Never. Never make me no underdog. And never talk about who's gonna stop me. Well, there ain't nobody gonna stop me. I must be the greatest. I shook up the world. I shook up the world. I shook up the world." A much older Ali then sits in front of the young boy and encourages him to "shake things up," thereby associating Linus and Linux with the underdog who won the fight and ushered in a technical revolution.[10] While the money behind IBM's advertising machine makes its take on F/OSS especially prominent, the company holds no monopoly on the interpretation of F/OSS's meaning and importance, as the next example illustrates.

ALTERNATIVES TO CAPITALISM: IMCs

Also bearing a three-letter acronym, the IMC once represented the vibrant epicenter of a grassroots, people-based digital media journalism, whose mission and spirit could not be more antithetical to the goals of a corporate mammoth like IBM.[11] A worldwide volunteer collective of loosely affiliated grassroots media Web sites and centers, IMC activists make and disseminate locally generated media using various Web applications and tools. Indymedia emerged out of historic struggles against corporate neoliberal globalism policies. In the mid- to late 1990s, opposition against corporate globalization began to take shape among various groups across the globe. Ya Basta!, the Direct Action Network, and the Zapatista National Liberation Army were notable players, while the World Trade Organization protests in the streets of Seattle on November 30, 1999, registered a potent, distilled version of this dissent in an area of the world where spectacular street demonstrations had been in extended hibernation. Aware that the mainstream media would rarely report on these denunciations by diverse constituents (or would distort and sensationalize the protests), local activists decided to self-disseminate the news and thus established the first IMC (Anderson 2012; Pickard 2006)

Politically minded geeks who were bred during the era of cheaper personal computers, homeschooled programming, and virtual interactions chose to use or write free software for the technical components of the IMCs. Mailing lists and IRC, both widely available in free software versions at the time, were used in many of the same ways as in F/OSS projects. They were the main communication tools that facilitated conversation between dispersed tech activists establishing centers in different locations like Washington, DC, Boston, London, and Seattle. Unlike most F/OSS projects, however, the IMC movement articulated itself as a primarily political endeavor seeking to tackle broad structural problems:

> It is our goal to further the self-determination of people underrepresented in media production and content, and to illuminate and analyze local and global issues that impact ecosystems, communities and individuals. We seek to generate alternatives to the biases inherent in the corporate media controlled by profit, and to identify and create positive models for a sustainable and equitable society.[12]

As part of their mission, the IMCs made a conscious choice to use and develop free software to further their goals. Unlike IBM—which conceptualizes F/OSS production as a flexible means by which to extend market presence and emphasize individual, consumerist messages of openness— these activists saw it as a radical and independent alternative to the existing corporate-driven market, and they used it to advance explicitly anticorporate political aims (Milberry 2009).

For example, the IMC tech working group (the segment of the IMC that makes technical decisions about software choices, development, and licensing, and implements and maintains the technical infrastructure of the IMC) gave significant weight to licenses when choosing a particular piece of software. After a lengthy discussion through IRC, it was decided that copyleftstyle licenses (such as the GNU GPL) were preferable to noncopyleft free software licenses (such as the Berkley Software Distribution license, which do not require modified versions to remain open), which in turn were preferable to proprietary software. If the free software was not functional or presented a security risk, then consideration of potential alternatives, along a gradated list of software with increasingly less free licenses, was deemed appropriate. These two quotes from the IRC discussion exemplify understandings of how F/OSS can be used as a revolutionary tool to further the political goals of IMCs:

> <leda>: I assume it is safe to say that we are making this choice in order to try to choose the thing which has the least chance of benefiting any corporation, or any other form of hoarding in any way
> <ozzy>: There is a wonderful pool of very well-developed free software out there. Earlier, someone said that IMC is a revolutionary project, and free software is a revolutionary tool for it. I stan[d] very firmly behind using free software first

In 2001, the IMCs formalized this commitment to F/OSS by including it as one of the provisions in their networkwide Principles of Unity: "All IMCs shall be committed to the use of free source code, whenever possible, in order to develop the digital infrastructure, and to increase the independence of the network by not relying on proprietary software."[13]

Despite their official stance on licensing, some leftists have trouble accepting the formulation of nondiscrimination lying at the heart of F/OSS legal agreements. Some express discomfort or dismay that nondiscrimination, as articulated in F/OSS licensing, bars the type of control that would allow Indymedia to keep its work from being exploited for purposes of oppression (by the military, say) or corporate profit. In this guise, they echo the Marcusian critique of liberalism's "pure tolerance" of free speech (Marcuse 1965). In the IRC conversation mentioned earlier, one Indymedia participant expressed her anxiety about the decision to use free software: "I disagree strongly with the [Debian] social contract: you can't deny use of your software to army, etc, in it." Though the activist confuses the provision of nondiscrimination as specific to Debian (when in fact it is the underlying logic of all F/OSS licenses), her concern captures some of the incompatibilities between leftist and more liberal notions of freedom and equality that underwrite so much of free software's legal culture.

Just as IBM is unlikely to foreground certain messages of freedom (in particular, those critical of intellectual property), leftist activists such as those from the Indymedia collectives tend to downplay or express concern about the reality that F/OSS's flexibility can be used to any end, even the very instruments of oppression and discrimination (like the military or corporation) they are trying to dismantle.

Along with activists, left-leaning academic writers, such as Michael Hardt and Antonio Negri (2004), Alex Galloway (2004), and Johan Söderberg (2007), are inspired by what they see as the radical political potential of free software, and treat it as a living, breathing icon to refine their political sensibilities and projects. Galloway, for instance, locates political potential in the hacker capacity to leverage change by altering technology, code, and protocols. In *Multitude*, Hardt and Negri (2004, 340) deploy the concept of open source to clarify the democratic underpinnings of the political category of multitudes:

> We are more intelligent than any one of us is alone. Open source collaborative programming does not lead to confusion and wasted energy. It actually works. One approach to understanding the democracy of the multitude, then, is an open-source society, that is, a society whose source code is revealed so that we can work collaboratively to solve its bugs and create new, better social programs.

Just as at IBM, the adoption, use, and support of F/OSS by activists and its academic rearticulations give F/OSS much greater visibility within a completely different domain of production. In particular, it has extended the networks where developers code into the spheres of activism and academics. And just as some F/OSS developers work full-time on F/OSS, blurring their volunteer pastime with their day job, other F/OSS developers have entered the world of anticorporate political activism through the spread of F/OSS into these channels (or vice versa).

It is also important to note that many IMC geeks are themselves hackers, and a number of them are involved with free software projects such as Debian. They may attend developer conferences or larger hacker gatherings, such as HOPE or the European outdoor festivals held every four years. They represent a small but growing population among the technological elite of overt political aficionados who direct their love of and passion for technology toward leftist political transformation as well as activism (B. Coleman 2005; Juris 2008; Milberry 2009). Although more common in Italy, Spain, and eastern Europe (often aligning with homegrown anarchist politics), these leftist hackers have established hacker collectives across North America, Latin America, and Europe. Through their exposure to the Left, some hackers have come to appreciate their own role in F/OSS development and advocacy as part of a wider leftist political sensibility (even if they are reluctant to project these intentions onto other F/OSS developers, as this is discouraged—sometimes vehemently—in traditional F/OSS projects). Nonetheless, the use of F/OSS as both a technology and icon to justify other political projects has led some hackers to come to inhabit new political subjectivities.

Liberal Commons and Limits to Capital

In the course of the last decade, an explicit campaign calling for the creation as well as protection of a knowledge commons and free culture has emerged in certain parts of the globe, including North America, Europe, Latin America (especially Brazil), and parts of Asia, among others. The main actors within this movement and sociopolitical debate—students, lawyers, geeks, and other activists—construe access to public goods as the basis by which to further create and extend the commons, a collective pooling of resources made publicly accessible to many. The commons is often articulated as a pool of shared resources that then acts as the fertilizer for further vibrant cultural production and at times a healthy democracy. Among moderate proponents, the commons is understood as compatible with private property and a capitalist market, although certainly acting as a bulwark against some of their worst abuses.[14] The more liberal facet of the commons endeavor is but one moment within a broader liberal critique of the neoliberal face of capitalism. In an *Atlantic Monthly* article, reformed financial tycoon (now also philanthropist) George Soros (1997) enunciated the basic terms of this liberal critique: "the untrammeled intensification of laissez-faire capitalism and the spread of market values into all areas of life is endangering our open and democratic society."

The most influential articulations and organizations within this nascent commons movement have been those founded by Lessig (1999, 2001b; Creative Commons) and David Bollier (2002, 2009; Public Knowledge). These in turn have helped spawn offshoots, such as the Students for Free Culture movement, which is organized into clubs on colleges across North America. These thinkers used the messages and example of F/OSS to build institutions that support the production of open knowledge. In both writings and public talks, Lessig and Bollier frequently refer to F/OSS as a source of inspiration as well as justification for their visions and projects.

For instance, in his enormously influential book *Code and Other Laws of Cyberspace*, Lessig (1999, 7) justifies his argument that "the lack of ownership, the absence of property, the inability to direct how ideas will be used—in a word, the presence of a commons—is key to limiting, or checking, certain forms of governmental control," and does so by relying heavily on the example of "open code." The nonprofit organization he founded, Creative Commons, has developed licenses and Web tools that are used by individuals and organizations to "build an intellectual property conservancy."[15] The model he drew from, unsurprisingly, was the GNU GPL:

> Taking inspiration in part from the Free Software Foundation's GNU General Public License (GNU GPL), Creative Commons has developed a Web application that helps people dedicate their creative works to the public domain—or retain their copyright while licensing them as free for certain uses, on certain conditions.[16]

While Lessig and Creative Commons may represent the most prominent of these liberal translations, there are many others. Bollier's book *Silent Theft* (the title plays off Rachel Carson's *Silent Spring*, which crystallized much thinking about the movement), for instance, contends that the establishment of a commons can limit the multinational plundering of knowledge and culture. One example of an existing commons is F/OSS, which he treats as an independent gift economy that is seen to coexist productively with the market, although also providing protections against some of its least savory elements. Benkler (2006), a legal theorist, has published a thorough account of what he calls peer-to-peer production, liberally using the illustration of F/OSS to make an argument about the vibrancy of a new networked economy—a mode of production that helps sustain and nourish classical liberal political ideals, such as autonomy and freedom.

But more than any other actor, Lessig's individual role in translating the meanings of F/OSS deserves attention. He acted as a "spokesperson" for many years—a role conceptualized in the work of Latour (1987, 1988) as a prominent person who enrolls allies, builds institutions, changes perceptions, and translates the message of free software in ways that appeal to a wider constituency. Just as Louis Pasteur served as the spokesperson who made the germ theory of illness compelling and intelligible to wider publics (Latour 1993), Lessig has worked assiduously, passionately, and diligently to bring out and successfully translate the artifacts and messages of F/OSS from the confines of the hacker lab out to the field. He took a highly technical, sometimes-esoteric set of concerns shared among geeks and reenvisioned them in a language accessible to wider groups: academics, lawyers, Silicon Valley entrepreneurs, policymakers in Washington, DC, and activists.

As part of these efforts, Lessig spoke hundreds of times to various audiences (including geeks), has written dozens of articles and four books, built the Creative Commons organization that provides alternative licensing schemes to copyright, argued in the Supreme Court case *Eldred v. Ashcroft* over copyright extensions heard in January 2003, personally taught a cadre of lawyers at Harvard and Stanford universities about open code, and has made the politics of technical architectures, once a fringe interest in academic circles, into a publicly relevant (and more intelligible) issue.

Of the ten times I have seen Lessig give lectures, the first was the most indicative of the set of transformations that he helped initiate. At that meeting, in 1999 in a packed room of University of Chicago law students, Lessig spoke of his then-recently published book *Code*. In it, he discussed the "emergent" übergeeky technical movement called free software that relies on different licensing mechanisms than those of intellectual property law. Lessig had to proceed at the time with great caution with his argument that open code, as he calls it, had come across a profound and important insight. His idea that there were limits and alternatives to intellectual property law was scandalous (and seen as just plain wrong), *especially* at the University of Chicago law school—home to neoliberals, like Richard Epstein (2004), who are deeply committed to private property and thus have been quite skeptical of open source.[17] When I spoke of the example of free software between 1999 and 2001, I routinely encountered similar skepticism or at least confusion, with most people unable to even grasp how developers gave away their code for free and asking me to repeat my description of free software multiple times.

Today, Lessig and those who follow in his footsteps no longer have to walk on eggshells. The discourse has so radically transformed that open source is accepted as a social fact, known to many outside technological circles. Lessig has helped utterly redefine the terms of engagement, such that law students now learning about computer law and intellectual property are compelled to cast their skepticism aside (at least for a short while) and confront the existence of intellectual property alternatives.

Part of his success can be attributed to the fact that he, like F/OSS geeks, is reluctant to portray his work as political; instead, he prefers to articulate his position either in terms of a constitutionality that sits above the fray of politics (Lessig 1999, 2001b) or in terms of the importance of cultural preservation (Kelty 2004). In an arena where politics has acquired negative connotations, Lessig's avoidance of the term has allowed him to garner a diverse audience and build the many alliances that have extended his work around the globe. Like many of the developers I studied, he clearly operates from a social imaginary that emphasizes one form of liberty—that represented by the Millian tradition stressing self-development and free speech—over a more libertarian or even classic liberal position, in which the most important value is protecting individual autonomy and private property. While certainly not antithetical to property, Lessig (1999, 85) elevates what he calls "Mill's method" to identify all forms of coercion (government, markets, and norms) that impinge on an individual's liberty.

Given Lessig's own brand of political agnosticism, articulation of Millian liberal values, and active presence in the geek public (speaking at rallies and events, writing articles, and serving on the board of the Electronic Frontier Foundation), it is not surprising that Lessig's message has taken at least partial hold in the geek community. Lessig relied on an accessible and compelling vocabulary—such as the commons, public goods, and code is law—that has been used by hackers to understand the nature of F/OSS knowledge along with its broader social significance. In large part because of Lessig's claims and analysis, developers can no longer deny the political effects of their work, even if they do not fully accept Lessig's politics, and even if some of them are still unwilling to hinge their labor on grand narratives of justice, socialism, and anticapitalism.

Lessig has also had a subtle though no less profound effect on the political consciousness of some individual hackers. Largely by way of his work, and in part bolstered by the dramatic dot-com bust of the late 1990s, he has reined in the libertarian inclinations of some hackers, leading them toward more liberal grounds that mirror his own personal biography. Lessig, raised in a conservative family, was a faithful member of the Republican Party in his youth. Placing enormous faith in the power of the individual and the free market, he held a corollary distrust of the government. Much of this changed during the early 1980s when he went to study at Cambridge University at the height of Margaret Thatcher's neoliberal rule. As he explained in a *Wired* article, "I remember going to Cambridge as a very strong libertarian theist," and "by the time I left I was not a libertarian in that sense, and no longer much of a theist" (quoted in Levy 2002). Identifying with workers' rights, Lessig shed his "theism" to cast a critical eye toward markets and came to place more faith in the role of constitutional governments as safeguards of democratic liberty.

The F/OSS movement has not yet been completely engulfed by Lessig's political claims of the commons. There have even been some important critiques of Creative Commons among advocate-lawyers and F/OSS developers who note how Creative Commons' promotion of choice dilutes the clear standard of freedom found in F/OSS (Elkin-Koren 2006; Hill 2005), and edges quite close to neoliberal territory in advocating a language of choice. Despite these differences, there is an affinity between the two, and they act to mutually reinforce each other's goals, interests, and visions. In chartering a new nonprofit that curates licenses modeled along the lines of F/OSS, high-profile academic lawyers like Lessig have raised the credibility of the idea of software freedom. Conversely, the success of F/OSS has served to demonstrate the plausibility of Creative Commons' idea. Through a process of cross-pollination, many hackers have been inspired by the aims and actions of Lessig, particularly those concerning the notion of a commons.

THE POLITICS OF DEFAMILIARIZATION

"Free software may have started as mere software," explains Bollier (2009, 37), "but it has become [. . .] proof that individual and collective goals, and the marketplace and the commons, are not such distinct arenas." Despite the fact that versions of this statement are routine, much less has been written about the social mechanisms and political conditions under which F/OSS could serve as such a powerful icon. In the previous section, I examined how and under what conditions F/OSS has served as transposable model. I now offer a few concluding thoughts about the effects of its adoption across a wide domain of social arenas.

As already noted, a central feature of F/OSS is its political agnosticism (or alternatively, its narrowly defined politics), which has facilitated its visible spread and adoption in distinct arenas of life, allowing it to attain a position where it can perform a political message. Because the practices of F/OSS challenge economic incentive theory—assumptions that buttress intellectual property law—it works as a form of cultural critique, tacit assumptions converted to an explicit state of affairs. The moment that "any set of values, and material forms comes to be explicitly negotiable," observe Comaroff and Comaroff (1992, 29), signals "the end of its naturalized state."

Jacques Derrida's work on language, culture, and law provides insight into the realization and practice of copyleft. Along with a string of other theorists, Derrida has demonstrated that any naturalized proposition (like heterosexuality) or social fact both presupposes and ultimately propagates what it excludes (Butler 1997; Derrida 1978; Graeber 2001, 2004). It is just this structural quality of language and cultural concepts that Stallman exploited when he established the first F/OSS license, the GPL. What is important to highlight here, though, is that while mainstream copyright discourse and related intellectual property laws necessarily presuppose their opposition, they lack any metapragmatic indication of this presupposition. Most of copyright's recent legal history in fact represents a vehement disavowal, through economic incentive theory, of oppositional entailment of the copyright. The GPL more clearly speaks a metapragmatic commentary on its oppositional existence—an awareness even built into its informal name, copyleft, which explicitly calls into being and thus points to its counterpart, copyright.

Noting this asymmetry is crucial if we are to understand how copyleft licenses provide not only an alternative but also one that critically points to the shortcomings of its inverted cousin—copyright. We might even push this further, again with the help of Derrida, this time using insights from an essay titled "Force of the Law: The Mystical Foundation of Authority." Derrida (1990, 12) identifies what he calls the "performative" (and circular) nature of liberal law, in which law gains its authority by virtue of being sanctioned as law: "Laws keep up their good standing," explains Derrida, "not because they are just, but because they are laws." By its very definition, law is endowed with authority, as a force nonetheless sustained by the monopoly use of state-sanctioned violence.

One might add that constitutional laws (like those of the First Amendment and intellectual property in the United States) are often revered and cherished, for being the foundational laws of nations, they carry with them the extra weight of widespread patriotic respect, and are commonly invoked during times of national crisis and rituals of commemoration. What is important to keep in mind is that Stallman, in the process of creating a legal alternative to a constitutional mandate, bypassed the usual channels (the courts and judges) by which one would question or change a law, especially constitutional law. In so doing, he also partially punctured the authority of the law, laying bare the assumption that only institutions of legal authority (the courts and congress) have the right to alter the law. To be sure, lawyers and legal council were and still are essential to making free software law legally binding. The point, however, I am trying to convey is that Stallman did bypass some traditional routes, such as lawsuits, in order to challenge patents and copyrights, instead devising a license that cleverly reformatted copyright by its very use.

The GNU GPL and similar copyleft licenses hence rupture the naturalized form of intellectual property by inverting its ossified, singular logic through the very use of intellectual property.[18] Let's recall how F/OSS licenses work: they simultaneously use *and* defy the core tenets of copyright law. To make software open source or free software, one first applies a copyright and then adds any one of a number of F/OSS licenses, which then disables the restrictive logic of copyright law. In this capacity, the use of these F/OSS legal artifacts behave as a "destructive analysis of the familiar" (Sapir 1921, 94), to use an old but famous anthropological phrase.

This move is not unlike Marx's inversion of Hegelian idealism, which retained Georg Wilhelm Friedrich Hegel's dialectical method to repose history not as an expression of the "Absolute Idea" but instead as humanity's collective creation through labor. Using copyright as its vehicle, the copyleft turns copyright on its head and in the process demystifies copyright's "absolute" theory of economic incentive. In other words, free software practices denaturalize the assumption that intellectual property instruments hold a singular relationship between means and ends—a relationship that can only be established by institutions of authority, notably courts and governments.

Without question, F/OSS hackers are prominent actors in a contemporary debate, yet one that speaks to a longer history of contention over the definitions of individualism, free speech, property, and freedom within liberal thought and practice. Probably more than any other current site of labor, F/OSS production makes legible the present-day frictions between free speech and intellectual property regulations that have grown so markedly pronounced, in part because both sets of rights have undergone such significant expansions over the last hundred years. If courts have altered the provisions of intellectual property law so as to sanction and facilitate the conversion of knowledge into private property, they have also altered the definition of free speech laws so as to accord new protections to categories of expression such as political speech and, in some instances, source code. Hackers have spoken clearly in this debate, but primarily in their capacity as producers of free and open software: they demonstrate in material action that they value the right to express themselves, learn, and create technology over the right to privatize the fruits of their labor—a site of labor that became particularly prominent as other groups and actors, from radical anticapitalists to capitalist giants, have deployed free software.

Nested within this liberal conundrum is another closely related friction over the definition of liberal individualism: What does it mean to be a *free individual*? In the mid-nineteenth century, Mill helped to clearly define the debate when he reformulated the utilitarian philosophy of his upbringing that also dominated the political landscape of Britain by infusing the utilitarian concept of selfhood with overtones of Romanticism. Unwilling to reduce individuals to pleasure seekers of utilitarian theory, he redefined individuals as rational actors who cultivate their capacity for thought and discrimination. This self-refashioning required a specific set of social and affective conditions (judgment, critical debate, and the freedom to speak); it engendered a stance of skepticism and justified the political liberty to speak freely. In the United States, John Dewey continued to give further shape to Mill's concerns. He launched a critique of "rugged individualism" and laissez-faire liberalism. Dewey (1935, 88) insists that "the ultimate place of economic organization in human life is to assure the secure basis for an ordered expression of individual capacity and for the satisfaction of the needs of man in non-economic directions." Today hackers are entangled in as well as voice this dilemma over personhood, the meaning of freedom, markets, and property, asserting that not every object of knowledge falls under a neoliberal property regime.

Certainly the debate over the direction and limits of intellectual property law is not over simply because of the rise of the F/OSS legal alternatives; the mere existence of a material practice such as F/OSS has not fully muted contentions based on universal principles or theories of human nature. In some respects we can say that because of the forceful appearance of F/OSS, a formidable politics has taken hold in the last decade, fueled by the rise of technologies like peer-to-peer systems that encourage copying, translation, and reconfiguration. The politics of intellectual property law have over the past ten years reached a contentious point—a political debate that cannot fully or at least comfortably rely on abstractions, universal principles, or naturalized rationalities but instead must entertain more local, pragmatic stakes along with the reality of what people do, can do, or desire to do.

Under threat, these principles may clamor for more attention. For example, in March 2005, on the eve of an important Supreme Court deliberation over the legality of peer-to-peer technologies, the *New York Times* ran an editorial stating its position on intellectual property law by way of arguments couched in a vocabulary of doom, liberal progress, and naturalization: "If their work is suddenly made 'free,' all of society is likely to suffer. [. . .] The founders wrote copyright protections into the Constitution because they believed that they were necessary for progress."[19] By invoking the country's founders and tropes of progress, this message sought to reassert the naturalness of these propositions precisely when they were most under threat.

The battle over the proper scope of intellectual property law thus continues to rage worldwide. Nonetheless, by virtue of the fact that one can point to a living practice that unsettles arguments based on abstract principles, the latter tend to lose some of their efficacy. On this basis, policy and law can perhaps be more easily channeled away from universal claims, and entertain local, pragmatic stakes while addressing the reality of what people do, can do, or desire to do. As Helen Nissenbaum (2004, 212) has maintained, we are drawn to the example of hacker activity because hackers "represent a degree of freedom, an escape hatch from a system that threatens to become overbearing."

Rendered visible, the F/OSS example has been utilized by many scholars and lawyers as a powerful justification for balancing the current system, even as other activists and educators shore up their own claims not within the pages of books but instead by building alternatives (Benkler 2006; Bollier 2002; Lessig 1999). The formal attributes of this critical politics of defamiliarization should immediately strike a resonant chord with anthropologists, whose work is often conceptualized in terms of a politics of denaturalization. For most of the last century, anthropological knowledge has been marshaled to unsettle essentialist and universal assumptions about human behavior through cross-cultural and comparative examination (Benedict 1959; Marcus and Fisher 1986; Mauss 1954; Sahlins 1976). The disciplinary vehicle for this is a work of speech: the narrative of ethnography. What I find interesting is that F/OSS, among many other things, functions as a form of critical ethnography writ large. It exemplifies what George E. Marcus and Michael Fisher (1986, 139) call "defamiliarization" [. . .] by "cross-cultural juxtapositioning." In the case of F/OSS, such juxtaposition arises from an accidental cultural practice and not a discursive anthropological one.

In emphasizing this performative and critical dimension of F/OSS, I am echoing a common theme within a rich body of anthropological and sociological theory (Comaroff 1985; Gilroy 1993; Hebdige 1979; Martin 1998; Ong 1987; Scott 1985; Taussig 1980, 1987). This literature has compellingly shown that the scope of political transformation far exceeds intentional political action, which has been the traditional focus of political theory, activists' perceptions, governmental programs, and even much of critical democratic thought. F/OSS hackers, in other words, have not helped usher in social change primarily by organizing in order to change the world, standing and speaking on the political soapbox, or demanding legislative changes (although some free software developers do engage in these political forms). Instead, as noted above, they speak primarily in their capacity as F/OSS producers.

Following the work of theorists of publics, politics, and carnival (Stallybrass and White 1987; Warner 2002), the important question to consider is: Under what conditions can nonrhetorical, embodied action speak effectively, become public, captivate an audience, offer critical insight, and move an audience to join in its carnival of possibilities?

The answer does not lie in the formal or a priori nature of performativity; it requires us to assess the interrelationship between a dominant political climate and the pragmatic, semiotic elements specific to a phenomenon under investigation. In the case of F/OSS, I have argued that its political ambiguity and replicable nature facilitate its ability to captivate a diverse audience, which is then provoked into action because it has confronted a living piece of evidence and a model for organizing similar endeavors. Sometimes language alone is not capable of inspiring action, and, under certain historical conditions, language is often *robbed* of the potential it holds to imagine alternative realities.

Indeed, the F/OSS case reveals broader insights about what is possible in the prevailing political atmosphere, especially in the United States, where the media and other actors can dismantle, literally in the blink of an eye, the import of a message or politics through spin, insufficient attention, or spectacle (Kellner 2003; Postman [1985] 2006). The mass media, closely aligned with imperatives of capital (McChesney 1997), routinely reduce events to well-established ideological categories (in the United States, this is usually along the lines of liberal versus conservative, and since 9/11, patriotic versus antipatriotic, with red baiting also being a common tactic).[20]

While F/OSS was certainly covered extensively in this news, the media, for the most part, did not reduce it to any simplistic ideological binaries. Indeed, early media reports featured in the *New York Times* and *Wired*, for example, seemed so surprised at the economic logic of free software, that they faithfully and extensively reported as well as conveyed the very surprise and even wonder that was also expressed by many individuals, including hackers themselves, about this phenomenon, noting the pleasures and difficulties of using open-source software.

Much of the early history of F/OSS in fact demanded a certain level of skeptical and open experimentation on the part of developers and hackers, and eventually other adopters of the software and legal ideas of F/OSS.

Initially, hackers themselves collaborated with each other without complete conviction (or even a vocabulary) that such an approach could realistically compete with software built under proprietary or "cathedral" models of development. Only through the course of small progressions, partial successes, frustrations, and a series of translations that expanded the F/OSS network was this form of production apprehended temporally as a viable technical modus operandi. Ultimately, when it gained visibility with wider publics (in part through the circuits of capital and its politically agnostic character), a range of actors turned to F/OSS to fuel other imaginaries outside the geek public.

In drawing attention to F/OSS's portability and lack of political affiliation as two elements that facilitate its politics of visibility, I am admittedly raising a host of difficult questions that should be of interest to both academics and activists. For anthropologists and those interested in capturing these processes of cultural critique represented by the F/OSS example, there are a host of conundrums to be contemplated. The politics of defamiliarization that arises through the cultural practice is quite ephemeral, leaving few traces. The shock waves induce a process of cultural rethinking and transform practices in other arenas of social life. The nature of this shock is to lose its shock value and sink back into the natural state of affairs as soon as a set of practices are more or less stabilized. Thus, the task of a critical anthropology is to keep a mindful orientation toward these powerful yet elusive processes of cultural contrast as they are unfolding so that the politics of cultural defamiliarization can be more effectively known, acknowledged, and perhaps even directed.

A number of other pressing questions about politics are provocatively raised by the example of F/OSS's politics: Must a politics of visibility rely on the circuits of capital to make itself known in a public sense, and is the law a political friend or foe? Can we realistically work outside these channels? If so, how? And if we work within these channels, are there ways to be flexible about some convictions, but firmer about others, and secure the vision or values being heralded, as the copyleft does? This of course is the copyleft's most striking element. It allows knowledge to travel and gain new meanings, but since it is protected by a clever legal mechanism from the commodification of dissent (Frank and Weiland 1997) and other viral corruptions, the knowledge stays intact and accessible, recursively returning to its source, the developer, and user community. Here I won't provide answers to these questions, but since they are so strongly suggested by the F/OSS case, I raise them for further thought.

How to Proliferate Distinctions,
Not Destroy Them

⌀⌀⌀

In 2006, *Time* magazine crowned social media and "you" as the person of the year. Typical of many mainstream media representations, *Time* not only latched on to the moniker Web 2.0 but celebrated it with breathless hyperbole too:

> It's a story about community and collaboration on a scale never seen before. It's about the cosmic compendium of knowledge Wikipedia and the million-channel people's network YouTube and the online metropolis MySpace. It's about the many wresting power from the few and helping one another for nothing and how that will not only change the world, but also change the way the world changes. (Grossman 2006)

This quote treats Wikipedia, YouTube, and Myspace not only as interchangeable examples of community and collaboration but also as moral solvents with the power to melt away existing power structures. Although the hype may be more pronounced in this piece, the simple conflation of these distinct digital domains is not unique to *Time* or even other journalistic pieces; it is simply one example of how Internet technologies between 2005 and the present have been imagined by academics, journalists, policymakers, and activists.

Starting in 2005, but continuing unabated today, many commentators and critics alike have placed a range of digital phenomenon, including free software, under the umbrella of Web 2.0. This term was first coined in 2005 by O'Reilly to differentiate contemporary technologies (wikis, blogs, and embedded videos) from their immediate predecessors, such as email and static Web pages. These second-generation technologies, he claimed, allowed for more interactivity, flexibility, and participation than the earlier ones. Since the term's invention, it has not only become *the* governing metaphor by which to understand contemporary Internet technologies and the social practices that cluster around them. It also has been stretched so far and so wide that it now encompasses software (blogs and wikis), corporate platforms (Flickr, Twitter, Facebook, YouTube, and Myspace), projects and nonprofits (Wikipedia, Debian, and Creative Commons), and collaborative techniques (remixing and crowdsourcing).

There are certainly points of connection to be made between these domains, technologies, practices, and projects. Yet this constant conflation obscures far more than it reveals. When used in celebratory terms, Web 2.0 puts on equal footing a user who uploads a video on YouTube or a photo on Flickr (corporate-owned, proprietary platforms) and a free software developer or even a Wikipedian who is part of a nonprofit, collective effort. Many academics and journalists who are critical of Web 2.0 often accept the assumption smuggled within this discourse—namely, that these disparate phenomenon belong in the same analytic frame in the first place. "It breaks my heart," writes one of the fiercest critics of contemporary computer currents, Jaron Lanier (2010, 70), "when I talk to energized young people who idolize the icons of the new digital ideology, like Facebook, Twitter, Wikipedia and free/open/Creative mashups." Lanier might be less perturbed if he knew that those who embrace F/OSS and Wikipedia are frequently the fiercest critics of the privacy violations and copyright policies of social network platforms like Facebook.

Among other effects, this rampant lumping together obscures the complex sociology and history of some digital projects—a surprising omission given that a number of quite prominent citizen media and free software projects, like Indymedia and Debian, were at the forefront of organizing themselves into institutional forms years before the rise of so-called Web 2.0, by 2000 and as early as 1998. It was not simply that most journalists, pundits, and many academics ignored this fact, though. This omission was replaced with a countervailing story that suggested otherwise, alleging that knowledge was being created by forces of mild disorganization whereby individuals, acting in loose coordination with each other, led to novel forms of collaboration. This vision reached prominence for the way it so perfectly meshes with, and thus supports, dominant understandings of freedom, agency, and individualism. There is no better example of this sentiment than the title of Shirky's enormously popular 2006 book *Here Comes Everybody: The Power of Organizing without Organizations*. Although many of his observations about digital dynamics are illuminating, and many of the examples he draws on, such as meet-up groups, remain informal, many others that he discusses, such as Wikipedia and Linux, were by 2006, organized, and as such, some type of organization.

These new institutions are not the large slumbering bureaucracies most often associated with governments, the post office, or big corporations. In building what are new institutional forms, open-source developers and Wikipedians usually seek to strike a balance between stability and open-ended flexibility. In the process of doing so, many engender particular forms of social value that include mutual aid, transparency, and complex codes for collaboration along with other ethical precepts that help guide technical production. In the case of Debian—explored in detail in this book—its policies, direction, and imperatives are decided by a collective that not only creates software but also has been innovative, quite successfully so, in terms of institution building. Just as significant is the fact that free software licensing ensures that the fruits of labor are equally available to all—a condition unmet by many forms of crowdsourced labor, much less ones that unfold on corporate and cloud-based platforms, such as Flickr, where collaboration is said to flourish, and yet where users can lose access to their data when and if the company folds or takes down a service.

The politics of F/OSS, narrowly defined though they may be, are obfuscated and severely distorted when they are lumped in with Web 2.0. When the organizational sociologies of these projects are ignored, it is far easier to collapse them into the category of more informal, less coordinated forms of production, thereby obscuring how these distinct forms of production ethically, politically, and economically function. "Observing participation without any guide to its diversity," argues Adam Fish and his colleagues (2011, 160), "is like watching birds with no sense of what distinguishes them other than that they fly and squawk (when of course, many do neither)." In recent times, scholars have started to unearth as well as describe the organizational dynamics at play with free software (Kelty 2008), Wikipedia (Fuster Morell 2010; O'Neil 2009; Reagle 2010), and hacker anticapitalist technology collectives (Anderson 2009; Juris 2008; Milberry 2009), and insist on analytically disaggregating the lumping that is so common when analyzing digital media (Gillespie 2010; Fish et al. 2011).[1]

Many, however, continue to conflate different digital domains. For instance, despite the astounding plurality exhibited by digital activism, it is treated in starkly singular terms. Take, say, the widely circulated (and much discussed) critique of the politics of digital media in a 2010 *New Yorker* article titled "Small Change: Why the Revolution Will Not Be Tweeted," where author Malcolm Gladwell (2010) notes, "the evangelists of social media seem to believe that [. . .] signing up for a donor registry in Silicon Valley today is activism in the same sense as sitting at a segregated lunch counter in Greensboro in 1960." I share Gladwell's deep skepticism of the hype that envelops mainstream understandings of many social networking platforms like Twitter and Facebook. I think it is imperative to discuss the limits of activism based on weak social ties and the security risks in using corporate platforms. Yet his critique only works by way of silencing a number of historical and contemporary examples. Digital interaction and activism are not, as Gladwell suggests, inherently grounded in weak ties but also can be the basis for socially deep ties, such as is the case for much of F/OSS production—a domain that has fundamentally altered the politics of access and intellectual property. Digital media has also played a critical role in fomenting and helping sustain more traditional social movements like the counterglobalization protests (Bennett 2003; Juris 2008). To take a more recent case, the digital entity Anonymous, part digital direct action, part human rights technology activism, and part performance spectacle, while quite organizationally flexible, is perhaps one of the most extensive movements to have arisen almost directly from certain quarters of the Internet (Coleman 2012a). Instead of differentiating between types and forms of digital activism, Gladwell, like so many, paints digital activism in starkly singular terms, in the process relegating existing forms that do not conform to "slacktivism" into the dustbin of history, and unable to distinguish in the most basic ways between forms of activism with distinct roots, forms of organization, and effects.

Attention to these basic, sometimes-fundamental differences in digital sociality and activism can help foster greater understanding of what digital politics mean along with the range of possibilities they might have to offer and their limits. We must be ruthless in how we differentiate the social dynamics and formats of digital activism in order to more fully glean the public as well as political lessons afforded by these worlds.

In the end, it is worth taking a cue from the world of free software in two regards. It is, for one, a domain where developers balance forms of sociality and forces often treated as mutually exclusive: individualism and social cooperation, utility and artistry, altruism and self-interest, organization and disorganization, populism and elitism, and especially individualism and social cooperation. Hackers who are seen (and at times portray themselves) as quintessentially individualistic often live this individualism through remarkably cooperative channels. This should not make us question the reality of individualism, which is also culturally incarnated, but instead encourage us to examine the assumption that this individualism precludes cooperation. In fact, individualism frequently results in more cooperation, on a larger scale than would otherwise exist. Second, what makes these projects so interesting is not how they engender democracy writ large, or fundamentally change the warp and woof of economic and social structures, but that collaborators make technology at the same time that they experiment in the making of a social commonwealth; it is there where the hard work of freedom is practiced.

NOTES

⌒⊙⌒

INTRODUCTION: A TALE OF TWO WORLDS

1. https://www.gnu.org/copyleft/gpl.html (accessed September 22, 2011).
2. It is now routine for anthropologists to unpack the effects of liberal formations by attending to the fraught politics of multiculturalism and secularism, the establishment of publics, the coconstruction of markets, marketing, and consumer desire, and the political changes wrought by new national constitutions and neoliberal policies (see Comaroff and Comaroff 2000, 2003; Ferguson and Gupta 2002; Haydn 2003; Mahmood 2004; Ong 2006; Povinelli 2002, 2006; Scott 2011). Despite this rich literature, the influence of liberal values in the context of Anglo-European societies still tends to figure thinly or inconsistently, either as an external economic influence that shapes cultural expressions, or more richly, as relevant to the discussion of secularism, religion, publics, and most especially, multiculturalism. The study of privacy and free speech, for instance, has tended to come in normative, philosophical, and legal terms (Bollinger and Stone 2002; Nissenbaum 2009; Rule 2009; Solove 2010). There is, however, a small but growing body of anthropological literature on liberalism and technology (Helmreich 1998; Malaby 2009) as well as the anthropology of the press and free speech (Boyer 2010; Keane 2009). For an enlivening historical account on liberalism as a lived set of principles in mid-Victorian Britain, see Hadley 2010.
3. Because the bulk of my research was conducted on Debian, a free software project, and with developers involved with other free software projects, my analysis also tilts in the direction of free over open-source software. And given how much attention has already been placed on open-source over free software, it is key to add this neglected perspective. But much of this book clearly applies to open source, for while even if open-source developers and projects de-emphasize a moral language of freedom (Chopra and Dexter 2007), they still routinely advance liberal ideals in, for example, their commitments to meritocracy and rational, public debate.
4. I am indebted to the stellar cultural analysis of liberalism offered by Stuart Hall (1986), who makes the compelling case that liberalism is not only a set of political creeds but also exists as cultural common sense composed of a set of interconnected principles that "hang together." Hall's definition is useful because he highlights some core features (such as a mistrust of authority and an accentuated commitment to individualism), yet he is careful not to pose a single logic to liberalism. He also argues that in its historical and lived dimensions, liberalism has incarnated into what he calls "variants of liberalism," replete with differences and contradictions. These differences and contradictions are still part and parcel of liberalism's life, and are evident among hackers.
5. A less humorous consequence of this ambivalence is the limited funding options available to students and researchers who choose to remain in North America for fieldwork (with the exception of those studying indigenous communities). Not only are existing funds nearly impossible to live on; there are few overall funding sources as well. So

even if we have managed to enlarge our field of inquiry, this is a case in which economic constraint works to discourage researchers from walking down a recently opened path.

6. For thoughtful contemplations on the method of participant observation and fieldwork, see Clifford and Marcus 1986; Comaroff and Comaroff 1992; Faubion and Marcus 2009.

7. Digital Millennium Copyright Act, 17 U.S.C. 1201(a)(1)(a).

8. One of the most crystalline examples of this utilitarian justification is provided in *Harper and Row, Publishers, Inc. v. Nation Enterprises*, a Supreme Court case deliberated in 1985. The question at hand was whether the magazine, the *Nation*, was entitled under the fair use doctrine to publish a three-hundred-word excerpt, in a thirteen-thousand-word article, from President Gerald R. Ford's twenty-thousand-word memoir published by Harper and Row. The court ruled in favor of Harper and Row, upholding the ideal that property rights promote a public benefit by inducing creation. Sandra Day O'Connor delivered the majority opinion portraying copyright as "the engine of free expression." Versions of this utilitarian rationale, in which Internet protocol (IP) is the basis for harvesting "knowledge," continue to be expressed and hold sway within the context of an heightened neoliberal expansion of intellectual property rights, making existing tensions between expressive and IP rights more palpable and acute than ever.

9. The Silicon Valley geek entrepreneur, who I am not addressing in this book, aligns quite closely with neoliberal aspirations. For a discussion of Web 2.0 technologies, entrepreneurs, and neoliberalism, see Marwick 2010.

10. http://mbrix.dk/files/quotes.txt (accessed April 10, 2007).

11. http://www.loyalty.org/~schoen/ (accessed March 19, 2007).

12. http://www.gnu.org/gnu/manifesto.html (accessed July 30, 2007).

13. https://upload.wikimedia.org/wikipedia/commons/b/b7/Anti-sec_manifesto.png (accessed, March 26, 2012).

14. Editorial, "The Victor Spoiled," *2600: The Hacker Quarterly* 15, no. 4 (1998–99): 4.

15. Although my exploration remains hemmed to free software and may not be relevant to *all* domains of hacking, there is certainly some overlap between what I describe and instances of hacking unrelated to the world of free software.

16. Gender also receives only cursory attention. The reasons for this omission are multiple, but foremost, I believe far more substantial research on the topic is needed before qualified and fair judgments as to the complicated dynamics at play can be posed, especially since analyses must interrogate wider social dynamics such as education and childhood socialization that have little to do with free software projects. In the last two years, a series of vibrant initiatives around diversity and gender have proliferated in the context of free software, with tremendous support from the wider developer community— something I have not been able to research adequately.

17. While this book attends to a number of translocal aspects of F/OSS development, it by no means captures the reality of all different places where free software has taken hold, such as India, Vietnam, Peru, and Brazil. For instance, many free speech commitments explored in this book are shared by Brazilian developers I worked with, even while the general story of free software in Brazil and other parts of Latin America looks quite distinct from what happened in the United States given how entwined it became with national politics (Chan 2008; Schoonmaker 2009; Murillo 2009).

18. The region, despite being dominated by high-tech capitalism, is by no means monolithic. It is home to a range of distinct values, stretching from staid engineering commitments

(English-Leuck 2002), to countercultural expressions (Turner 2006) and new age currents (Zandbergen 2010), to undoubtedly liberal (Malaby 2009) and neoliberal orientations (Marwick 2010).

CHAPTER 1: THE LIFE OF A FREE SOFTWARE HACKER

1. Most of the developers I interviewed were between the ages of eighteen and thirty-five, although there were a number over thirty-five years old (there were some under eighteen who I interacted with but did not formally interview due to provisions in my Institutional Review Board application). Thus, this life history is located very much in time, with the narrative spanning the period between the late 1970s until the present.
2. Warez typically refers to commercial or proprietary software that has been cracked or pirated, and therefore illegally circulated to the larger public (in the past on BBSs and currently on the Internet). For this to happen, the software's copy protection measure must be deactivated. In contrast, shareware is copyrighted software that is released by its author initially for free on a trial basis or under some other set of conditions.
3. For decades, computer science was a branch of mathematics or class offerings were scattered in different departments. Although MIT was home to many important computer projects, for instance, it only began offering an undergraduate computer science course in 1969. The first computer science department was established in 1962 at Purdue University, and it was not until the mid- to late 1970s and early 1980s when many US universities started to establish stand-alone computer science departments (Ensmenger 2010, 120–21). See also "History of the Department of Computer Sciences at Purdue University," http://www.cs.purdue.edu/history/history.html (accessed October 23, 2011).
4. These quotes are culled from my life history interviews.
5. Efficiency can mean various things for programming/software, including running faster, using less computing resources, or both.
6. For a comprehensive history of the BBS era, see the excellent eight-part documentary *BBS: The Documentary* by Jason Scott (2005).
7. BBSs also played a prominent role among phreaks and underground hackers (Thomas 2003; Sterling 1992). Usenet, a large newsgroup service, was significant for hackers as well (Pfaffenberger 1996).
8. FidoNet, established in 1984, was an independent mail and information transport system that connected BBSs together.
9. IRC happens on IRC servers (EFnet, Freenode, etc.) that run software that allow users to set up "channels" and connect to them. There are a number of major IRC servers around the world that are linked to each other. Anyone can create a channel, and once created and populated with users, all others in the channel can see anything anyone types in a given channel. Using IRC client software, a user can connect to multiple servers at once, and join multiple channels, switching conversations by switching tabs or windows. While conversation on the channel is public, one can also initiate multiple private conversations. IRC has grown tremendously since it was first created in 1988. In July 1990, IRC averaged at 12 users on 38 servers. Now there are thousands of servers, and over 100,000 users on some servers. To give a sense of its growth, one of the more

popular servers, EFnet, had 38,000 users in 1998, growing to 106,976 in 2004. For current statistics, see http://www.hinner.com/ircstat/ (accessed August 2, 2011).

10. For a detailed history of the relationship between Unix and Linux, see Kelty 2008.

11. As a number of developers noted, the actual number ranged from twelve to forty depending on whether one was doing a base install or a more elaborate one as well as the size of the floppy (3.5 inch/1.44MB floppies, or 5.25 inch/1.2MB floppies).

12. This is no longer a problem, but was potentially one in the 1990s. See the Linux reference guide for installing X window: "Be careful if manually editing values in the Monitor section of /etc/X11/xorg.conf. Inappropriate values can damage or destroy a monitor. Consult the monitor's documentation for a listing of safe operating parameters." http://www.linuxtopia.org/online_books/centos_linux_guides/centos_linux_reference_guide/s1-x-server-configuration.html (accessed September 20, 2010).

13. http://www.outpost9.com/reference/jargon/jargon_27.html (accessed June 5, 2009).

14. http://web.bilkent.edu.tr/Online/Jargon30/JARGON_S/SUIT.HTML (accessed June 5, 2009).

15. Email on file with the author.

16. Email on file with the author.

17. While in the early to mid-1990s the number of noncommercial free software applications was growing, many of the early Linux distributions were actually commercially produced. In the early 1990s, one of the most popular was SLS, which many considered to taint the good name of free software because it was riddled with bugs and false advertising. Murdock wrote that "these 'distributors' have a disturbing tendency to misleadingly advertise non-functional or extremely unstable 'features' of their product. Combine this with the fact that the buyers will, of course, expect the product to live up to its advertisement and the fact that many may believe it to be a commercial operating system (there is also a tendency not to mention that Linux is free nor that it is distributed under the GNU General Public License). To top it all off, these 'distributors' are actually making enough money from their effort to justify buying larger advertisements in more magazines; it is the classic example of unacceptable behavior being rewarded by those who simply do not know any better. Clearly something needs to be done to remedy the situation" (quoted in "A Brief History of Debian," http://www.debian.org/doc/manuals/project-history/ap-manifesto.en.html [accessed August 28, 2010]).

18. http://www.debian.org/doc/manuals/project-history/ap-manifesto.en.html (accessed July 29, 2011).

19. For example: "Apache is an organic entity; those who benefit from it by using it often contribute back to it by providing feature enhancements, bug fixes, and support for others in public newsgroups. The amount of effort expended by any particular individual is usually fairly light, but the resulting product is made very strong. This kind of community can only happen with freeware—when someone pays for software, they usually aren't willing to fix its bugs. One can argue, then, that Apache's strength comes from the fact that it's free, and if it were made 'not free' it would suffer tremendously, even if that money were spent on a real development team" (http://httpd.apache.org/ABOUT_APACHE.html [accessed July 12, 2006]).

20. The Bay Area Linux Events Web site, for example, listed eight different meetings/events between March 1 and 8, 2005. See http://www.linuxmafia.com/bale/ (accessed August 2, 2009). In the last five years, hacker workshop spaces, such as Noisebridge in San Francisco, have been established in cities across Europe and North America.

21. Some of the first hacker cons were the Hackers Conference held in California (1984), the Computer Chaos Club Congress held in Germany (1984), and Summercon held in Saint Louis (1987).

22. While no hacker con can be called a tame affair, they do, however, exist on a spectrum, ranging from the large and wild, to more subdued and intimate affairs. Most hacker cons mix socializing with hacking, gaming, and talks/panels, which span from the purely technical to the fabulously silly, with many legal, political, and historical oddities and talks in between.

23. http://gravityboy.livejournal.com/35787.html (accessed July 2, 2009).

24. The experience is quite different for organizers, of course, which I myself had the "pleasure" of experiencing when I was on the local team for Debconf10, held at Columbia University in New York in August 2011. As an organizer, the conference was still enjoyable, and even more intense, but also frustrating, frenetic, and much more exhausting.

25. A BOF is an informal discussion group session scheduled during a conference. Multiple people have told me that the bird reference is meant to signify that hackers, like birds, flock together. I have also been told that it may also refer to the fable by Hans Christian Andersen to denote how an informal conversation can transform something small (like vague or incipient ideas) into mature and well-formed ideas. See http://www.underthesun.cc/Classics/Andersen/ThereIsNoDoubt (accessed July 29, 2011).

26. During the course of my research, I attended Defcon 2002 (Las Vegas), Codecon 2002 (San Francisco), Debconf 2002 (Toronto), Debconf 2004 (Porto Alegre), Debconf 2006 (Oaxtepec, Mexico), Debconf 2007 (Edinburgh), Debconf10 (New York), LinuxWorld 2000/2001/2002 (Bay Area), Annual Linux Showcase 2001 (Oakland, CA), Usenix 2002 (San Francisco), Computer, Freedom, and Privacy 2002 (San Francisco), HOPE 2002/2004/2010 (New York), Forum Internacional Software Livre 2004 (Porto Alegre), and What the Hack 2005 (Boxtel, Netherlands). I helped to organized Debconf11, held in New York. Compared to many geeks I know, my attendance record on the conference circuit was fairly light to moderate. The following account is primarily based on fieldwork during the many Debconfs that I attended, although it draws from some of the other conferences as well.

27. http://media.debconf.org/dc7/report/ (accessed August 2, 2011).

28. http://bugs.debian.org/cgi-bin/bugreport.cgi?bug=252171 (accessed March 25, 2005).

29. For the purposes of full disclosure, I organized this informal history roundtable as a BOF, attended by twenty-five people. I was inspired to do so, however, based on the fact that so many informal conversations between developers over meals were precisely on the "exchange of memory." Debian developers also archive their history into a software package that comes with Debian.

30. Email on file with the author.

31. http://blog.madduck.net/debian/2007.06.25_debconf7 (accessed October 12, 2010).

32. http://media.debconf.org/dc7/report/ (accessed October 12, 2010).

33. https://gallery.debconf.org/main.php (accessed October 12, 2010).

34. http://media.debconf.org/dc7/report/ (accessed August 2, 2011).

35. http://media.debconf.org/dc7/report/ (accessed August 2, 2011).

36. http://listas.softwarelivre.org/pipermail/debconf4/2004-June.txt (accessed August 2, 2011).

37. http://listas.softwarelivre.org/pipermail/debconf4/2004-June.txt (accessed August 2, 2011).
38. http://media.debconf.org/dc6/report/ (accessed August 2, 2011).

CHAPTER 2: A TALE OF TWO LEGAL REGIMES

1. For accounts of the rise of free software, see Kelty 2008; Moody 2001; Wayner 2000.
2. This, however, does not mean that access makes ethical or pragmatic sense for all cultural material and knowledge. For a discussion of the limits of access and circulation, see Christen 2006, 2009; Coleman 2010.
3. To be more specific, privacy is everywhere in shambles (Nissenbaum 2009; Rule 2009); free labor is expropriated from many Net participants, and an ethic of play is easily co-opted for the sake of profit (Scholz 2008; Terranova 2000); and a more exploitative side of informational capitalism can be found among the global body shoppers and immigrant programmers who are rarely given voice in mainstream depictions of digital media (Amrute 2008; Biao 2006). Closest to this project, the copyright alternatives proposed by free software and free culture advocates should also not be elevated as a universal alternative to be adopted by cultural groups worldwide given the different regimes around knowledge access as well as circulation (Christen 2006, 2009; Coombe and Herman 2004; Ginsburg 2008).
4. New technologies, such as the photocopying machine, raised many concerns in the publishing industries over copyright law, leading President Ford in 1974 to establish the National Commission on New Technological Uses of Copyrighted Works (CONTU) to prepare guidelines on photocopying policy. Two years later, the copyright act was amended to include many of the commission's recommendations.
5. http://digital-law-online.info/CONTU/ (accessed March 25, 2012).
6. These changes granted five exclusive rights to copyright owners: the rights to make copies of the work, make derivative works, distribute the work, publicly perform the work, and display the work publicly. These exclusive rights were subject to narrowly defined exceptions, such as fair use provisions. Along with these provisions, the copyright term was extended to the life of the author plus fifty years.
7. This reversal was made possible by a combination of significant changes in patent policy and practices in conjunction with landmark legal decisions (Jaffe and Lerner 2004). For instance, the court in charge of hearing patent cases, the Court of Appeals for the Federal Circuit formed in 1982, proved to be consistently propatent. By frequently upholding patents, the courts also encouraged patent litigation, which increased nearly 50 percent in the 1980s and became a significant source of revenue for at least some technology firms (Boyle 1996, 133).
8. The monetary value provided by patents for the computer industry has been and still is enormous. In the United States alone, the revenues from computer-related patents amount to one hundred billion dollars. In 1999, IBM, the largest patent holder in the world, made a profit of one billion dollars from patent licenses while it accrued a record-breaking 2,756 new patents (Gleick 2000). In 2003, IBM boasted on its Web site that it had earned 3,415 US patents, "breaking the record for patents received in a single year and extending its run as the world's most innovative company to eleven consecutive years" (http://www-03.ibm.com/ibm/history/history/year_2003.html [accessed September 8, 2011]).

9. Stallman, at the time still employed at MIT's artificial intelligence lab, was able to do this since MIT purchased the LISP OS from Symbolics. But he first had to reverse engineer the program to understand its functionality and devise new solutions as the recently revised copyright statute kept him from simply copying the source code. For a detailed history, see Moody 2001.

10. For a detailed history, see Kelty 2008. See also the conclusion in this book.

11. The first version of his license was the GNU Emacs GPL, and by 1989, the FSF devised a license that was not application specific: the GNU GPL. Don Hopkins, Stallman's friend and a user of FSF software, coined the term copyleft, which refers to a class of licenses (such as the GPL). For this particular history, see Brate 2002, 256.

12. http://www.usdoj.gov/criminal/cybercrime/CFAleghist.htm (accessed August 9, 2011). See also http://www.copyright.gov/title17/92appg.html (accessed August 9, 2011). For a detailed history of these transformations, see Marshall 1993.

13. Despite the magnitude and importance of TRIPS, with its crystal-clear message that a country's legal restrictions on goods and information were a central precondition for so-called free trade, much of its work had been accomplished earlier by the US-led bilateral regulations of the 1980s, notably the General System of Preferences and Section 301 (see especially Drahos and Braithwaite 2002, 134). Many nations have yet to fulfill all the mandates.

14. Commerce Department Information Infrastructure Task Force, "Intellectual Property and the National Information Infrastructure: The Report of the Working Group on Intellectual Property Rights," September 1995, 10; cited in Clark 1996, 988.

15. https://groups.google.com/forum/#!msg/comp.os.minix/dlNtH7RRrGA/SwRavC zVE7gJ (accessed July 20, 2011).

16. Robert Young, "Interview with Linus, the Author of Linux," http://www.linuxjournal .com/article/2736 (accessed November 8, 2010).

17. During much of the 1980s, hackers and programmers did work together over long distances, especially on various FSF and other Unix applications. For example, while different versions of Unix were largely developed within the bounds of one institution (such as Berkeley, Sun Microsystems, or Bell Labs), collaborative development was important. Changes were made through the trading of patches" on newsgroups or tapes were traded via the mail. The developments of Arpanet and Internet protocols through the request for comment documents also represent an important long-distance collaborative effort (DeNardis 2009; Gitelman 2006)

18. For a typical example, see Dobrzynski 1999. A group of *New York Times* reporters gathered with Silicon Valley CEOs to discuss the trials and thrills of managing companies in the "Internet era."

19. http://wp.netscape.com/newsref/pr/newsrelease558.html (accessed November 2002); http://blog.lizardwrangler.com/tag/netscape/ (accessed August 9, 2011).

20. http://www.catb.org/~esr/halloween/ (accessed September 25, 2010).

21. http://www.ussg.iu.edu/hypermail/linux/kernel/9904.0/0332.html (accessed August 9, 2011).

22. I would like to thank Andrew Leonard, who raised this point with me many years ago.

23. I first came across this quote in Litman 2001, 151 (emphasis added). Its original source is Philips 2000.

24. http://web.archive.org/web/20010917030022/http://www.bsa.org/usa/press/ newsreleases/2001-08-30.692.phtml (accessed July 12, 2008; on file with the author).

25. International Intellectual Property Alliance, *Special 301: Brazil*, February 18, 2010, 141.

CHAPTER 3: THE CRAFT AND CRAFTINESS OF HACKING

1. Here is a little more information about the code. The "tr" in this code is a function that translates all occurrences of the search characters listed, with the corresponding replacement character list. In this case, the slash character delimits the search list, so the list of what to search for is the asterisk character. The replacement list is the second asterisk character, so overall it is replacing the asterisk with an asterisk. The side effect of this code is that the "tr" function returns the number of search and replaces performed, such that by replacing all the asterisks in the variable $sky, with asterisks, the variable $cnt gets assigned the number of search and replaces that happen, resulting in a count of the number of stars in the $sky. What follows after the # symbol is a comment, a nonfunctional operator found in most programs, theoretically supposed to explain what the code does.

2. These were once blog entries and no longer exist. These texts are on file with the author. Python and Perl are computer languages.

3. The entries are judged on aesthetics, output, and incomprehensibility, and are only decipherable by the most accomplished of Perl experts, but can undoubtedly be aesthetically admired by all as a postmodern object of utter incomprehension and amusement. For an insightful discussion of obfuscation in code, see Monfort 2008.

4. In his engrossing ethnography, Graham Jones (2011) covers the way in which cunning, cleverness, and inventiveness are learned, performed, valued, and embodied among the magicians that he worked with in Paris.

5. For a discussion of some of the tensions in the corporate world that arose due to the perception of programmers as clever and idiosyncratic, and an excellent history of programmers, see Ensmenger 2010, especially chapter 3.

6. http://www.ingen.mb.ca/cgi-bin/news.pl?action=600&id=10383 (accessed November 20, 2007).

7. I would like to thank Jonah Bossewitch, who pushed me to think about humor in light of the rationality of the computer more deeply.

8. Some notable examples of populist formulations are *Computer Lib* by Ted Nelson (1974) and Stallman's "GNU Manifesto." For examples of the elitist manifestation, see Levy 1984; Sterling 1992; Borsook 2000.

9. http://osdir.com/ml/linux.debian.devel.mentors/2003-03/msg00272.html (accessed July 5, 2009).

10. http://osdir.com/ml/linux.debian.devel.mentors/2003-03/msg00225.html (accessed July 5, 2009).

11. This is quite similar in logic to liberal notions of states of nature that posit forms of individuality outside social relations. An interesting question to further explore is why this view still holds such appeal even though it is most often only conceptualized in these hypothetical terms.

12. http://osdir.com/ml/linux.debian.devel.mentors/2003-03/msg00225.html (accessed July 23, 2010). During interviews, this idea that programming could span the spectrum from unoriginal functionalism to high art came up again and again. For example, one programmer characterized it in the following way: "I think it can be art, but it is not always. [. . .] If I had to pick a comparison, I would pick carpentry because carpentry always has that range. You can start with just making a bookcase or something utilitarian all the way to creating something like creating a piece of art with wood." Developers explained their craft triangulated between math/science, engineering, and

art. Engineering was usually at the apex, respectively tending toward the side of art or science, depending on the idiosyncrasies and preferences of the programmer along with the nature of the project.

13. For instance, it is routine for project developers to thank users or nonmember developers for their contributions. By way of illustration, on the Subversion project, which develops code-tracking software, out of the approximately eighty-seven full and partial committees, fifty-five were thanked by name in a commit log message (that someone else committed) before they became a committee themselves (as of April 25, 2005).

14. Luser is a common intentional misspelling of loser. "A luser is a painfully annoying, stupid, or irritating computer user. The word luser is often synonymous with lamer. In hackish, the word luser takes on a broader meaning, referring to any normal user (i.e. not a guru), especially one who is also a loser (luser and loser are pronounced the same). Also interpreted as a layman user as opposed to power user or administrator" (http://en.wikipedia.org/wiki/Luser [accessed September 9, 2011]).

15. http://www.thinkgeek.com/tshirts/frustrations/3239/ (accessed March 21, 2006).

16. http://lists.debian.org/debian-vote/2005/03/msg00610.html (accessed July 5, 2009).

17. http://www.mail-archive.com/debian-vote@lists.debian.org/msg08500.html (accessed July 17, 2010).

18. http://svn.red-bean.com/repos/kfogel/trunk/.emacs (accessed July 5, 2009).

19. http://evans-experientialism.freewebspace.com/barthes06.htm (accessed September 17, 2011).

20. I would like to thank Martin Langhoff, who suggested the name palimpsest for the authorial tracking that occurs on these version control systems.

21. Those hackers who use Berkeley Software Distribution licenses place more value on "freedom of choice" than necessarily recursively feeding modified code back into the community of hackers. I would still like to point out, however, that by using a Berkeley Software Distribution license, a hacker has still made a deliberate choice to keep their code open and accessible to others. The difference is that the license does not mandate this choice for others and thus adheres to a more negative/libertarian notion of liberty than that of Mill's.

CHAPTER 4: TWO ETHICAL MOMENTS IN DEBIAN

1. A prolific literature in the sociology and anthropology of science fruitfully dissects how professional identities along with ethical commitments are established during periods of training (Good 1994), vocational practice (Gusterson 1998; Luhrmann 2001; Rabinow 1996), and are sustained by the coded and metaphoric language of professions that work to elide ethical concerns (Cohn 1987). All these works have pushed me to think about how ethical commitments are forged by a range of micropractices, many of them narrative based.

2. For the history and working of consensus among Internet engineers, see Kelty 2008; Gitelman 2006; DeNardis 2009.

3. For an analysis of similar dynamics among programmers, see Helmreich 1998; Levy 2011.

4. The analysis of trust in the context of digital media interactions has so far been sporadic, but it is starting to gain momentum. For an edited collection exclusively dedicated

to the subject, see Ess and Thorseth 2011. For a discussion of trust and feelings of fellowship in the context of gaming, see Malaby 2007.

5. One can maintain a software package that one did not program from scratch. The person who is the developer for the software is called the upstream author. In many cases, the upstream author and maintainer are the same person, although there is no term to mark this differentiation.

6. The etiquette surrounding how to proceed with an NMU is more complicated than I am able to elaborate here. There are policy guidelines that explain best practices, and from time to time, the release manager can strongly encourage NMUs for the sake of focusing attention on release critical bugs that must be fixed before a release can happen. For a telling example of such exhortations, see Towns 2002.

7. Perens was considered too much of a micromanager, but was respected for putting in so much time and dedication, especially in guiding the project through the creation of the Social Contract and DFSG.

8. Since at the time the procedures were not well established or clear, they ran into procedural problems, so one leader basically dropped out of the race, leaving the other runner as the de facto Debian project leader.

9. In addition to these more formalized positions, decisions made by informal ad hoc groups permeate the entire organization.

10. This is a complicated topic, but it is worth stating that one of the reasons that the Debian project leader is discouraged from changing positions is because it would smack too much like politics (i.e., bringing in your own cronies at the expense of those already doing a good enough job).

11. FTP refers to file transfer protocol and used to be the main method by which developers uploaded pieces of software to the repository. It is no longer the case that this is the only method used, but the name FTP master has stuck.

12. See Usenet Cabal FAQ, http://www.subgenius.com/bigfist/hallscience/computers/X0012_Internet_History.html (accessed July 26, 2011).

13. http://lists.debian.org/debian-devel/2005/03/msg02062.html (accessed July 10, 2011).

14. http://www.mail-archive.com/debian-vote@lists.debian.org/msg08500.html (accessed July 26, 2011).

15. http://lists.debian.org/debian-project/2005/03/msg00142.html (accessed July 26, 2011).

16. http://www.debian.org/devel/tech-ctte (accessed July 26, 2011).

17. Ibid.

18. To contain the sprawling size of this chapter, I am not providing an example of one of these legendary bugs or how debate over technical issues becomes a place where questions of authority are raised. This must be left for another time. For two such legendary Debian bugs, see http://bugs.debian.org/cgi-bin/bugreport.cgi?bug=97671 (accessed July 28, 2011); http://bugs.debian.org/cgi-bin/bugreport.cgi?bug=143825 (accessed July 28, 2011). The first one was over an obscure file that violated the file system hierarchy standard (a policy detailing where pieces of programs should be placed in the file system) and whether it needed to be fixed in time for the impending release. This turned into a lengthy, acrimonious debate between a famous package maintainer and the release manager, and had as much to do with whose decisions should stand, the maintainer or the release manager. As the maintainer observed in one part of the voluminous writing dedicated to this one bug: "The issue is for me is twofold: about the

package maintainer being empowered to manage his own bug list for triage purposes, and about the limits of the release manager's or another developer's power to make decisions for another developer." The Technical Committee refused to hear the case, the release manager did not budge on his recommendation, and finally the maintainer proceeded to ask for help to fix the problem.

19. Many of the conversations over this "dis-ease" occurred over the private mailing list, and as such, I am unable to quote any of the exact conversations. The mailing list is only supposed to be used for sensitive material—for example, for announcing when a developer will be on vacation. From time to time, some of the more interesting discussions unfold there, and then someone suggests moving them to a public list. I have been told about many such conversations, and some individuals have allowed me to see their own personal posts to get some clarity over the issues. In 2005, the project voted to move toward declassifying debian-private, but the process by which to do so has still not been fully worked out. See "Debian Declassification Delayed," https://lwn.net/Articles/394660/ (accessed October 25, 2011).

20. While I emphasize some of the ethical and social elements of the NMP, it is important to note that it is just as much a method of displaying technical proficiency as well as a process of technical mentoring. In the final step of the NMP, applicants usually demonstrate that they have the technical wherewithal to be trusted with the ability to integrate software into the Debian archive and represent Debian to the world. This test is often filled with the presentation of a clean, policy-compliant piece of software and a bug-free example of the type of work the applicant aims to put within the Debian distribution (e.g., a package), although this is complemented by a significant series of technical questions.

21. Email on file with author.

22. http://article.gmane.org/gmane.linux.debian.devel.announce/605 (accessed July 31, 2011).

23. Bakhtin, as Greg Nielsen (1998) argues, does not entirely repudiate Kant's theory of ethics but instead rejects his theory of action.

CHAPTER 5: CODE IS SPEECH

1. http://www.cs.cmu.edu/~dst/DeCSS/Gallery/decss-haiku.txt (accessed October 22, 2009).

2. This comparison can only be made to do so much work. The law, being written in a natural language, contains all sorts of nuance, assumptions, and linguistic flexibility not present in the much more formal and rigid language of software. And although programmers can acquire legal knowledge, they do not necessarily make good lawyers—a profession that requires many other skills on top of a formal comprehension of the law.

3. Email on file with the author.

4. Ibid.

5. Email on file with the author.

6. http://lists.debian.org/debian-news/2002/msg00015.html (accessed September 10, 2011).

7. http://lists.debian.org/debian-news/2002/msg00029.html (accessed September 10, 2011).

8. http://www.debian.org/News/weekly/2002/48/ (accessed September 10, 2011).

9. http://www.debian.org/News/weekly/2002/39/ (accessed September 10, 2011).

10. *Bernstein v. U.S. Department of Justice*, 176 F.3d 1132 (1999).

11. *DVD Copy Control Association, Inc. v. Bunner*, 116 Cal. App. 4th 241, 10 Cal. Rptr. 3d 185 (2004); *Pavlovich v. Superior Court*, 29 Cal. 4th 262, 268, Cal. Rptr. 2d 329, 334 (2002).

12. *Universal City Studios Inc. v. Reimerdes*, 82 F. Supp. 2d 211 (2000).

13. http://web.archive.org/web/20031124051048/cyber.law.harvard.edu/archive/dvd-discuss/msg00000.html (accessed November 10, 2008).

14. http://slashdot.org/comments.pl?sid=3644&cid=1340340 (accessed August 15, 2008).

15. http://lwn.net/2000/0727/bigpage.php3 (accessed November 20, 2008).

16. http://www.pigdog.org/decss/ (accessed February 5, 2009).

17. http://www-2.cs.cmu.edu/?dst/DeCSS/Gallery/ (accessed November 10, 2008).

18. Ibid.

19. http://cryptome.org/mpaa-v-2600-bac.htm (accessed April 23, 2009).

20. I recorded the speech and transcribed it. Speech on file with the author.

21. *Universal City Studios Inc. v. Reimerdes*, 82 F. Supp. 2d 211 (2000). This case was appealed by one of the defendants, Corley. In the subsequent case, *Universal City Studios Inc. v. Corley* (273 F. Supp. 3d 429 [2001]), the presiding judges also affirmed the importance of this view insofar as they highlighted and quoted a longer version of this statement.

22. http://www.loyalty.org/~schoen/haiku.html (accessed September 10, 2011).

CONCLUSION: THE CULTURAL CRITIQUE OF INTELLECTUAL PROPERTY LAW

1. http://emoglen.law.columbia.edu/publications/berlin-keynote.html (accessed August 22, 2011).

2. By beer, I mean strictly the source code. Even if source must be made available for free, F/OSS is frequently bought and sold in the open market, but companies usually are charging for the service, support, and labor as opposed to the knowledge.

3. http://lists.debian.org/debian-legal/2003/03/msg00494.html (accessed August 10, 2010).

4. Email on file with the author.

5. Email on file with the author.

6. For a rich intellectual history of the liberal free speech concept, see Peters 2005.

7. See, for instance, Penenberg 2005.

8. http://www.ibm.com/news/us/2002/01/10.html (accessed January 23, 2003).

9. As of 2005, 90 percent of the top twenty-five kernel developers were paid to work on the kernel. See http://www.newsfactor.com/story.xhtml?story_id=34392 (accessed October 10, 2008). A large number of Apache developers also work for pay. In Debian, a majority of developers are volunteers because of its large size.

10. http://www.youtube.com/watch?v=sYT5VcPSjSg (accessed March 15, 2012).

11. Although they no longer command the type of singular attention they once did, the IMCs in fact inspired many others to follow in their direct footsteps and initiated countless other grassroots, citizen-led journalism projects (Anderson 2012).

12. http://seattle.indymedia.org/contact.php3 (accessed August 24, 2011).

13. http://doc.indymedia.org/view/Global/PrinciplesOfUnity (accessed July 25, 2006).

14. There is also a radical and leftist embrace of commons discourse that deserves more attention than I can provide here. Some of these thinkers have also drawn on the example of free software. For some prominent articulations of this work, see Caffentzi 2010; Federici 2004; Linebaugh 2010; Hardt and Negri 2009.

15. Creative Commons, http://www.creativecommons.org/ (accessed December 20, 2010).

16. http://creativecommons.org/about/history (accessed August 25, 2011).

17. In his article "Why Open Source Is Unsustainable" in the *Financial Times*, Epstein (2004) mulls over various reasons why open source will fail. Largely painting it as a "commune" phenomenon, he maintains that it cannot scale and launches other criticisms. His editorial was followed by a response from another lawyer, James Boyle, which in turn produced yet another set of objections by Epstein.

18. The justifications for intellectual property law are not singular but instead encompass various competing theories, from commitments to moral rights, common in France, to utilitarian justifications, common in the United State. Nonetheless, what they share is the idea that these instruments in some form are necessary to induce creation.

19. See "When David Steals Goliath's Music," March 28, 2005, http://www.nytimes .com/2005/03/28/opinion/28mon1.html?ex=1115179200&en=2e53e0eca0c1d9 ac&ei=50 (accessed August 25, 2011). In addition to this, in the last couple years, two think tanks, the Alexis de Tocqueville Institution (http://adti.net/) and the Progress Freedom Foundation, have attacked open source on the grounds that intellectual property law is *necessary* for freedom and a vital economy.

20. For an analysis of how red baiting was successfully used to disable progressive US-based media reform in broadcasting in the 1940s, see Pickard 2011.

EPILOGUE: HOW TO PROLIFERATE DISTINCTIONS, NOT DESTROY THEM

1. On the importance of recognizing and theorizing the diversity of digital media forms and formats, see Fish et al. 2011.

REFERENCES

Abbate, Janet.
1999. *Inventing the Internet*. Cambridge, MA: MIT Press.

Abu-Lughod, Janet L.
1991. Writing against Culture. In *Recapturing Anthropology: Working in the Present*, ed. Richard Gabriel Fox, 137–54. Santa Fe, NM: School of American Research Press.

Akera, Atsushi.
2001. Voluntarism and the Fruits of Collaboration: The IBM User Group, Share. *Technology and Culture* 42 (4): 710–36.

Amrute, Sareeta.
2008. Producing Mobility: Indian ITers in an Interconnected World. PhD diss., University of Chicago.

Anderson, C. W.
2009. Breaking Journalism Down: Work, Authority, and Networking Local News, 1997–2009. PhD diss., Columbia University.
2012. *Networking the News: The Struggle to Rebuild Metropolitan Journalism in the Web Era, 1997–2011*. Philadelphia: Temple University Press.

Anonymous.
n.d. Anatomy of a Pirate. http://www.textfiles.com/piracy/anatomy.txt (accessed July 25, 2004).

Arendt, Hannah.
1998. *The Human Condition*. Chicago: University of Chicago Press.

Asad, Talal, ed.
1973. *Anthropology and the Colonial Encounter*. London: Ithaca Press.

Bakhtin, Mikhail.
1981. *The Dialogic Imagination: Four Essays*. Austin: University of Texas Press.
1984. *Rabelais and His World*. Bloomington: Indiana University Press.
1993. *Toward a Philosophy of the Act*. Austin: University of Texas Press.

Barthes, Roland.
1975. *The Pleasure of the Text*. New York: Hill and Wang.

Beebe, Barton.
2010. Intellectual Property Law and the Sumptuary Code. *Harvard Law Review* 123 (4): 809–89.

Bellah, Robert N., Richard Madsen, William M. Sullivan, Ann Swidler, and Steven
    M. Tipton.
1985. *Habits of the Heart: Individualism and Commitment in American Life.*
    Berkeley: University of California Press.

Benedict, Ruth.
1959. *Patterns of Culture.* Boston: Houghton Mifflin.

Benjamin, Walter.
(1933) 1999. On the Mimetic Faculty. In *Walter Benjamin: Selected Writings, Vol.
    2: 1927–1934*, ed. Michael W. Jennings, 720–22. Cambridge, MA: Belknap
    Press of Harvard University.
(1936) 2005. The Work of Art in the Age of Mechanical Reproduction. http://www
    .marxists.org/reference/subject/philosophy/works/ge/benjamin.htm (accessed
    January 4, 2011).
1969. Theses on the Philosophy of History. In *Illuminations: Essays and Reflec-
    tions*, ed. Hannah Arendt, 253–64. Berlin: Schoken.

Benkler, Yochai.
1999. Free as the Air to Common Use: First Amendment Constraints on Enclosure
    of the Public Domain. *New York University Law Review* 74:354–446.
2006. *The Wealth of Networks: How Social Production Transforms Markets and
    Freedom.* New Haven, CT: Yale University Press.

Bennett, W. Lance.
2003. Communicating Global Activism: Strengths and Vulnerabilities of Net-
    worked Politics. *Information, Communication, and Society* 6 (2): 143–68.

Berger, Peter L., and Thomas Luckmann.
1967. *The Social Construction of Reality: A Treatise in the Sociology of Knowl-
    edge.* New York: Anchor.

Berry, David M.
2008. *Copy, Rip, Burn: The Politics of Copyleft and Open Source.* London: Pluto
    Press.

Biao, Xiang.
2006. *Global "Body Shopping": An Indian Labor System in the Information Tech-
    nology Industry.* Princeton, NJ: Princeton University Press.

Black, Maurice Joseph.
2002. The Art of Code. PhD diss., University of Pennsylvania.

Bollier, David.
2002. *Silent Theft: The Private Plunder of Our Common Wealth.* New York: Rout-
    ledge.
2009. *Viral Spiral: How the Commoners Built a Digital Republic of Their Own.*
    New York: New Press.

Bollinger, Lee, and Geoffrey Stone, eds.
2002. *Eternally Vigilant: Free Speech in the Modern Era.* Chicago: University of
    Chicago Press.

Borsook, Paulina.
2000. *Cyberselfish: A Critical Romp through the Terribly Libertarian Culture of High Tech*. New York: Public Affairs.

Bourdieu, Pierre.
1977. *Outline of a Theory of Practice*. Cambridge: Cambridge University Press.

Boyer, Dominic.
2010. Digital Expertise in Online Journalism (and Anthropology). *Anthropological Quarterly* 83 (1): 73–96.

Boyle, James.
1996. *Shamans, Software, and Spleens: Law and the Construction of the Information Society*. Cambridge, MA: Harvard University Press.
2003. The Second Enclosure Movement and the Construction of the Public Domain. *Law and Contemporary Problems* 66 (Winter–Spring): 33–75.

Brate, Adam.
2002. *Technomanifestos: Visions from the Information Revolutionaries*. New York: Texere.

Brown, Bill.
2001. Thing Theory. *Critical Inquiry* 28 (1): 1–22.

Brown, Wendy.
2006. *Regulating Aversion: Tolerance in the Age of Identity and Empire*. Princeton, NJ: Princeton University Press.

Butler, Judith.
1997. *Excitable Speech: A Politics of the Performative*. New York: Routledge.

Caffentzis, George.
2010. A Tale of Two Conferences: Globalization, the Crisis of Neoliberalism, and the Question of the Commons. *Commoner*. http://www.commoner.org.uk/wp-content/uploads/2010/12/caffentzis_a-tale-of-two-conferences.pdf (accessed August 25, 2011).

Campbell-Kelly, Martin.
2003. *From Airline Reservations to Sonic the Hedgehog: A History of the Software Industry*. Cambridge, MA: MIT Press.

Carneiro da Cunha, Manuella.
2009. *"Culture" and Culture: Traditional Knowledge and Intellectual Rights*. Chicago: Prickly Paradigm Press.

Castells, Manuel.
2001. *The Internet Galaxy: Reflections on the Internet, Business, and Society*. Cambridge: Oxford University Press.

Ceruzzi, Paul E.
1998. *A History of Modern Computing*. Cambridge, MA: MIT Press.

Chan, Anita
2008. Retiring the Network Spokesman: The Poly-Vocality of Free Software Net-
    works in Peru. *Science Studies* 20 (2): 78–99.

Chopra, Samir, and Scott Dexter.
2007. *Decoding Liberation: The Promise of Free and Open Source Software*. Ox-
    ford: Routledge.

Christen, Kimberly.
2006. Tracking Properness: Repackaging Culture in a Remote Australian Town.
    Cultural Anthropology 21 (3): 416–46.
2009. Access and Accountability: The Ecology of Information Sharing in the Digi-
    tal Age. *Anthropology News* (April): 4–5.

Clark, Charles C.
1996. Clashing over Copyright: Is Intellectual Property Safe in the Age of the Inter-
    net? *CQ Researcher* 6 (42): 985–1008.

Clifford, James.
1986. On Ethnographic Allegory. In *Writing Culture: The Poetics and Politics of
    Ethnography*, ed. James Clifford and George E. Marcus, 98–121. Berkeley:
    University of California Press.
1988. *The Predicament of Culture: Twentieth-Century Ethnography, Literature,
    and Art*. Cambridge, MA: Harvard University Press.

Clifford, James, and George E. Marcus, eds.
1986. *Writing Culture: The Poetics and Politics of Ethnography*. Berkeley: Univer-
    sity of California Press.

Cohn, Carol.
1987. Sex and Death in the Rational World of Defense Intellectuals. *Signs* 12 (4):
    687–718.

Cohn, Cindy, and James Grimmelmann.
2003. Seven Ways in Which Code Equals Law. In *Code: The Language of Our
    Time*, ed. Christine Schipf and Gerfried Stocker, 20–25. Berlin: Hatje Cantz.

Coleman, Biella.
2005. Indymedia's Independence: From Activist Media to Free Software. http://
    journal.planetwork.net/article.php?lab=coleman0704&page=1 (accessed
    November 28, 2010).

Coleman, E. Gabriella.
1999. The Politics of Survival and Prestige: Hacker Identity and Global Production
    of an Operating System. Master's thesis, University of Chicago.
2004. The Political Agnosticism of Free and Open Source Software and the Inad-
    vertent Politics of Contrast. *Anthropology Quarterly* 77 (3): 507–19.
2010. Ethnographic Approaches to Digital Media. *Annual Review of Anthropology*
    39: 487–505.
2012a. Our Weirdness Is Free: The Logic of Anonymous—Online Army, Agents of
    Chaos, and Seeker of Justice. *Triple Canopy*. http://canopycanopycanopy.com/
    15/our_weirdness_is_free (accessed March 20, 2012).

2012b. Phreaks, Hackers, and Trolls: The Politics of Transgression and Spectacle. In *The Social Media Reader*, ed. Michael Mandiberg, 99–119. New York: New York University Press.

Coleman, E. Gabriella, and Alex Golub.
2008. Hacker Practice: Moral Genres and the Cultural Articulation of Liberalism. *Anthropological Theory* 8 (3): 255–77.

Collier, Jane, Bill Maurer, and Liliana Suarez-Navaz.
1997. Sanctioned Identities: Legal Constructions of Modern Personhood. *Identities* 2 (1–2): 1–27.

Collins, Randall.
2004. *Interaction Ritual Chains*. Princeton, NJ: Princeton University Press.

Comaroff, Jean.
1985. *Body of Power, Spirit of Resistance: The Culture and History of a South African People*. Chicago: University of Chicago Press.

Comaroff, Jean, and John Comaroff.
1992. *Ethnography and the Historical Imagination*. Boulder, CO: Westview Press.
2000. Millennial Capitalism: First Thoughts on a Second Coming. *Public Culture* 12 (2): 291–343.
2003. Reflections on Liberalism, Policulturalism, and ID-ology: Citizenship and Difference in South Africa. *Social Identities* 9 (3): 445–74.

Coombe, Rosemary J.
1998. *The Cultural Life of Intellectual Properties: Authorship, Appropriation, and the Law*. Durham, NC: Duke University Press.

Coombe, Rosemary J., and Andrew Herman.
2004. Rhetorical Virtues: Property, Speech, and the Commons on the World Wide Web. *Anthropology Quarterly* 77 (3): 559–74.

Cover, Robert.
1993. Nomos and Narrative. In *Narrative, Violence, and the Law: The Essays of Robert Cover*, ed. Martha Minow, Michael Ryan, and Austin Sarat, 95–172. Ann Arbor: University of Michigan Press.

Critchley, Simon.
2002. *On Humor: Thinking in Action*. New York: Routledge.

Crowston, Kevin, and James Howison.
2005. The Social Structure of Free and Open Source Software Development. *First Monday* 10 (2). http://firstmonday.org/htbin/cgiwrap/bin/ojs/index.php/fm/rt/printerFriendly/1478/1393 (accessed July 18, 2011).

Csikszentmihalyi, Mihaly.
1990. *Flow: The Psychology of Optimal Experience*. New York: Harper and Row.

DeNardis Laura.
2009. *Protocol Politics: The Globalization of Internet Governance*. Cambridge, MA: MIT Press.

Derrida, Jacques.
1978. *Writing and Difference*. Chicago: University of Chicago Press.
1990. Force of Law: The Mystical Foundation of Authority. *Cardozo Law Review*
11 (5–6): 921–1045.

Dewey, John.
1935. *Liberalism and Social Action*. New York: G. P. Putnam's Sons.

Dibbell, Julian.
2006. *Play Money: Or, How I Quit My Day Job and Made Millions Trading Virtual Loot*. New York: Basic Books.

Dickson, David.
1988. *The New Politics of Science*. Chicago: University of Chicago Press.

Dirks, Nicholas.
1992. Introduction to *Colonialism and Culture*, ed. Nicholas Dirks, 1–26. Ann Arbor: University of Michigan Press.

Dobrzynski, Judith.
1999. Online Pioneers: The Buzz Never Stops. *New York Times*, November 21, section 3. http://www.nytimes.com/1999/11/21/business/ceo-round-table-online-pioneers-the-buzz-never-stops.html (accessed August 10, 2011).

Donner, Wendy.
1991. *The Liberal Self: John Stuart Mill's Moral and Political Philosophy*. Ithaca, NY: Cornell University Press.

Douglas, Mary.
1975. *Implicit Meanings: Essays in Anthropology*. London: Routledge.

Downey, Gary.
1998. *The Machine in Me: An Anthropologist Sits among Computer Engineers*. London: Routledge.

Drahos, Peter, with John Braithwaite.
2002. *Information Feudalism: Who Owns the Knowledge Economy?* London: Earthscan.

Elkin-Koren, Niva.
2006. Exploring Creative Commons: A Skeptical View of a Worthy Pursuit. In *The Future of the Public Domain: Identifying the Commons in Information Law*, ed. Lucie Guibault and P. Bernt Hugenholtz, 325–46. Leiden, Netherlands: Kluwer Law International.

Elliott, Carl.
2003. *Better Than Well: American Medicine Meets the American Dream*. New York: W. W. Norton and Company.

Ellison, Ralph.
1964. *Shadow and Act*. New York: Vintage.

English-Leuck, J. A.
2002. *Cultures@SiliconValley*. Stanford, CA: Stanford University Press.

Ensmenger, Nathan L.
2010. *The Computer Boys Take Over: Computers, Programmers, and the Politics of Technical Expertise*. Cambridge, MA: MIT Press.

Epstein, Richard.
2004. Why Open Source Is Unsustainable. *Financial Times*, October 21. http://www.ft.com/cms/s/2/78d9812a-2386-11d9-aee5-00000e2511c8.html (accessed August 25, 2011).

Ess, Charles, and May Thorbeth, eds.
2011. *Trust and Virtual Worlds: Contemporary Perspectives*. New York: Peter Lang.

Ewick, Patricia, and Susan Silbey.
1998. *The Common Place of the Law: Stories from Everyday Life*. Chicago: University of Chicago Press.

Faubion, James D., and George E. Marcus, eds.
2009. *Fieldwork Is Not What It Used to Be: Learning Anthropology's Method in a Time of Transition*. Ithaca, NY: Cornell University Press.

Federici, Silvia.
2004. *Caliban and the Witch: Women, the Body, and Primitive Accumulation*. Brooklyn: Autonomedia.

Ferguson, James, and Akhil Gupta.
2002. Spatializing States: Toward an Ethnography of Neoliberal Governmentality. *American Ethnologist* 29 (4): 981–1002.

Fish, Adam, Luis F. R. Murillo, Lilly Nguyen, Aaron Panofsky, and Christopher M. Kelty.
2011. Birds of the Internet: Towards a Field Guide to the Organization and Governance of Participation. *Journal of Cultural Economy* 4 (2): 157–87.

Fish, Stanley.
1994. *There's No Such Thing As Free Speech: And It's a Good Thing, Too*. Oxford: Oxford University Press.
2002. The Dance of Theory. In *Eternally Vigilant*, ed. Lee C. Bollinger and Geoffrey Stone, 198–231. Chicago: University of Chicago Press.

Fischer, Michael J.
1999. Worlding Cyberspace: Towards a Critical Ethnography in Time, Space, and Theory. In *Critical Anthropology Now: Unexpected Contexts, Shifting Constituencies, Changing Agendas*, ed. George Marcus, 261–304. Santa Fe: School of American Research Press.

Florin, Fabrice, dir.
1986. *Hackers: Wizards of the Electronic Age*. 26 min. http://www.hackersvideo.com (accessed July 19, 2011).

Fortun, Kim.
2001. *Advocacy after Bhopal: Environmentalism, Disaster, New Global Orders*. Chicago: University of Chicago Press.

Frank, Thomas, and Matt Weiland, eds.
1997. *Commodify Your Dissent: Salvos from the Baffler*. New York: W. W. Norton and Company.

Free Software Foundation.
(1996) 2010. Free Software Definition. http://www.gnu.org/philosophy/free-sw.html (accessed November 28, 2010).

Freiberger, Paul, and Michael Swaine.
2000. *Fire in the Valley: The Making of the Personal Computer*. New York: McGraw-Hill.

Friedman, Ted.
2005. *Electric Dreams: Computers in American Culture*. New York: New York University Press.

Fuller, Matthew, ed.
2008. *Software Studies: A Lexicon*. Cambridge, MA: MIT Press.

Fuster Morell, Mayo.
2010. Governance of Online Creation Communities. Provision of Infrastructure for the Building of Digital Commons. PhD diss., European University Institute.

Gallaway, Terrel, and Douglas Kinnear.
2004. Open Source Software, the Wrongs of Copyright, and the Rise of Technology. *Journal of Economic Issues* 38 (2): 467–75.

Galison, Peter.
1997. *Image and Logic: A Material Culture of Microphysics*. Chicago: University of Chicago Press.

Galloway, Alexander R.
2004. *Protocol: How Control Exists after Decentralization*. Cambridge, MA: MIT Press.

Gancarz, Mike.
1995. *The Unix Philosophy*. Boston: Digital Press.

Gardiner, Michael.
2004. Wild Publics and Grotesque Symposiums: Habermas and Bakhtin on Dialogue, Everyday Life, and the Public Sphere. *Sociological Review* 52 (s1): 28–48.

Gates, William Henry, III.
1976. An Open Letter to Hobbyists. http://www.blinkenlights.com/classiccmp/gateswhine.html (accessed July 19, 2011).

Geertz, Clifford.
1977. *The Interpretation of Culture*. New York: Basic Books.
1983. *Local Knowledge: Further Essays In Interpretive Anthropology*. New York: Basic Books.

Ghosh, Rishab Aiyer.
1998. Cooking Pot Markets: An Economic Model for the Trade in Free Goods and Services on the Internet. *First Monday* 3 (3). http://firstmonday.org/htbin/cgiwrap/bin/ojs/index.php/fm/article/view/580/501 (accessed July 27, 2011).

Gillespie, Tarleton.
2007. *Wired Shut: Copyright and the Shape of Digital Culture*. Cambridge, MA: MIT Press.
2009. Characterizing Copyright in the Classroom: The Cultural Work of Anti-Piracy Campaigns. *Communication, Culture, and Critique* 2 (3): 274–318.
2010. The Politics of Platforms. *New Media and Society* 12 (3): 347–64.

Gilroy, Paul.
1993. *The Black Atlantic: Modernity and Double Consciousness*. Cambridge, MA: Harvard University Press.

Ginsburg, Faye.
2008. Rethinking the Digital Age. In *The Media and Social Theory*, ed. David Hesmondhalgh and Jason Toynbee, 127–44. London: Routledge.

Gitelman, Lisa.
2006. *Always Already New: Media, History, and the Data of Culture*. Cambridge, MA: MIT Press.

Gladwell, Malcolm.
2010. Small Change: Why the Revolution Will Not Be Tweeted. *New Yorker*, October 4. http://www.newyorker.com/reporting/2010/10/04/101004fa_fact_gladwell (accessed August 25, 2011).

Gleick, James.
2000. Patently Absurd. *New York Times Sunday Magazine*. http://www.nytimes.com/2000/03/12/magazine/patently-absurd.html (accessed March 24, 2012).

Gluckman, Max.
1963. *Order and Rebellion in Tribal Africa: Collected Essays*. New York: Macmillan.

Goffman, Erving.
1967. *Interaction Ritual: Essays in Face-to-face Behavior*. New York: Anchor Books.

Good, Byron J.
1994. *Medicine, Rationality, and Experience: An Anthropological Perspective*. Cambridge: Cambridge University Press.

Goriunova, Olga and Shulgin, Alexei.
2008. Glitch. In *Software Studies: A Lexicon*, ed. Matthew Fuller, 110–19. Cambridge, MA: MIT Press.

Graeber, David.
1997. Manners, Deference, and Private Property in Early Modern Europe. *Comparative Studies in Society and History* 39 (4): 694–728.

2001. *Toward an Anthropological Theory of Value: The False Coin of Our Own Dreams*. New York: Palgrave.

2004. *Fragments of an Anarchist Anthropology*. Chicago: Prickly Paradigm Press.

2007. *Possibilities: Essays on Hierarchy, Rebellion, and Desire*. Oakland, CA: AK Press.

Gramsci, Antonio.
1971. The Modern Prince. In *Selections from the Prison Notebooks*, ed. Quintin Hoare and Nowell Smith, 313–41. London: Lawrence and Wishart.

Greene, Thomas C.
2001. Ballmer: Linux Is a Cancer. *Register*, June 2. http://www.theregister.co.uk/2001/06/02/ballmer_linux_is_a_cancer/ (accessed November 8, 2011).

Grossman, Lev.
2006. You—Yes, You—Are Time's Person of the Year. *Time*, December 25. http://www.time.com/time/magazine/article/0,9171,1570810,00.html (accessed August 25, 2011).

Gupta, Akhil, and James Ferguson.
1997. Discipline and Practice: The "Field" as Site, Method, and Location in Anthropology. In *Anthropological Locations: Boundaries and Grounds of a Field Science*, ed. Akhil Gupta and James Ferguson, 1–46. Berkeley: University of California Press.

Gusterson, Hugh.
1998. *Nuclear Rites: A Weapons Laboratory at the End of the Cold War*. Berkeley: University of California Press.

Habermas, Jürgen.
1981. *The Theory of Communicative Action: Reason and the Rationalization of Society*. London: Beacon Press.

1987. *The Philosophical Discourse of Modernity*. Cambridge, MA: MIT Press.

1989. *The Structural Transformation of the Public Sphere: An Inquiry into a Category of Bourgeois Society*. Cambridge, MA: MIT Press.

Hadley, Elaine.
2010. *Living Liberalism: Practical Citizenship in Mid-Victorian Britain*. Chicago: University of Chicago Press.

Hakken, David.
1999. *Cyborgs@Cyberspace? An Ethnographer Looks at the Future*. London: Routledge.

Hall, Jon "maddog."
2000. My Life and Free Software. *Linux Journal* (June), 114–18. http://www.linux journal.com/article/4047 (accessed July 14, 2011).

Hall, Stuart.
1986. Variants of Liberalism. In *Politics and Ideology: A Reader*, ed. James Donald and Stuart Hall, 34–69. Milton Keynes, UK: Open University Press.

Halliday, Richard J.
1976. *John Stuart Mill*. London: Routledge.

Haraway, Donna J.
1997. *Modest_Witness@Second_Millennium.FemaleMan©_Meets_OncoMouse™*. New York: Routledge.

Hardt, Michael, and Antonio Negri.
2000. *Empire*. Cambridge, MA: Harvard University Press.
2004. *Multitude: War and Democracy in the Age of Empire*. New York: Penguin.
2009. *Commonwealth*. Cambridge, MA: Harvard University Press.

Harvey, David.
2005. *A Brief History of Neoliberalism*. Oxford: Oxford University Press.

Haydn, Cori.
2003. *When Nature Goes Public*. Princeton, NJ: Princeton University Press.

Hebdige, Dick.
1979. *Subculture: The Meaning of Style*. London: Methuen.

Heidegger, Martin.
(1927) 2008. *Being and Time*. New York: HarperCollins.

Helmreich, Stefan.
1998. *Silicon Second Nature: Culturing Artificial Life in a Digital World*. Berkeley: University of California Press.

Henderson, Scott.
2007. *The Dark Visitor: Inside the World of Chinese Hackers*. http://onlinebooks .library.upenn.edu/webbin/book/lookupid?key=olbp49128 (accessed February 15, 2012).

Hesse, Carla.
2002. The Rise of Intellectual Property, 700 B.C.–A.D. 2000: An Idea in the Balance. *Daedalus* 131 (Spring): 26–45.

Hill, Benjamin Mako.
2005. Freedom's Advanced Standard. *Mute: Culture and Politics after the Net*, November 23. http://www.metamute.org/en/Freedoms-Standard-Advanced (accessed November 3, 2011).

Himanen, Pekka.
2001. *The Hacker Ethic and the Spirit of the Information Age*. New York: Random House.

Hindman, Matthew.
2008. *The Myth of Digital Democracy*. Princeton, NJ: Princeton University Press.

Hoffman, Paul.
2011. The Tao of IETF: A Novice's Guide to the Internet Engineering Task Force. http://www.ietf.org/tao.html (accessed July 27, 2011).

Hogle, Linda F.
2005. Enhancement Technologies and the Body. *Annual Review of Anthropology*
    34:695–716.

Hunter, Dan.
2005. Culture War. *Texas Law Review* 83 (4): 1106–136.

Jackson, Michael.
1996. Introduction: Phenomenology, Radical Empiricism, and Anthropological Cri-
    tique. In *Things as They Are: New Directions in Phenomenological Anthro-
    pology*, ed. Michael Jackson, 1–50. Bloomington: Indiana University Press.

Jaffe, Adam.
1999. The U.S. Patent System In Transition: Policy Innovation and the Innovation
    Process. National Bureau of Economic Research Working Paper 7280. http://
    www.nber.org/papers/w7280 (accessed July 19, 2011).

Jaffe, Adam, and Joshua Lerner.
2004. *Innovation and Its Discontents: How Our Broken Patent System Is Endan-
    gering Innovation and Progress, and What to Do about It*. Princeton, NJ:
    Princeton University Press.

Johns, Adrian.
1998. *The Nature of the Book: Print and Knowledge in the Making*. Chicago:
    University of Chicago Press.
2006. Intellectual Property and the Nature of Science. *Cultural Studies* 20 (2–3):
    145–64.
2010. *Piracy: The Intellectual Property Wars from Gutenberg to Gates*. Chicago:
    University of Chicago Press.

Jones, Caroline A., and Peter Galison, eds.
1998. *Picturing Science, Producing Art*. New York: Routledge.

Jones, Graham.
2011. *Trade of the Tricks: Inside the Magician's Craft*. Berkeley: University of
    California Press.

Jordan, Tim.
2008. *Hacking: Digital Media and Technological Determinism*. Cambridge, UK:
    Polity Press.

Joyce, Patrick.
2003. *The Rule of Freedom: Liberalism and the Modern City*. New York: Verso.

Juris, Jeffrey S.
2008. *Networking Futures: The Movements against Corporate Globalization*. Dur-
    ham, NC: Duke University Press.

Karanovic, Jelena.
2010. Contentious Europeanization: The Paradox of Becoming European through
    Anti-Patent Activism. *Ethnos: Journal of Anthropology* 75 (3): 252–74.

Kawamoto, Dawn.
1998. Netscape Earnings Take a Big Hit. C-Net, January 27. http://news.cnet.com/
    Netscape-earnings-take-big-hit/2100-1001_3-207526.html (accessed Novem-
    ber 3, 2011).

Keane, Webb.
2009. Freedom and Blasphemy: On Indonesian Press Bans and Danish Cartoons.
    Public Culture 21 (1): 47–76.

Kellner, Douglas.
2003. *Media Spectacle*. London: Routledge.

Kelty, Christopher M.
2004. Punt to Culture. *Anthropological Quarterly* 77 (3): 547–58.
2005. Geeks, Social Imaginaries, and Recursive Publics. *Cultural Anthropology* 20
    (2): 185–214.
2008. *Two Bits: The Cultural Significance of Free Software*. Durham, NC: Duke
    University Press.

Kenigsberg, Amos.
2001. Peace, Love, and Marketing. *Mother Jones*, July 20. http://motherjones.com/
    politics/2001/07/peace-love-and-marketing (accessed August 24, 2011).

Kidder, Tracy.
1981. *The Soul of a New Machine*. Boston: Little, Brown and Company.

Klein, Naomi.
2008. *The Shock Doctrine: The Rise of Disaster Capitalism*. New York: Henry
    Holt and Company.

Kollock, Peter.
1999. The Economies of Online Cooperation: Gifts and Public Goods. In *Commu-
    nities in Cyberspace*, ed. Marc A. Smith and Peter Kollock, 219–39. London:
    Routledge.

Knuth, Donald.
1998. *The Art of Computer Programming, Vol. 1*. New York: Addison-Wesley.

Lakoff, George.
2004. *Don't Think of an Elephant! Know Your Values and Frame the Debate*.
    White River Junction, VT: Chelsea Green.
2006. *Whose Freedom? The Battle over America's Most Important Idea*. New
    York: Farrar, Straus, Giroux.

Lancashire, David.
2001. Code, Culture, and Cash: The Fading Altruism of Open Source Develop-
    ment. *First Monday*, October 3. http://firstmonday.org/htbin/cgiwrap/bin/ojs/
    index.php/fm/rt/printerFriendly/1488/1403 (accessed July 18, 2011).

Lanier, Jaron.
2010. *You Are Not a Gadget: A Manifesto*. New York: Alfred A. Knopf.

Latour, Bruno.
1987. *Science in Action: How to Follow Scientists and Engineers through Society.* Cambridge, MA: Harvard University Press.
1993. *The Pasteurization of France.* Cambridge, MA: Harvard University of Press.

Latour, Bruno, and Steve Wooglar.
1979. *Laboratory Life: The Social Construction of Scientific Facts.* Beverly Hills: Sage Publications.

Lea, Graham.
1999. US versus Microsoft: The Twelfth Week. http://news.bbc.co.uk/2/hi/special _report/1998/04/98/microsoft/262488.stm (accessed March 23, 2012).

Leonard, Andrew.
1998. The Saint of Free Software. Salon.com. http://archive.salon.com/21st/feature/ 1998/08/cov_31feature.html (accessed July 17, 2011).

Lerner, Josh, and Mark Schankerman.
2010. *The Comingled Code: Open Source and Economic Development.* Cambridge, MA: MIT Press.

Lerner, Josh, and Jean Tirole.
2001. The Open Source Movement: Key Research Questions. *European Economic Review* 45 (4–6): 819–26.

Lessig, Lawrence.
1999. *Code and Other Laws of Cyberspace.* New York: Basic Books.
2001a. *The Future of Ideas: The Fate of the Commons in a Connected World.* New York: Random House.
2001b. Jail Time in the Digital Age. *New York Times*, July 30. http://www.nytimes .com/2001/07/30/opinion/jail-time-in-the-digital-age.html (accessed July 17, 2011).

Levy, Steven.
1984. *Hackers: Heroes of the Computer Revolution.* New York: Dell.
2002. Lawrence Lessig's Supreme Showdown. *Wired.* http://www.wired.com/wired/ archive/10.10/lessig_pr.html (accessed August 25, 2011).
2011. *In the Plex: How Google Thinks, Works, and Shapes Our Lives.* New York: Simon and Schuster.

Linebaugh, Peter.
2010. Meandering on the Semantical-Historical Paths of Communism and the Commons. *Commoner.* http://www.commoner.org.uk/wp-content/uploads/ 2010/12/meandering-linebaugh.pdf (accessed August 25, 2011).

Litman, Jessica.
2001. *Digital Copyright: Protecting Intellectual Property on the Internet.* Amherst, NY: Prometheus Books.

Lovink, Geert.
2005. *The Principles of Notworking: Concepts in Critical Internet Culture.* Amsterdam: HvA Publicates.

2007. *Zero Comments: Blogging and Critical Internet Culture*. Oxford: Routledge.

Luhrmann, Tanya M.
2001. *Of Two Minds: The Growing Disorder in American Psychiatry*. New York: Alfred A. Knopf.

Macpherson, C. B.
1962. *The Political Theory of Possessive Individualism: Hobbes to Locke*. Oxford: Oxford University Press.

Mahmood, Saba.
2005. *Politics of Piety: The Islamic Revival and the Feminist Subject*. Princeton, NJ: Princeton University Press.

Malaby, Thomas.
2007. Beyond Play: A New Approach to Games. *Games and Culture* 2 (2): 95–113.
2009. *Making Virtual Worlds: Linden Lab and Second Life*. Ithaca, NY: Cornell University Press.

Marcus, George E., and Michael Fischer.
1986. *Anthropology as Cultural Critique: An Experimental Moment in the Human Sciences*. Chicago: University of Chicago Press.

Marcuse, Herbert.
1965. Repressive Tolerance. In *A Critique of Pure Tolerance*, ed. Robert Paul Wolff, Barrington Moore, and Herbert Marcuse, 95–118. Boston: Beacon Press.

Marshall, Patrick.
1993. Software Piracy: Can the Government Help Stop the Drain on Profits? *CQ Researcher* 3 (May 21): 19.

Martin, Randy.
1998. *Critical Moves: Dance Studies in Theory and Practice*. Durham, NC: Duke University Press.

Marwick, Alice.
2010. Status Update: Celebrity, Publicity, and Self-Branding in Web 2.0. PhD diss., New York University.

Marx, Karl, and Friedrich Engels.
1978. *The Marx-Engels Reader*. Edited by Robert C. Tucker. New York: W. W. Norton and Company.

Mauss, Marcel.
1954. *The Gift*. London: Cohen and West.

McGill, Meredith L.
2002. *American Literature and the Culture of Reprinting, 1834–1853*. Philadelphia: University of Pennsylvania Press.

McGowan, David.
2001. The Legal Implications of Open Source Software. *University of Illinois Law Review* 1:241–304.

McLeod, Kembrew.
2007. *Freedom of Expression®: Resistance and Repression in the Age of Intellectual Property*. Minneapolis: University of Minnesota Press.

Merleau-Ponty, Maurice.
1962. *Phenomenology of Perception*. London: Routledge and Kegan Paul.

Mezey, Naomi.
2001. Law as Culture. *Yale Journal of Law and the Humanities* 13:35–67.

Milberry, Kate.
2009. Geeks and Global Justice: Another (Cyber)World Is Possible. PhD diss., Simon Fraser University.

Mill, John Stuart.
(1857) 1991. *On Liberty*. Edited by H.B. Acton. London: Dent.

Miller, Daniel, and Don Slater.
2000. *The Internet: An Ethnographic Approach*. London: Berg.

Mitnick, Kevin D.
2011. *Ghost in the Wires: My Adventures as the World's Most Wanted Hacker*. New York: Little, Brown and Company.

Monfort, Nick.
2008. Obfuscated Code. *In Software Studies: A Lexicon*, ed. Matthew Fuller, 193–99. Cambridge, MA: MIT Press.

Moody, Glyn.
1997 The Greatest OS that (N)ever Was. Wired August. Available at http://www.wired.com/wired/archive/5.08/linux.html, accessed July 20, 2011.
2001. *Rebel Code: The Inside Story of Linux and the Open Source Revolution*. Cambridge, MA: Perseus Publishing.

Morozov, Evgeny.
2011. *The Net Delusion: The Dark Side of Internet Freedom*. New York: Public Affairs.

Mowery, David C.
1999. The Computer Software Industry. In *Sources of Industrial Leadership: Studies of Seven Industries*, ed. David C. Mowery and Richard R. Nelson, 133–68. Cambridge: Cambridge University Press.

Mulkay, Michael.
1988. *On Humor: Its Nature and Its Place in Modern Society*. Boston: Blackwell.

Murillo, Luis Felipe Rosado.
2009. Technologia, Política e Cultura Na Comunidade Brasileira de Software Livre e de Código Aberto. PhD diss., Universidade Federal do Rio Grande do Sul.

Nelson, Ted.
1974. *Computer Lib/Dream Machines*. Self-published.

Netanel, Neil Weinstock.
2008. *Copyright's Paradox*. Oxford: Oxford University Press.

Nielsen, Greg.
1998. The Norms of Answerability: Bakhtin and the Fourth Postulate. In *Bakhtin and the Human Sciences*, ed. Michael Bell and Michael Gardiner, 214–30. London: Sage.

Nissenbaum, Helen.
2004. Hackers and the Contested Ontology of Cyberspace. *New Media and Society* 6 (2): 195–217.
2009. *Privacy in Context: Technology, Policy, and the Integrity of Social Life*. Stanford, CA: Stanford University Press.

Nimmer, Melville B.
1970. Does Copyright Abridge the First Amendment Guarantees of Free Speech and Press? *UCLA Law Review* 17:1180–1204.

Nussbaum, Martha C.
2004. Mill between Aristotle and Bentham. *Daedalus* 133 (2): 60–68.

O'Mahony, Siobhán, and Fabrizio Ferraro.
2007. The Emergence of Governance in an Open Source Community. *Academy of Management Journal* 50 (5): 1079–106.

O'Neil, Mathieu.
2009. *Cyberchiefs: Autonomy and Authority in Online Tribes*. London: Pluto Press.

Ong, Aihwa.
1987. *Spirits of Resistance and Capitalist Discipline: Factory Women in Malaysia*. Albany: State University of New York Press.
2006. *Neoliberalism as Exception: Mutations in Citizenship and Sovereignty*. Durham, NC: Duke University Press.

Orr, Julian E.
1996. *Talking about Machines: An Ethnography of a Modern Job*. Ithaca, NY: Cornell University Press.

Passavant, Paul A.
2002. *No Escape: Freedom of Speech and the Paradox of Rights*. New York: New York University Press.

Patterson, Lyman Ray.
1968. *Copyright in Historical Perspective*. Nashville: Vanderbilt University Press.

Penenberg, Adam L.
2005. Red Herring: Don't Listen to Bill Gates. The Open-Source Movement Isn't Communism. *Slate*, November 22. http://www.slate.com/id/2130798/ (accessed August 24, 2011).

Peters, John Durham.
2005. *Courting the Abyss: Free Speech and the Liberal Tradition*. Chicago: University of Chicago Press.

Pfaffenberger, Bryan.
1996. "If I Want It, It's OK": Usenet and the (Outer) Limits of Free Speech. *Information Society* 12:365–88.

Philips, Chuck.
2000. Piracy: Music Giants Miss a Beat on the Web. *Los Angeles Times*, July 17. http://articles.latimes.com/2000/jul/17/news/mn-54359 (accessed August 10, 2011).

Pickard, Victor.
2006. United yet Autonomous: Indymedia and the Struggle to Sustain a Radical Democratic Network. *Media, Culture, and Society* 28 (3): 315–36.
2011. The Battle over the FCC Blue Book: Determining the Role of Broadcast Media in a Democratic Society, 1945–1948. *Media, Culture, and Society* 33 (2): 171–91.

Plato.
n.d. *The Republic*. Translated by Benjamin Jowett. http://classics.mit.edu/Plato/republic.html (accessed November 2, 2011).

Polanyi, Michael.
1966. *The Tacit Dimension*. New York: Doubleday.

Postigo, Hector.
2010. Information Communication Technologies and Framing for Backfire in the Digital Rights Movement: The Case of Dmitry Sklyarov's Advanced e-Book Processor. *Social Science Computer Review* 28 (2): 232–50.

Postman, Neil.
(1985) 2006. *Amusing Ourselves to Death: Public Discourse in the Age of Show Business*. New York: Penguin.

Povinelli, Elizabeth A.
2002. *The Cunning of Recognition: Indigenous Alterities and the Making of Australian Multiculturalism*. Durham, NC: Duke University Press.
2006. *The Empire of Love: Toward a Theory of Intimacy, Genealogy, and Carnality*. Durham, NC: Duke University Press.

Prakash, Gyan.
1999. *Another Reason: Science and the Imagination of Modern India*. Princeton, NJ: Princeton University Press.

Rabinow, Paul.
1996. *Making PCR: A Story of Biotechnology*. Chicago: University of Chicago Press.

Radcliffe-Brown, A. R.
1952. *Structure and Function in Primitive Society*. New York: Free Press.

Ratto, Matt.
2005. Embedded Technical Expression: Code and the Leveraging of Functionality. *Information Society* 21 (3): 205–13.

Raymond, Eric S.
1999. *The Cathedral and the Bazaar: Musings on Linux and Open Source by an Accidental Revolutionary*. Sebastopol, CA: O'Reilly.

Reagle, Joseph Michael.
2010. *Good Faith Collaboration: The Culture of Wikipedia*. Cambridge, MA: MIT Press.

Rheingold, Howard.
1993. *The Virtual Community: Homesteading on the Electronic Frontier*. New York: Harper Perennial.

Ricoeur, Paul.
1996. Reflections on a New Ethos for Europe. In *Paul Ricoeur: The Hermeneutics of Action*, ed. Richard Kearney, 3–14. London: Sage.

Riemens, Patrice.
2003. Some Thoughts on the Idea of "Hacker Culture." *Multitudes* 8 (2). http://multitudes.samizdat.net/Some-thoughts-on-the-idea-of.html (accessed January 27, 2009).

Rose, Nick.
1999. *Powers of Freedom: Reframing Political Thought*. Cambridge: Cambridge University Press.

Rosenberg, Scott.
2007. *Dreaming in Code: Two Dozen Programmers, Three Years, 4,732 Bugs, and One Quest for Transcendent Software*. New York: Three Rivers Press.

Rosenblum, Nancy L.
1987. *Another Liberalism: Romanticism and the Reconstruction of Liberal Thought*. Cambridge, MA: Harvard University Press.

Ross, Andrew.
2006. Technology and Below-the-Line Labor in the Copyfight over Intellectual Property. *American Quarterly* 58 (3): 743–66.

Rossiter, Ned.
2007. *Organized Networks: Media Theory, Creative Labour, New Institutions*. Rotterdam: Nai Publishers.

Rule, James B.
2009. *Privacy in Peril: How We Are Sacrificing a Fundamental Right in Exchange for Security and Convenience*. New York: Oxford University Press.

Sahlins, Marshall.
2000. Sentimental Pessimism and Ethnographic Experience, or Why Culture Is Not a Disappearing Object. In *Biographies of Scientific Objects*, ed. Lorraine Daston, 158–202. Chicago: University of Chicago Press.

Said, Edward.
1978. *Orientalism*. New York: Vintage Books.

Salin, Peter.
1991. Freedom of Speech in Software. http://www.philsalin.com/patents.html (accessed November 12, 2003).

Salus, Peter.
1994. *A Quarter Century of Unix*. Reading, MA: Addison-Wesley.

Sapir, Edward.
1921. *Language: An Introduction to the Study of Speech*. New York: Harcourt Brace.

Schoen, Seth.
2001. How to Decrypt a DVD: In Haiku Form. http://www.cs.cmu.edu/~dst/DeCSS/Gallery/decss-haiku.txt (accessed October 2, 2008).

Scholz, Trebor.
2008. Market Ideology and the Myth of Web 2.0. *First Monday* 13 (3). http://firstmonday.org/htbin/cgiwrap/bin/ojs/index.php/fm/article/view/2138/1945 (accessed July 27, 2011).

Schoonmaker, Sara.
2009. Software Politics in Brazil: Toward a Political Economy of Digital Inclusion. *Information, Communication, and Society* 12 (4): 548–65.

Schutz, Alfred.
1967. *The Phenomenology of the Social World*. Evanston, IL: Northwestern University Press.
1970. *On Phenomenology and Social Relations*. Chicago: University of Chicago Press.

Schweik, Charles M., and Robert English.
2012. *Internet Success: A Study of Open Source Software Commons*. Cambridge, MA: MIT Press.

Scott, James C.
1985. *Weapons of the Weak: Everyday Forms of Peasant Resistance*. New Haven, CT: Yale University Press.

Scott, Jason.
2005. *BBS: The Documentary*. http://www.archive.org/details/BBS.The.Documentary (accessed July 28, 2011).

Scott, Joan Wallach.
2009. *The Politics of the Veil*. Princeton, NJ: Princeton University Press.

Sell, Susan.
2003. *Private Power, Public Law: The Globalization of Intellectual Property Rights*. Cambridge: Cambridge University Press.

Sennett, Richard.
2008. *The Craftsman*. New Haven, CT: Yale University Press.

Sewell, William.
2005. *Logics of History: Social Theory and Social Transformation*. Chicago: University of Chicago Press.

Shapin, Steven.
1994. *A Social History of Truth: Civility and Science in Seventeenth-Century England*. Chicago: University of Chicago Press.

Shirky, Clay.
2008. *Here Comes Everybody: The Power of Organizing without Organization.*
New York: Penguin Press.

Silverstein, Michael.
2004. "Cultural" Concepts and the Language-Culture Nexus. *Current Anthropology* 45 (5): 621–52.

Söderberg, Johan.
2007. *Hacking Capitalism: The Free and Open Source Software Movement.* Oxford: Routledge.

Solove, Daniel J.
2010. *Understanding Privacy.* Cambridge, MA: Harvard University Press.

Soros, George.
1997. The Capitalist Threat. *Atlantic Monthly.* http://www.theatlantic.com/past/docs/issues/97feb/capital/capital.htm (accessed March 25, 2012).

Stallman, Richard.
1985. The GNU Manifesto. *Dr. Dobb's Journal of Software Tools* 10 (3): 30–35.

Stallybrass, Peter, and Allon White.
1997. From Carnival to Transgression. In *The Subcultures Reader*, ed. Ken Gelder and Sarah Thorton, 293–301. London: Routledge.

Star, Susan Leigh, and James R. Griesemer.
1998. Institutional Ecology, "Translation," and Boundary Objects: Amateurs and Professionals in Berkeley's Museum of Vertebrate Zoology. In *The Science Studies Reader*, ed. Mario Biagioli, 505–24. New York: Routledge.

Stephenson, Neal.
1999. *In the Beginning Was the Command Line.* New York: Avon Books.

Sterling, Bruce.
1992. *The Hacker Crackdown: Law and Disorder on the Electronic Frontier.* New York: Bantam.

Streeter, Thomas.
2011. *The Net Effect: Romanticism, Capitalism, and the Internet.* New York: New York University Press.

Swedin, Eric G., and David L. Ferro.
2005. *Computers: The Life Story of a Technology.* Westport, CT: Greenwood Press.

Taussig, Michael.
1980. *The Devil and Commodity Fetishism in South America.* Chapel Hill: University of North Carolina Press.
1987. *Shamanism, Colonialism, and the Wild Man: A Study in Terror and Healing.* Chicago: University of Chicago Press.

Taylor, Charles.
1992. *Sources of the Self: The Making of the Modern Identity*. Cambridge, MA: Harvard University Press.
2004. *Modern Social Imaginaries*. Durham, NC: Duke University Press.

Taylor, T. L.
2006. *Play between Worlds: Exploring Online Game Culture*. Cambridge, MA: MIT Press.

Terranova, Tiziana.
2000. Free Labor: Producing Culture for the Global Economy. *Social Text* 18 (2): 33–58.

Thomas, Douglas.
2003. *Hacker Culture*. Minneapolis: University of Minnesota Press.

Thompson, E. P.
1963. *The Making of the English Working Class*. New York: Vintage Books.

Tilly, Charles, and Sidney Tarrow.
2006. *Contentious Politics*. Boulder, CO: Paradigm.

Towns, Anthony.
2002. It's Huntin' Season. http://lists.debian.org/debian-devel-announce/2002/01/msg00014.html (accessed July 28, 2011).

Trouillot, Michel-Rolph.
2003. *Global Transformations: Anthropology and the Modern World*. New York: Palgrave Macmillan.

Turkle, Sherry.
1984. *The Second Self: Computers and the Human Spirit*. New York: Simon and Schuster.

Turner, Fred.
2006. *From Counterculture to Cyberculture: Steward Brand, the Whole Earth Network, and the Rise of Digital Utopianism*. Chicago: University of Chicago Press.

Turner, Victor.
1967. *The Forest of Symbols: Aspects of Ndembu Ritual*. Ithaca, NY: Cornell University Press.
1969. *The Ritual Process: Structure and Anti-Structure*. Chicago: Aldine.
1986. *The Anthropology of Performance*. New York: PAJ Publication.

Tushnet, Rebecca.
2004. Copy This Essay: How Fair Use Doctrine Harms Free Speech and How Copying Serves It. *Yale Law Journal* 114:535–90.

Ullman, Ellen.
1997. *Close to the Machine: Technophilia and Its Discontents*. San Francisco: City Lights.
2003. *The Bug*. New York: Nan A. Talese.

Vaidhyanathan, Siva.
2001. *Copyrights and Copywrongs: The Rise of Intellectual Property and How It Threatens Creativity*. New York: New York University Press.
2004. *The Anarchist in the Library: How the Clash between Freedom and Control Is Hacking the Real World and Crashing the System*. New York: Basic Books.

Vetter, Greg R.
2004. The Collaborative Integrity of Open-Source Software. *Utah Law Review* 563–700.
2007. Open Source Licensing and Scattering Opportunism in Software Standards. *Boston College Law Review* 48 (1): 225–49.

von Hippel, Eric.
2005. *Democratizing Innovation*. Cambridge, MA: MIT Press.

von Hippel, Eric, and Georg von Krogh.
2003. Open Source Software and the "Private-Collective" Innovation Model: Issues for Organization Science. *Organization Science* 14 (8): 208–23.

Wark, McKenzie.
2004. *A Hacker Manifesto*. Cambridge, MA: Harvard University Press.

Warner, Michael.
2002. *Publics and Counterpublics*. New York: Zone Books.

Wayner, Peter.
2000. *Free for All: How Linux and the Free Software Movement Undercut the High-tech Titans*. New York: Harper Business.

Weber, Steven.
2004. *The Success of Open Source*. Cambridge, MA: Harvard University Press.

Weizenbaum, Joseph.
1976. *Computer Power and Human Reason: From Judgment to Calculation*. San Francisco: W. H. Freeman.

Wittgenstein, Ludwig.
1953. *Philosophical Investigations*. Oxford: Blackwell.

Yngvesson, Barbara.
1989. Inventing Law in Local Settings: Rethinking Popular Legal Culture. *Yale Law Journal* 98 (8): 1689–1709.

Yuill, Simon.
2008. Concurrent Versions Systems. In *Software Studies: A Lexicon*, ed. Matthew Fuller, 64–69. Cambridge, MA: MIT Press.

Zandbergen, Dorien.
2010. Silicon Valley New Age: The Co-Constitution of the Digital and the Sacred. In *Religions and Modernity: Relocating the Sacred to the Self and the Digital*, ed. Stef Aupers and Dick Houtman, 161–85. Leiden: Brill

INDEX

Adobe, 8, 72, 85, 179–181
aesthetics. *See* hacking: aesthetic dimensions of
Allen, Paul, 65, 66
Altair, 65, 76
anarchism, 19, 191, 196
Anonymous, 210
anthropology, 4–6, 205. *See also* ethnography; fieldwork
antiglobalization movements, 8, 83, 186, 210
antisec, 19
Apache, 39, 44, 75, 78, 82
Apple, 33, 59, 170, 191
Arendt, Hannah, 76
AT&T, 36, 68. *See also* Bell Laboratories
authority, 117, 121, 126–27, 130, 135–40, 154–55; legal vs. meritocratic, 179, 201
authorship, 95, 116–17

Bakhtin, Mikhail, 48, 57, 104, 157, 190
Barthes, Roland, 13, 117
BASIC, 29, 65
Bayh-Doyle Act, 66
BBDB, 101–2
Beebe, Barton, 15
Bell Laboratories, 36, 76. *See also* Unix
Benjamin, Walter, 29, 64, 104
Benkler, Yochai, 62, 63, 82, 83, 85, 123, 197, 203
Bernstein, Daniel J., 169, 182
Bernstein v. U.S. Department of Justice, 169–70, 171–72, 182
BIND, 39, 78
Blandy, Jim, 115
BOF (Birds of a Feather) session, 48, 215n25
Boing Boing, 26, 163
Bollier, David, 197, 200, 203
Bourdieu, Pierre, 51, 100
Boyle, James, 10, 62, 66, 82, 89
Brazil, 20, 87, 196, 212n17, 217n25
bug tracking system, 43, 128–29, 132, 140
Bulletin Board System (BBS), 25, 30–33, 58, 213n6, 213n7
Bush, George Herbert Walker, 72, 73, 103
Business Software Alliance (BSA), 71, 85–86, 89
Byte, 28

cabal, 122, 127, 136–38, 155, 220n12
carnival, 48, 204
Castells, Manuel, 45
Clark, David, 125
Clark, Erinn "helix," 52
cleverness, in hacking, 7, 16, 17, 36, 93–95, 100–101, 140–45, 116, 173, 176, 218n4
Clifford, James, 4, 20
Clinton, Bill, 73, 84
code: code is law, 27, 199; code is speech, 8, 161ff., 170, 173; writing of, as poetry, 13, 92, 94, 97, 175, 176, 178. *See also* authorship
collaboration, 29, 43–44, 53, 75–76, 83, 95, 106–7, 116–18, 128–29, 191, 209
collectivism, 44, 94–95, 116. *See also* individualism
Comaroff, Jean and John, 184, 200, 203
command line, 35, 36. *See also* Linux; Unix